The Lessons of
Israel's Great Inflation

The Lessons of
Israel's Great Inflation

HAIM BARKAI

Westport, Connecticut
London

Library of Congress Cataloging-in-Publication Data

Barkai, Haim, 1925–
  The lessons of Israel's great inflation / Haim Barkai.
    p.   cm.
  Includes bibliographical references and index.
  ISBN 0–275–95146–4 (alk. paper)
    1. Inflation (Finance)—Israel.   2. Monetary policy—Israel.
  3. Economic stabilization—Israel.   4. Economic history—1971–1990.
  5. Israel—Economic policy.   I. Title.
  HG1210.B37   1995
  332.4'1'095694—dc20   95–7984

British Library Cataloguing in Publication Data is available.

Library of Congress Catalog Card Number: 95–7984
ISBN: 0–275–95146–4

First published in 1995

Praeger Publishers, 88 Post Road West, Westport, CT 06881
An imprint of Greenwood Publishing Group, Inc.

Printed in the United States of America

The paper used in this book complies with the
Permanent Paper Standard issued by the National
Information Standards Organization (Z39.48–1984).

10 9 8 7 6 5 4 3 2 1

Contents

Figures and Tables

FIGURES (PART II)

TABLES (PART II)

Preface

The common theme of the two parts of this volume is Israel's "great inflation." Though significantly lower in the early 1990s than in the preceding two decades, having finally made it to the threshold of a single-digit rate, the adjective "great" describes its comparative momentum and duration when compared with the "standard" inflationary experiences of the industrial countries, which during the 1970s and 1980s were subject to inflationary processes of varying intensity.

At the same time, the adjective "great" also refers to Israel's (and Palestine's) preceding price history between the advent of World War II and 1970. During these three decades, which included two clear-cut lulls (lasting two to three years) of almost stable prices, inflation rates never reached three digits—the defining feature of the economy over six years between the end of the 1970s and the mid-1980s. Indeed, with the exception of 1954, when the economy was put through the pressure cooker of a (successful) stabilization process designed to eliminate (suppressed) inflation generated by Israel's War of Independence and mass immigration, inflation never reached an annual rate of 50 percent. In the three decades of endemic inflation preceding 1970, inflation remained in the single-digit range, whereas the following two decades were an era of two- and three-digit inflation.

The two parts of this study focus on two well-defined units of observation (actually the two ends of a lengthy process): the 45 months of the take-off of inflation, from early 1970 through October 1973, and the all-out effort to halt and rapidly reverse its momentum, implemented by the July 1985 Economic Stabilization Program and strictly adhered to since. The common thread linking the analysis of these two episodes is the view that a similar set of interlocking factors, which can clearly be identified as the determinants of that process, was at work in both cases. Their relative importance during these two periods, though, was different.

The same analytical scaffolding is therefore applied to the two episodes: the macroeconomic conceptual reformulation of the 1970s and 1980s, which allows for explicit integration of the traditional Keynesian effective demand model, with the cost (push) component. This model, now known as the Aggregate Demand–Aggregate Supply (reduced form) model, also permits the explicit integration and study of the impact of inertial factors, dormant when prices are stable, that grow in importance as inflation gains momentum.

In Part I of the study we show that the take-off of inflation can be identified as a clear-cut case of classical, demand-generated inflation, initiated by a highly expansionary fiscal policy and a loose (and later expansionary) monetary policy. Cost effects were hardly discernible, and in any case were miniscule, even at a later stage of the take-off. The relevance of inertial factors was initially negligible, growing in significance in the last stage of the take-off when inflation was already running at an annual rate of 20 percent.

The comparatively small impact of inertial and especially cost factors on the 1970–73 take-off, due to the fact that prices were fairly stable during the four preceding years or so, is now, after a 15-year bout of high and accelerating inflation and almost a decade of a relatively stable inflation rate in the 10–18 percent range, a matter of record. But once inflation crossed the three-digit threshold in 1979 and remained there for over six years, and with an annual rate of 400–500 percent in the two last quarters before the July 1985 Economic Stabilization Program was launched, both inertial and cost factors became painfully apparent. The program therefore had to apply instruments that could address these factors and forces if it hoped to achieve its prime target—to immediately reduce inflation to annual rates of 15–20 percent.

Because of the identity in their timing, the comings and goings in Israel's 1985 stabilization program could be compared with two conterminously implemented programs in Argentina and Brazil. This is carried out in Part II of the book, in which it is shown that the contrast between the success of the Israeli program and the failure of the Latin American programs can be explained in terms of the different models underlying their implementation. The Latin American programs followed the extreme heterodox model, with emphasis on cost and inertia as the dominating factors during a prolonged period of inflation; the Israeli economic stabilization policy of 1985 put proper emphasis on aggregate demand determinants and its implementation involved a restrictive fiscal policy supporting a highly restrictive monetary policy, with the latter maintained for several years.

The message of Part II is therefore fully in line with that of Part I: whereas the first part underlines the major—almost exclusive—responsibility of aggregate demand factors for the take-off of inflation, the second part proves that the sine qua non condition for an attempt to stem the tide of inflation, and to hold it within a range in which its elimination could be attempted, is strict aggregate demand discipline, hence, fiscal and monetary restraint. The message of the second part lies in pointing out the pitfalls of the heterodox recipe, which, to the political community, seems to offer a "quick fix" for inflation without recourse to politically unpalatable treatment. It explains why attempts to march to the tune of heterodoxy have, so far, ended in dismal failure.

Acknowledgments

Part I of this volume had quite a long gestation period. A preliminary draft, planned as an article-length study, was presented in a public lecture in Jerusalem in the spring of 1987. The lively discussion at that meeting suggested that the subject, labeled "The Take-off of the Great Inflation," was of substantial significance to an evaluation of the whole 18-year (at that time) pattern of inflation. It also indicated that the proposed period, from about the first quarter of 1970 to the outbreak of the Yom Kippur War early in October 1973, was, indeed, a unique and well-defined unit of observation.

With the exception of newspaper columns, notably from the *Ma'ariv Economic Panel* published during this time interval, very little literature and quantitative data with a focus on that period are available. I was therefore forced to construct a database for this study from primary sources—CBS *Statistical Annuals,* monthly bulletins, and supplementary reports, Bank of Israel *Annual Reports* and data from other Bank publications and unpublished data from its database, and data from National Insurance Institute publications. The quantitative foundation of this study is the set of 30 tables—Tables 1–30.

Delving into the real and monetary statistical series, I soon ran into a major obstacle: the frequent revision of series with frequent changes in definitions. The construction of consistent time series from the mid-1960s to 1974 sometimes proved quite a headache. The paucity of data, mainly on the 1960s, also imposed constraints. Nevertheless, the benefit gained from digging into the quantitative material, and the work put into setting up this comprehensive body of data offered many insights on the workings of the economy and underlined the problems facing policymakers who had to rely on inadequate data—especially fiscal data.

I owe much to the comments of my colleagues, Michael Beenstock and Joseph

Zeira, who read the whole draft of Part I of this book. Their detailed criticism and suggestions were helpful in the preparation of the final draft. Due to their suggestion to spell out the theoretical model underlying the analysis, I have considerably expanded the third section of Chapter 1, in which I attempt to spell out clearly, and with reference to the specific features of the Israeli economy, the standard aggregate demand and supply framework used nowadays for the study of macroeconomic issues. The scope of the introduction to Part I, in which I attempt to summarize my findings and make explicit their message for the economic issues of today, was expanded and rewritten in response to these readers' challenge to state the central message simply and clearly at the outset and clarify its relevance to the specification of Israel's economic policy of today.

A draft of Part II of this volume was prepared while I was a Visiting Scholar in the European Department of the International Monetary Fund, and was circulated as an IMF working paper (WP/90/29, April 1990). The views expressed in this part are those of the author and do not necessarily represent those of the Fund. I am indebted to M. Russo, Director of the European Department, for inviting me to work on that subject. The comments of H. Schmidt and G. Bélanger, both members of that department, on the first draft of Part II of the book were highly significant and very helpful in clarifying several major points at issue and improving the presentation. Thanks are due also to D. Kochau and D. P. O'Brien for comments on the second draft of Part II. Remaining errors and omissions are, of course, entirely my responsibility.

I am grateful to the sponsors of Part I of this study—The Jerusalem Institute and the Maurice Falk Institute for Economic Research in Israel—for their patience while it was in the works, and to IMF-European Department for offering research facilities and advice for the work on Part II. Thanks are also due to Avi Simhon and Danny Krivaa, research assistants, for collecting and processing the database, and to Sharon Simmer and Hyla Berkowitz for deciphering my almost illegible handwriting. It goes without saying that were it not for the critical judgment of Maggie Eisenstaedt, the Falk Institute's excellent editor and draftsperson, this volume in its two parts would have been in an altogether different shape.

A note on the bibliographical references is in place here. Owing to the many references to the Bank of Israel's *Annual Reports* and *Economic Reviews,* and to the Central Bureau of Statistics' *Statistical Abstract of Israel,* these sources are referred to as *Report, Review,* and *Abstract,* respectively. Page numbers cited refer to the Hebrew editions unless otherwise specified.

—— PART I ——

The Take-Off of Israel's Great Inflation

Introduction

The unfolding events in these chapters tell a sad story. The rise of inflation from a negligible rate in the late autumn months of 1969 to 10 percent at the end of 1970, and to 20 percent and more in the last three quarters before the October 1973 Yom Kippur surprise, bespeaks a major failure of economic policy. Of course, exogenous factors also played a role. Specifically, the leap in the oil revenues of the Arab members of OPEC and the all-out forward policy of the Soviet Union, which poured state-of-the-art armaments in quantities affordable only to major powers and financed most of the cost of rearming the confrontation states, imposed a heavy burden on the Israeli economy to allow a corresponding buildup of Israel's defense posture. Nevertheless, all inflations are man-made, and this is no less true of the take-off. It was the clear product of a demand-pull effect, and it reflects an attempt to avoid a politically painful reordering of priorities, replete with errors in the estimation of the quantitative impact of their policy and a misunderstanding and misjudgment of the economic momentum of inertial factors (dormant between 1966 and 1969), once these are turned loose as inflation gets going.

In what follows, we show that highly expansionary fiscal and monetary policies pursued throughout that period of about 45 months share the main responsibility for what might perhaps be described as the Yom Kippur fiasco of the Israeli economy. The fiscal and monetary expansion did indeed gain stride several years before that, somewhat before the unexpected political crisis that led to the 1967 war; it was actually initiated in an economic environment of a severe slowdown, involving a 10 percent unemployment rate. The Six Day War and its aftermath, the War of Attrition, inevitably led to further fiscal expansion. The existence of substantial excess capacity and a major increase in import surplus, financed by a leap of contributions by Jewish communities in the diaspora, allowed non-inflationary, rapid growth in the immediate aftermath of the war, in spite of a significant devaluation (late in 1967). Yet, as these high rates of growth should have suggested, with an economy moving toward its capacity ceiling at the end of the 1960s, the expansionary clout of these determinants of aggregate demand should have been reined in. This, however, did not happen.

A reduction in the onslaught of money, mainly due to the loss of reserves, was indeed visible in the two closing quarters of 1969. But this was soon reversed. The characteristic feature of the financial system from mid-1970 onward was rather like a monetary avalanche (Tables 15, 16, and Chapter 2). Fiscal policy, too, was all but oblivious to the fact that the capacity constraint, which indeed may not have been relevant through 1969, was clearly resurfacing by 1970 at the latest. The domestic fiscal figures do show an improvement for 1970, implemented by a major leap of gross taxation. But even this move, which involved a much smaller rise in net taxes, was reversed by 1971.

Yet even in 1970, the only year of relative (insufficient) fiscal restraint, the direct impact of government on resources at the disposal of the economy grew by 11 percent—several percent more than the significant growth rate of the economy in that year. It kept growing at that rate, and at even higher rates through 1973, although the system had clearly been operating beyond its capacity since 1971 at the latest. The 1970 dip in the domestic deficit disappeared in the following year, as a major expansion of social (spending) policy was put into place. The corresponding rise in transfer payments and the leap in (effective) credit subsidies to households and firms, directly linked to the jump of inflation to 10 percent in 1970, meant that the 1970 gain in net fiscal absorption was completely eroded in 1971 (Tables 3, 5, and 6). The Bank of Israel's accommodation of these growing deficits, its policy of pegging the price of government bonds, and its failure to reduce an inflow of hot money all generated explosive increases in monetary aggregates—by about 30 percent in 1971 and in the following years (Tables 15 and 16). The combined effect of these expansionary policies, generating massive increases in aggregate demand, battering against the dam of capacity constraint, found release in the price sluice in the significant inflationary swell of the take-off.

This view of the events, which puts the focus on demand factors as the instigators and main perpetrators of that bout of inflation, is obviously not in line with what was the conventional wisdom of the late 1980s. The dramatic disappearance in the 1970s of the straightforward notion of an inflation–employment trade-off in the wake of the "OPEC one" and "two" price shocks, put cost push on the agenda of macroeconomic theory. Some economists, especially those brought up in the tradition of the Latin American school of political economy and the Prebisch lore of structural inflation, were prone to opt for the extreme position: to identify cost-push and inertial factors operating on the cost dimension as the exclusive determinants of the (almost) perennial inflation in Latin American countries.

It goes without saying that the explicit integration of cost factors and expectations into both dimensions of the standard macroeconomic models of the 1970s and 1980s—the profession's response to the challenge of the collapse of the oversimplified original Phillips Curve notion—offered important new insights into the workings of the macroeconomy and the dynamics of the inflationary process. The study of the events in the Israeli economy accordingly relied on this model, with its two dimensions—aggregate demand (AD) and aggregate supply (AS) (Chapter 1). The notion that the very loose fiscal and monetary policies, pulling aggregate demand, were responsible for the inflation fiasco is thus not due to an a priori rejection of cost and inertial elements as possible initiators and propellants of inflation. My claim that it was the demand dimension that initiated and was the main feeder of the process throughout the take-off is based on a close empirical study of the demand, cost, and inertial factors operating during these 45–48 months. In my opinion, this analysis clearly shows that cost factors were, at most, of minor significance for most of that interval. The same applies to the inertial factors at the first stages of the process, although these gained significance at the very last phase—the "Releasing of the Brakes" phase, preceding the outbreak of the 1973 war.

The presumption that an unwarranted boost to wages, the most famous component of the well-known first "package deal" of January 1970, initiated the inflationary process and fanned it (via COLA adjustments of January 1971 and 1972) has long since made its way into popular perception. It has apparently also crept into the professional literature. Yet once the major increases in productivity in the relevant period are taken into consideration, it is quite clear that nominal wage increases did not overcompensate for productivity gains. The unit-cost data for 1970–72 clearly demonstrate this (see p. 13 and pp. 26–28). The microeconomic evidence of the wage cost per unit of output is supported by the overall indicators of the situation in the labor market; during that whole interval there is not even a whiff of a slowdown in the expansion of employment. In spite of the massive expansion of the labor force due to increased immigration and the inflow of labor from the administered areas, unemployment rates declined over the entire 45–48 months of the take-off, clearly indicating overfull employment from late 1970 onward at the latest. Thus, although the celebrated "pathbreaking" 1970 package deal on wages, profits, and taxes, and particularly its cost-of-living component, had the (unfortunate) appearance of a cost-push device, both the micro- and macroeconomic data show conclusively that a "wage-push" hypothesis as even a minor factor explaining the initiation and acceleration of inflation is widely off the mark.

The impression that the professional literature had identified "wage push" as a factor contributing to the take-off is quite prevalent. This is presumably due to a wrong interpretation of the significance of the analytical framework underlying several studies of the inflationary process over the long run—a stretch of about two decades from the mid-1960s onward. Thus, the Bruno and Fischer (1986) study *The Inflationary Process: Shocks and Accommodation* specifies an

AS function involving the rate of change of real wages as a determinant of inflation, and gives an estimate of the value of its positive coefficient (1986, pp. 348, 351, 357). But these authors never suggest that the 1970–73 take-off (they did not use that term) could be attributed to a wage push. Indeed, the real wage data which they display in their table 17 for the period (p. 355), which they describe as the "Boom of 1971–73," indicates that in this specific interval a wage hike, generating a (unit) cost shock was not on the books. Their discussion of wage indexation (p. 367) suggests that they do not identify wage indexing as a wage-push factor under the Israeli rules of the game.

In his "External Shocks" paper, which covers a slightly different period, and in which Bruno refers to a similar analytical and empirical specification of the AS function (Bruno, 1986, pp. 285, 297), he is even more explicit in effectively rejecting the wage-push hypothesis for the period which is the subject of our study. He says that "real wages were downward flexible in 1967–72" and, in a table representing "Supply and Demand Shifts" for 1965–81, he shows that "product wages" (unit costs) were negative in the two overlapping intervals 1969–72 and 1972–75 (Bruno, 1986, pp. 290–91). Similarly, Kleiman's data (Kleiman, 1986, table 15 and figures 15-3 and 15-4) lead him to an even more far-reaching conclusion, applying to the 1968–82 interval: "It is doubtful whether wage increases of any kind constituted the main cost-push mechanism." These studies, which treated the take-off interval as only one segment in a longer-run vista, thus fully support the rejection of a wage-push proposition as a significant factor initiating inflation from scratch and propelling it to 20 percent and beyond during the take-off interval (see Chapters 2, 3, and 4).

This leaves two other possible cost-push factors: an escalation of world market prices and/or an upward adjustment of the exchange rate—a devaluation. In an economy as open as Israel's, with imports and exports around 50 percent of GDP, the economy had indeed been quite vulnerable to a cost shock administered to its tradables by either one of these events. Yet the price series do not show a significant rise in the dollar cost of imports for two consecutive years through 1971. These costs rose slowly in 1972, yet the inflation rate in that year stayed just beyond the single digit; and in 1973 the rising commodity prices in the world market could have made only a minor contribution to the leap of inflation to 20 percent and beyond (see Table 2, and pp. 13 and 44). A dollar import price shock as a meaningful contributor to inflation was thus not relevant, nor was it mentioned in the literature.

The claim made in this study (see especially pp. 13–14) that the two devaluations of (August) 1970 and 1971 were not relevant to the initiation of the take-off nor to the acceleration of inflation is, prima facie, inconsistent with the Liviatan–Piterman hypothesis: that the Israeli economy displayed an "empirical one-to-one correspondence between BOP crises and sharp accelerations in inflation" (Liviatan and Piterman, 1986, p. 334). Accordingly, the balance-of-payment crisis had forced the government to perform repeated substantial devaluations, subjecting the system to major price shocks, and, in its wake, to the well-known jumps of Israel's inflation rate during the high inflation period of the 1970s and mid-1980s. Whatever the merit of that proposition for the period from the outbreak of the Yom Kippur War onward—this balance-of-payments theory of inflation acceleration is not inconsistent with my findings. From the very first sentence of their paper, Liviatan and Piterman restrict their proposition to "the inflationary process in Israel in 1974–83" (1986, p. 331). For better or for worse, the theory is attributed to a time interval which begins at the end of the take-off period. Thus, whatever its merit, it obviously does not apply to the take-off interval itself.

The exclusion of the very beginning of the great inflation from an attempt to find a "general" strain underlying Israel's great inflation is puzzling. A closer look at the data and timing indicates, however, that the "balance-of-payments crisis" proposition comes to grief when applied to the take-off interval. The strain on the balance of payments, underlined by the loss of international reserves, was already a fact of life early in 1969 (Tables 9 and 10). Yet, when the effective devaluation designed to reduce that strain was implemented in August 1970, the take-off of inflation was already underway. In the first two quarters of 1970, inflation was already running at an annual rate of close to 20 percent in terms of the GDP deflator. Indeed, the impact of the effective devaluation on the GDP deflator is hardly visible in its immediate aftermath; it *does* show up in terms of the consumer price index, whose basket is much more amenable to government fiat.

The theory fares no better on the next occasion, when a 20 percent formal (and effective) devaluation was implemented in August 1971. By that time, annual inflation had already passed the single-digit level, but had not leaped in the wake of that devaluation, which in this case (in contrast to 1970) applied across the board. Through the end of 1972, that is, for about 16 months after the August 1971 devaluation, the inflation rate did not budge. Indeed, in (calendar year) 1972 inflation was slightly less than the 1971 inflation (Table 1). This clearly contradicts the balance-of-payments hypothesis for the take-off. When, early in 1973, inflation finally leaped beyond the 20 percent annual rate, the impact of that devaluation on prices had clearly been spent (pp. 47–48).

This, in summary, disposes of the cost-shock hypothesis as a meaningful explanation of the take-off. There remain, however, the inertial factors. Yet although wages are one of the instruments through which inertial effects are transmitted into the system, they are not the only ones affecting the inflationary process. They directly affect aggregate demand too and, in the Israeli case, once inflation leaped to 10 percent and beyond, they had an immediate impact on real disposable income (and corresponding consumption expenditures) due to the significant capital gains of households and businesses on their non-linked (government) credits. Yet since inflation started from scratch, inertial factors were evidently not relevant, either on the cost or on the demand side, at what we refer to as the "Revving-up Phase," and somewhat beyond, through 1970

and early 1971. Later, particularly in 1973, inertial factors were already contributing to the acceleration of inflation.

The rejection of the cost-push hypothesis as an explanation for the inflationary
process during the entire take-off, and the exclusion of the relevance of inertial
factors to the initiation and early phase of the process, lie in the background to
the proposition made above that highly expansionary monetary and fiscal policies pursued throughout that period share the main responsibility for the leap of
inflation from almost zero to 20 percent and more in 45 months. This reading
of the omens identifies the Ministry of Finance and the central bank as the agents
responsible for the surfacing of an inflationary process whose momentum was
significantly greater than in other industrial countries, and also quite out of line
with Israeli experience since 1954. An error of omission—the refusal to sort
out the priorities—was undoubtedly at the root of the matter.

The demands made by the public sector on resources with which to maintain
a rapidly increasing defense effort, immigration absorption, and to finance a
major expansion of social policy overloaded a fully employed system by 1970–
71. The attempt made in 1970 to reduce the government deficit by raising taxes,
rather than by restraining real demand, was too little, came too late, and was
effectively given up just when the economy was reaching its capacity ceiling.
This premature relaxation of the attempt at restraint might have been partly due
to a misunderstanding: an error in the information at the disposal of the treasury,
in real time, on the actual fiscal situation. Due to an improper estimate of the
very large transfer and subsidy component of the budget, which excluded the
(implicit yet significant) subsidies on non-linked government credits, the treasury
overestimated the size of the fiscal restraint implemented in 1970. Relying on
the data at its disposal reflecting the government's cash flow, it erroneously also
believed that it was pursuing a restrictive policy in 1971 and 1972, when the
opposite was actually the case (Table 4 and pp. 30–32).

The personality of Minister of Finance Sapir, and his strong political standing—by that time 10 years at the economic helm after almost a decade as
Minister of Trade and Industry—dominated the scene in the natural tug-of-war
between the treasury and the Central Bank. Pointing to the monetary avalanche,
the Bank had indeed been remonstrating, both in private and, by means of its
periodic *Report on the Means of Payment,* even in public, but to no avail. The
changing of the guard at the Bank of Israel in the middle of the take-off period—
the outgoing governor ending 17 years in office, and his successor just appointed
by the government upon the recommendation of the Minister of Finance—offers
some explanation of both the poor performance of the Bank in its main mission
(the control of the volume of monetary aggregate) and the failure of its pleading
with the treasury for much more fiscal restraint.

Far more than the personalities involved, this failure reflected the constitu-
tionally weak position of the Bank, as set out in the Bank of Israel Law of
1954. This act provided for direct credit accommodation to the government,
removing any control of its volume by the Bank, even though government credit

was one of its main assets. The power to print base money was instead effectively vested in the Finance Committee of the Knesset.

In those days the committee was, to all intents and purposes, highly responsive (an understatement) to the demands of the treasury. The Law also stipulated that the Bank had to obtain the approval of the Economics Committee of the Cabinet before changing the liquidity ratios of commercial banks; hence, the Bank's control over the money multiplier was severely restricted. These two conditions meant that the Bank was not a master in its own house. Finally, the management of the Bank was entrusted to a governor, appointed for a fixed five-year term, but had no independent board of governors. The remedy for this curious lacuna was, and still is, an advisory committee, whose members are appointed coterminously for two-year terms of office. These (outwardly technical) arrangements had an enormous effect on the modus operandi of the fiscal and monetary sectors of the economy. They meant that the checks-and-balances framework, a mainstay of any democratic system of government, was effectively excluded from a highly sensitive function of "government"—the supply of money. Most features of the weak stance of the central bank in the inevitable power struggle built into a modern fiscal–monetary complex are, unfortunately, still in place to this very day. One significant component, though—the direct access of the treasury to central bank credit—was abolished by a 1985 amendment to the Bank of Israel Law. Yet some of the "banana-republic" features that have surfaced over the years in many facets of Israeli social and political life are unfortunately still evident in the government of the Bank as well: since 1982 the post of chairman of the advisory committee had been part and parcel of political coalition deals and its membership is overloaded with representatives of "special interest" lobbies.

Finally, the title of this part of the book and its main thrust suggest that although inflation accelerated to the three-digit level only toward the end of the 1970s, its first stage during the 45 months at the very beginning of this decade had a significant effect on its future pattern. This is not to say that every twist and turn along the road was preordained by what happened during the take-off. This would evidently amount to a belief in predestination—in a presumption that human and political volition expressed in terms of policy do not count.

On the other hand, the counterfactual proposition that the great inflation would have had the same pattern and timing in the wake of the major cost-push effect of OPEC I and the leap of commodity prices in late 1973 and early 1974, even if the take-off had not occurred, is not tenable. Macroeconomic theory clearly identifies the level of inflation rate in a given period as one of the determinants of the level of inflation in a subsequent period. This holds whether expectations are adaptive, reflecting strong inertial forces, or rational. It evidently made an enormous difference, when oil prices quadrupled and commodity prices rose by 30 percent, at one go, in the closing quarter of 1973, whether an economy was subject to an inflation running at an annual rate over and above 20 percent, or to an inflation at, say, around 5 percent. This is, of course, not merely an abstract illustration. These figures represent Israel's and the industrial countries' inflation rates in 1973, when OPEC I administered a major cost shock to the world economy. This shock accelerated inflation worldwide, and pushed the rate of inflation of the industrial countries from 7.5 percent in 1973 to about 12 percent in 1974 in terms of the GDP deflator (Table 19). In Israel, it pushed inflation by approximately the same rate. But in view of its 20 percent benchmark when subjected to the same shock, Israel's inflation rate immediately moved toward the 40 percent level.

This quantitative difference has, as we know, persuasive qualitative implications. One of the more important of these is its negative effect on the demand function for money, which had proven quite robust, notwithstanding single-digit and even 20 percent annual inflation rates. Yet the 40 percent rates of inflation were the final straw that broke the camel's back, reducing finally and significantly the demand for real balances. At least for that reason, and its implied effect on inertial forces, the high inflation rate toward the end of the take-off had far-reaching implications on the next turn of Israel's inflation wheel.

The available price series, specifically, though not exclusively, suggested the breakdown of the 45–48 months of the take-off of the great inflation into three (inevitably overlapping) periods. Each of the three core chapters of Part I (Chapters 2–4) is devoted to one of these phases of the process. The "Revving-Up Phase"—approximately nine months long—begins sometime at the turn of the decade and ends in the third quarter of 1970, immediately after the effective (though not formal) August 1970 devaluation. The "Lull," covering the next 24–27 months, ends in the fourth quarter of 1972. The third and final nine-month phase, "Releasing the Brakes," saw inflation leaping to an annual rate of 20 percent and beyond, and ends with the outbreak of war.

— 1 —

Backstage

More than two decades of inflation at annual rates of two and three digits have left an indelible mark on Israel's economy and society—on attitudes and expectations and on the modus operandi of the system. The adjective "great" in the title of this study refers not only to duration; it also points to the very high rates at which prices were rising—peaking at an annual average rate of 450 percent in 1984, after spending seven years in the three-digit range. The cumulative impact of these inflation rates, shown in the price curves of Figure 1, is no less significant than the annual rates of change presented in Figure 2. The data on this matter are clear-cut: inflation was indeed "great," even in terms of the chronic inflationary experience of the Israeli (and previously the Palestine) economy from 1940 to the mid-1960s. In only three of these 25 years (1951–53) did inflation rates exceed 20 percent, and these three years were the very period in which the pent-up pressures of tightly suppressed inflation were deflated by a once-and-for-all price "explosion." At that time the substantial rise in prices served both as a policy tool and as a signal heralding the transition from wartime universal price controls and rationing to a much more market-orientated system. Yet even the highest rate of price increase (about 66 percent in 1952) never came close to the three-digit threshold; in 1951 and 1953 the annual rate of price change did not exceed 20 percent (*Abstract 1971,* table 10-2). The same can be said of the 1940s—the World War II inflation during the mandatory period—and of the transition from the economic environment of the mandate to an Israeli economy.

A 20 percent rate of inflation is the "low" range, according to current notions, in which the Israeli economy has been operating since the launching of the 1985 stabilization program which pulled the economy back from the hyperinflation abyss. Before that watershed year, with inflation exceeding 10 percent annually for over two decades (1970–91) and exceeding 40 percent for over one decade (1974–85), the level of inflation—and especially its persistence—had become embedded in the very fiber of the social and political fabric, and hence in the concepts of a generation of economic agents, fashioning their attitudes, shaping their expectations, and affecting their behavior.

THE TAKE-OFF: 1970–73

An inspection of Figures 2 and 3 and Tables 1 and 2 suggests a breakdown of the extended pattern of rising prices into several stages. An obvious criterion for stage differentiation is the rate of inflation. This rate differed considerably over the entire 20-year period. In view of our subject—the take-off stage—it is the (approximate) delimitation of this take-off which we propose to consider here. Figure 3, which shows quarterly rates of change in prices, clearly suggests 1970 as the beginning of the take-off stage. With the 1974 rate of change twice as high as in 1973, these two years definitely belong to different chapters of the inflation story.

The quarterly data in Table 2 offer a closer look at the behavior of prices and allows a more specific identification of the take-off stage. An inspection of the implicit GNP deflator in the first quarter of 1970 shows a much higher rate of change than in any of the four preceding quarters. Though somewhat lower in the second quarter, the rate of change of this index in the second quarter of 1970 is still significantly higher than in any of the last three quarters of 1969, and than the mean rate for that year and for 1968. Similarly, we see much higher rates of change of the wholesale price index in 1970/I and in the last quarter of 1969 than in any preceding quarter. At about 1 percent, the quarterly rate of change in consumer prices in 1970/I is half the rate in 1969/IV, yet both the sign and the jump to a quarterly rate of almost 2 percent of these partly administered consumer prices in the next quarter is entirely consistent with the pattern observed in the other price indices. All of them, whether regarded separately or taken together, clearly identify the revving-up stage of the take-off as spanning the six months from the last quarter of 1969 to the first quarter of 1970.

The quarterly data in Table 2 and Figure 3 also allow a clear-cut identification of the end of the take-off stage in the fourth quarter of 1973. Both the consumer and wholesale price indices jump to quarterly rates of change of 7–8 percent (more than double the figures for the third quarter of 1973). Similarly, the implicit price deflator for 1974/I is 50 percent higher than the quarterly average for 1973. This identification of the end of the take-off stage is supported by exogenous factors. The most significant point in this context is the sudden plunge into a war economy, which totally transformed the economic scene. The war effort, requiring a highly expansionary fiscal policy and, inevitably, monetary accommodation, was superimposed on a system that was already at a very high level of economic activity (with overemployment and rapid inflation) by both domestic and international standards. At the same time, a major exogenous price shock administered by OPEC's first price coup hit late in October 1973 and was largely passed on to increase domestic energy prices. The substantial rise in world commodity prices administered a further price shock in the closing quarter of 1973 and throughout 1974. These exogenous, mainly unexpected factors—the outbreak of the war, its fiscal and monetary implications, and the price shocks in world commodity markets—pushed the economy into the next stage, with the annual inflation rate topping 40 percent.

All this clearly points to the end of the take-off stage of "the great inflation." From beginning to end this stage covers 45–48 months, from the last quarter of 1969 through the last quarter of 1973. It was during these four years that annual inflation rates rose from around 2 percent early in 1969, at first to 10 percent, then to somewhat above this figure for two years, and accelerated to an annual rate of 20 percent in the first three quarters of 1973, preceding the outbreak of the Yom Kippur War.

THE ECONOMIC AND POLITICAL ENVIRONMENT

A two-digit annual inflation rate, even if just past the single-digit threshold, does not materialize out of thin air; it might be set off by one or several endogenous and/or exogenous factors. But even if, say, expansionary demand or cost-shock factors are at work, this need not drive an economy—either all at once or even after a short while—onto an inflationary track. If the economic environment is not conducive to inflationary developments, the effect of demand-pull and cost-push factors could well peter out.

An obvious case in point is the trend of Israeli prices from 1967/II through 1969/III, when prices were rising at annual rates of 2 percent—virtual price stability by international and Israeli standards. During these 24 months, in the immediate aftermath of the Six Day War, fiscal policy was highly expansionary and monetary policy was fully accommodating (Tables 3, 7, 13, and 15). Furthermore, a 17 percent devaluation vis-à-vis the dollar and several European currencies was implemented in November 1967, almost at the very beginning of the period presently under review (Tables 2 and 11). Yet this cost shock, which raised sheqel-denominated import and export prices by about 13–14 percent in 1968 (Table 1) in an environment of rapidly expanding economic activity, hardly affected the general price indices.

A clear indication that these cost-push and demand-pull developments from late 1967 onward did not spark inflation is the complete absence of cost-of-living allowances (COLA) in this interval. Indeed, wages were not adjusted for changes in the cost of living for four years. The reason for these stable prices was the prevailing economic environment in those years—substantial excess capacity and high unemployment rates. After peaking at an annual rate of 10.4 percent in early 1967, unemployment was still only about 6 percent at the end of 1968 and 5 percent in the first quarter of 1969; the utilization rate of manufacturing capacity, though rapidly rising in 1968, was very low indeed.[1]

The economic environment of early 1970 was altogether different. Swiftly rising economic activity, which by that time had already been going on for almost three years, had effectively eliminated the entire unemployment overhang of 1967. With a rapidly increasing labor force, due to substantial immigration and the inflow of workers from the administered territories, an unemployment rate of 3.8 percent in the first half of 1970 (Table 7) gave clear indication of full employment. The manufacturing capacity slack of the mid-1960s was now fully utilized.

The high rates of growth of investment in manufacturing capacity and in farming, at average annual rates of 24 and 13 percent, respectively, in 1968–70, clearly support this reading of the omens.[2] The very high (and rising) level of activity, indicated by new housing starts from mid-1969 onward (Table 7), is a clear sign of the boom conditions into which the economy had been moving in the early months of 1970. The emergence of a seller's market in these years was given a further boost by external factors. The U.S. "Vietnam Inflation" had by that time spilled over into world markets, bringing in its wake a 10 percent rise in commodity prices and pushing inflation in the EEC (and even in Germany) to the two-digit threshold (Table 19). Thus, Israeli dollar-denominated import and export prices moved up 5 percent in 1969, just as the economy was approaching the full-employment ceiling. This could not but affect shekel prices, too (Tables 1 and 2).

But it was not purely economic endogenous and exogenous factors that impacted on the economic environment at the turn of the 1960s. The political situation, too, undoubtedly influenced economic management at the national level. Early in 1970, the War of Attrition along the Suez Canal and skirmishes with the Jordanian army and PLO infiltrators along the Jordan River (the latter had been going on for almost three years) were accelerating dangerously, claiming daily casualties. Unofficial Russian military activity in Egyptian airspace was intensifying. The economic boom, with growth rates of 10 percent or more, was therefore also a highly effective, morale-boosting device.

The partial opening of the emigration gates in the USSR, which accelerated the inflow of immigrants to an annual rate of 30 thousand from 1969 onward, was undoubtedly a major consideration in formulating economic policy. An inflow of that size involved a significant rise in the demand for housing and this, of course, was another factor preventing the government from trimming the sails of the construction sector, which had traditionally led the expansion. The tremendous rise in the defense budget—running at triple the 1966 level in 1970—involved, among other things, the rapid buildup of a major modern defense industry and naturally affected the government budget and aggregate demand in a similar direction.

Fresh memories of the mood that had prevailed during the slowdown preceding the Six Day War, with unemployment at about 10 percent, meant that in the first half of 1970 full employment took absolute priority. With the War of Attrition reaching its peak and cracks forming in the Unity Government's grand coalition on the handling of the war and the relations with the United States, the government was naturally reluctant to implement a restrictive policy. This was so in spite of the fact that by early 1969 the rising deficit in the current account balance of payments was already emitting a clear message on this score. However, in view of the considerations mentioned above, Finance Minister Sapir did not press for a change of course at this stage.

A CONCEPTUAL FRAMEWORK

The "classical" approach to an analysis of inflation focuses on factors affecting the aggregate demand of the private sector (i.e., of households and firms). Expansion fueled by a financial policy that reduces market interest rates and pulls up profit margins (thereby also raising business and household demand) is expected to create a sellers' market. These developments almost inevitably lead to price rises. The counterpart of such a scenario, with its focus on the workings of the non-government sector as the force generating inflation, cites the upswings of the business cycle between the second half of the nineteenth century and World War I. The "private-sector-generated" inflations and deflations were, however, an altogether different phenomenon; they were subject to endogenous correctives in the downswing of the cycle, and moreover, they were an altogether different species of inflation in terms of amplitude, momentum, and duration from the ones experienced after World War II.

These inflations were usually spurred by war, which, among other things, involved highly expansionary fiscal policies and a major shift in the size of the economy's public sector. Even when the effect of the size of the fiscal deficits was reduced in the aftermath of the two world wars, the second feature—the size of government—was hardly reduced. Rising public sector expenditures and the level of absorption by this sector, especially after World War II, were major determinants of aggregate demand and of chronic inflation.

The impact of the fiscal stance on the economy is reflected in the direct effect of the demand of the public sector on aggregate demand for goods and services. Its effect on liquidity has monetary implications, since by virtue of central government monopoly on the issue of high-powered money, deficits might be financed directly (or ultimately) by central bank operations in the money and capital markets. But even after World War II, monetary expansions were not due exclusively to government deficits. They could just as well have resulted from an expansionary monetary policy initiated and run by the central bank, or from its reluctance to sterilize short-term capital inflows and an understandable tendency to sterilize outflows. An analysis of monetary policy and its effects on liquidity and on interest rates is therefore an inseparable part of the approach which identifies inflation as a phenomenon reflecting mainly aggregate demand factors.

The business community, looking at the phenomenon from the viewpoint of enterprises in the real sector of the economy, has always been disposed to identify cost-push factors as fueling inflationary processes. This approach can be found in the literature as early as the controversy on "inflation" in the Napoleonic Wars—Tooke's *History of Prices* is an obvious case in point; the claims made by many professional German economists, who attributed the German post–World War I inflation to exchange-rate effects, is another example of cost-push factors being identified as the prime factor in a process that soon accelerated into hyperinflation. It was only toward the end of the 1960s that conventional macroeconomic theory finally absorbed the cost dimension into its model by incorporating the Phillips Curve notion, with Friedman's (1968, pp. 8–11) crucial distinction between its short-run and long-run characteristics, into the original (exclusively aggregate-demand-oriented) formal structure. The issue is still a controversial one, but there is no doubt that, especially in small economies such as Israel, cost-push shocks originating in the world market could be considered as entirely exogenous factors, initiating and/or accelerating an inflationary process. In our analysis of the take-off of the Israeli inflation we will attempt to identify the relevance of cost-push elements, whether completely exogenous (such as world prices) or partly endogenous (the exchange rate and wages) as determinants of this process.

The impact and workings of inertial forces are nowadays integrated into the conceptual framework applied to the study of inflationary processes. Awareness of the relevance of these forces surfaced during the controversy on the determinants of the German post–World War I inflation. Their significance is evident once inflation becomes a "state of nature" in terms of duration and rate. Although this might, prima facie, exclude the feasibility of their relevance at the take-off stage, the inflationary process that characterized Israel for 25 years might have created a framework allowing inertial forces to come rapidly to the fore in spite of the brief hiatus (1967–69) in which prices were stable. This suggests the application of the standard aggregate demand and aggregate supply model as a conceptual setup that can deal explicitly with the cost-push and inertial factors of the macroeconomic process.

The AD-AS Model in the Israeli Context

In what follows, we apply the standard Aggregate Demand (AD) and Aggregate Supply (AS) model of the 1970s and the 1980s to the analysis of the events in the Israeli economy during the take-off years. This analytical framework focuses on the relations between the price level and the aggregate level of activity—the level of GDP; its derivative dynamic version relates the *rate* of price change (inflation) to the *level* of product.

The analysis integrates the treatment of household consumption expenditures, gross investment, the impact of the current account of the balance of payment, the public sector's fiscal stance, and the workings of the monetary sector, subjected both to the requirements of government finance and to the flow of funds (including transactions on capital account) with the aggregate demand side of the AD–AS model. The impact of labor market factors on the system (affecting wages), of world market prices (affecting the cost of imports) and, finally, of the exchange markets are accordingly treated under the heading of aggregate supply.

These two complex constructs are by now the conventional tools of macro-economic analysis. But since the determinants of at least one of them are still being openly debated among economists, and the environment of each economy is likely to involve a specific twist of the particular features, I propose to summarize and spell out explicitly the features of the aggregate demand (AD) and supply (AS) functions which, in the specific Israeli context, have been applied to the analysis of the three stages of the take-off.

Aggregate Demand. The aggregate demand function derived from the IS/LM set up for an open economy specifies GDP (Y) as an increasing function of fiscal variables (including government expenditures and tax rates), an increasing function of the real exchange rate and of expectations about inflation, and an increasing function of real balances. The latter relation (and the positive relation between the real exchange rate and GDP) implies that Y is a decreasing function of the price level. On a conventional, two-dimensional diagram in which Y and P are measured on the horizontal and vertical axes, respectively, this relation is described as a negatively sloped curve. The slope of that curve depends, among other things, on the combination of coefficients specifying the Keynesian (open economy) multiplier, on the interest-rate coefficients of investment and consumption, on the income and interest-rate coefficients of the demand and supply functions of money, and on the real exchange-rate coefficients of exports and imports. The fiscal variables, the nominal quantity of money and nominal exchange rate, and price expectations determine the location of that curve in the two-dimensional plane. Changes in any one or in a combination of these variables generate a shift of the AD curve.[3]

As this study focuses on inflation, the discussion of the aggregate demand dimension is spelled out mainly by reference to the dynamic aggregate demand function derived from its "parent" which refers to *levels:* the relation of the level of output to the price level (see note 6). In this derived formula, the rate of inflation (π) replaces the price level (P), the rate of change of nominal balances (m) replaces the level of nominal balances (M), and the rate of change of the nominal rate of exchange (ρ) replaces the nominal rate of exchange (R). As in the parent function, however, GDP (Y_t) appears as a *level,* not as a rate of change, as does the GDP of the previous period (Y_{t-1}).

The derived formula shows Y_t (the current period's GDP) as an increasing function of (a) the output in the previous period Y_{t-1}, (b) the fiscal variables and the rate of change of the real rate of exchange, and (c) the rate of change of real balances and expected inflation. The positive sign of the relation between GDP and real balances (and also of GDP and the real rate of exchange) imply a negative relationship between Y_t and π, that is, between output and the rate of inflation.

This relationship is described by a negatively sloped aggregate demand curve in which the level of output Y is measured along the horizontal axis, and the rate of inflation ρ along the vertical axis. The slope of that curve and its location is determined by the same set of coefficients as in the parent equation—by the fiscal variables and expected inflation. The difference between the "derived" and the "parent" relation relates to money and the exchanges: it is the rate of change of the nominal quantity of money and the rate of change of the nominal exchange rates, rather than their *levels*, which here determine the location of the dynamic variant of the aggregate demand curve. Inflation is accordingly an increasing function of m and ρ, the rates of change of nominal money and nominal rate of exchange, respectively; an increasing function of the fiscal variables and of price expectations, an increasing function of previous period output, Y_{t-1}, and a decreasing function of current out Y_t.[4]

The fundamental structure and form of the aggregate demand function, described above, is not an issue among economists. It reflects the current orthodoxy on the demand dimension of macroeconomic theory. Specific to the Israel case in the early 1970s are two empirical features: the comparatively large size of the foreign trade sector in terms of GDP, and the dominance of the public sector in the market for goods and services. The first feature implies that changes in the trade account have a considerable effect on aggregate demand; hence, the impact of a change in the terms of trade, or a devaluation, on the resources at the disposal of the economy is highly significant. This means that the impact multiplier of the economy, a major determinant of φ in equation 1 and therefore of ϕ in equation 2, is smaller than in more closed economies, which acts as a depressant of demand and inflation. But the very characteristic which reduces the size of the impact multiplier—the small size of the economy—also implies high foreign price elasticities of demand for exports and high foreign supply elasticities of imports. These features are expressed by the value of φ in equation 2, and thus imply a strong impact on inflation of a depreciation of the domestic currency or a change in the level of world market prices. The significance of the dominant role of government in the goods and services markets, and, inevitably, in financial market, implies that even small changes in its fiscal stance translate into meaningful changes in aggregate demand.

Aggregate Supply. The conceptual underpinnings of the aggregate supply (AS) function are the subject of controversy among economists. The early notions of this formal construct were derived from an underlying empirical generalization (the Phillips Curve), a trade-off between unemployment and inflation, which became the hallmark of macroeconomics in the late 1950s and the 1960s—the so-called Neoclassical Synthesis. Supplemented by a (constant return) production function and a wage-cost markup, this synthesis implied a positively sloped aggregate supply curve, linking higher output with a higher price level. Following the Phelps-Friedman critique, the recent version of the aggregate supply (AS) function model—the "Expectations-Augmented Phillips Curve"—incorporates expectations as an inherent component of that formal construct. This generalized version indicates, however, that the inflation–employment trade-off, which had left a major imprint on the politics of industrial countries in the 1950s, 1960s, and 1970s, is only a short-run feature. In the longer run, as the labor market adjusts to the new price setup, there is no trade-off. The expectations-augmented Phillips Curve hypothesis yields a (long-run) vertical AS curve, whose location depends on the "natural rate" of unemployment, which identifies full employment in the specific socioeconomic context of each economy (Friedman, 1968, p. 11).

The basis for the reconstructed AS model, involving a positive slope of the short-run AS curve similar in shape to the original version, is the underlying assumption about (substantial) lags in the adjustment of wages to the level warranted by labor market conditions, and a lag in the adjustment of prices. These lags are due to wage contracts which set rates for specified intervals, and the staggering of these contracts between industries and even between firms in the same industry. Furthermore, price adjustments in the wake of changes in underlying costs, including wage costs, are also lagged. These lags reflect the cost of frequent price changes (itself a labor-intensive activity) and may also involve considerations related to the loss of sales to competition.[5]

The aggregate supply function derived from the premises spelled out above, similar to the aggregate demand curve, has two versions. The first specifies the price level (P) as the independent variable. The second variant, derived directly from the first, uses the rate of change of prices (π), inflation, rather than the price level. According to the parent function derived from the basic premises (Phillips Curve, production function and markup), the current price level is positively related to prices in the previous period and to the difference between current and full employment output.[6] The function involves a coefficient from the production function, and the markup coefficient for wages and other inputs. The positive slope of the AS curve in the two-dimensional diagram, in which output is measured on the horizontal and the price level on the vertical axis, reflects, however, only the short run, before full adjustment to the new labor market conditions. In the long run, reflecting wage adjustments due to labor market conditions, the short-run AS curve moves continuously up and to the left (if labor market conditions generate an upward move of nominal wages), tracing out a classical, vertical AS aggregate supply curve, which shows no employment–price level trade off.

When the basic Phillips Curve notion is spelled out in terms of rates of change, the dynamic version of the AS curve follows in straightforward fashion from the parent *level* formulation. It implies that the rate of change of prices (π)—inflation—is an increasing function of the difference between current and full employment output, and of expected inflation (π^e). The function involves the same coefficient as that of the parent price level equation. The AS curve with respect to inflation (π) can thus be drawn as a positively sloped curve in which inflation, π, is measured along the vertical and Y along the horizontal axis. This holds for the short run, in which an excess of current over full em-

ployment output is feasible. The long-run curve in which current and full employment output are equal is expressed in terms of the classical vertical curve
as full employment output.[7]

The expected-inflation component (π^e) in the dynamic version of the AS function allows the specification of alternative hypotheses on how expectations are
formed. The original adaptive-expectations hypothesis and the presumption that
the labor market (and other markets) do not clear over long time intervals imply
a comparatively small positive slope of the short-run AS curves. Over time, as
wages and prices adjust, the short-run AS curve moves slowly upward and to
the left, evolving into the long-run vertical curve. This view of the formation
of expectations (and hence the view of the labor market) has been challenged
by the new classical macroeconomics. The rational-expectations hypothesis,
which refers to expectations formulation and also assumes that markets, including the labor market, clear quite rapidly, undermines the Phillips Curve notion
underlying the AS function, especially the implication that short-run, positively
sloped AS courses are highly elastic, and the assumed drawn-out interval during
which, according to the lag and slow clearing of markets hypothesis, these
curves shift upward.

However, the market-clearing–rational-expectations approach (see Lucas,
1973) does not reject the proposition that the short-run AS curve has a positive
slope. Neither is it inconsistent with the notion of the direction of its adjustment
and approach to the long-run (vertical) configuration. The underlying hypothesis
that generated the Lucas AS curve focuses on imperfect information, or more
specifically, on the asymmetry of the information available to firms and workers
(which balances out over time). The output that firms are willing to supply is
therefore an increasing function of the ratio of the current to the expected price
level.[8] The error in prediction which, according to the Lucas hypothesis, led to
the temporary rise in output in the first place, is, however, soon corrected. The
rational-expectation hypothesis implies that workers react rapidly to the decline
in real wages (which allowed the expansion of output in the first place). Combined with the rapid market-clearance hypothesis, this means that real wages are
soon adjusted upward to reflect market reality, and the economy moves back
into the full employment configuration represented by the classical supply curve.

At this stage the choice between these two theoretical explanations of the AS
curve is an empirical matter. Factors onto which these two approaches are
pegged have undoubtedly been relevant in one or another extreme case, and in
different periods in the same economy. The argument presented below leans
more heavily toward the ''adaptive expectations,'' comparatively sticky wages,
and prices approach implied by the expectations-augmented Phillips Curve version than to its ''rational-expectations–market-clearing'' alternative. This choice
reflects my reading of the empirical evidence describing the events in the Israeli
economy during the period under review here, 1967–73, with focus on the last
four years of this interval.

The quarterly wage and price series (Tables 1 and 12) clearly indicated two years or so (1967–69) in which the labor supply curve and the corresponding AS curve (identified in terms of GDP and price data; Tables 1 and 9) were quite flat. This is evidently consistent with the Phillips Curve notion of an interval in which the economy does not operate at or near its full capacity output. The Phillips Curve implications of a significant lag in wage and price adjustments, as the system moves to and beyond its full employment output constraint, is further amplified by the wage price, employment, and output data for 1970–72, when the Israeli economy was clearly operating at top capacity (which, indeed, had been rapidly increasing).

The slow rise of real wages (Tables 9, 11, and 12) in this full employment period is fully in line with the Phillips Curve model assuming staggered and lagged contract-controlled wage adjustments. This reading of the omens receives further support from data on the inflation rate (Table 1): inflation had been marking time for about two years, at just beyond the single-digit level. In a standard two-dimensional diagram, with the inflation rate on the vertical axis, this shows up as a rather flat curve relating the rapidly growing levels of income in these years to a fairly stable inflation rate.

The move into the range in which the supply curve approaches a vertical configuration occurred in the last phase of the take-off—the first three quarters of 1973—when the economy had already been operating beyond its capacity constraints for more than a year. This lagged adjustment to the realities of the labor and goods market clearly reflects the adaptive-expectations–contract-controlled version of the AS model.

Finally, the wage-setting procedures in the highly unionized Israeli labor market and the institutional setup, which involves the government employers and the Histradrut in wage bargaining, leading to two-year contracts (with some lagged partial COL adjustments), supports the Phillips Curve version of the workings of the labor market. Furthermore, the influence of the public sector as the major employer in the labor market, the institutional price-setting powers of government affecting a substantial fraction of the consumer basket (25–30 percent in this period), and the prices of several major inputs (energy, animal feed, cement), suggest that the market-clearing presumption underlying the Lucas version of the aggregate supply model is inconsistent with what transpired in the Israeli economy in that period. Note also that the expectations-augmented Phillips Curve version of the aggregate supply model offers a better version of the impact of exogenous factors, such as a cost shock due to a deterioration in the terms of trade. Furthermore, the adaptive-expectations hypothesis, which clearly reflects the Israeli technique of COL adjustment used in that period, offers a better indication of the effect of inertial factors. These were indeed dormant initially, but became more and more relevant over time.

In what follows, the AD–AS formulation of the multidimensional macroeconomic model, with the latter in its (adaptive) expectations-augmented Phillips Curve version, serves as the scaffolding of our study of the dynamics of the take-off.

NOTES

1. The very high negative rate of growth of capital per employee in manufacturing (−11.5 percent in 1968, with capital stock increasing at 8.0 percent while employment was growing by almost 15 percent) suggests substantial excess capacity in this branch. The 1967 figures for the rate of change of capital stock per employee and of employment support this reading of the 1968 data. The data for the construction industry suggest even higher excess capacity. See *Report 1970*, table V-10, p. 95, and table XII-2, p. 215.

2. *Report 1973*, table V-4, p. 136. This is supported by the capital stock data for these two branches, *Report 1973*, table V-15, p. 149.

3. In terms of the notation and the specific functions used in Dornbusch and Fischer (1990), adapted here to an *open* system, the aggregate demand function, AD, can be written as:

$$\text{AD: } Y = \gamma \left[A + (V_x - V_n)\frac{R}{P} + \frac{b}{h}\frac{M}{P} + b\pi^e \right] \text{ where } \gamma = \frac{\alpha h}{h + \alpha b k}. \tag{1}$$

α is the Keynesian multiplier involving the propensity to consume, invest, import, and tax rate; b and h are interest-rate coefficients of the investment and money demand function respectively, and k is the income coefficient in the latter function. A represents the combination of fiscal variables, R is the nominal exchange rate, P, the price level, M the nominal quantity of money; π^e expected inflation, V_x and V_n are the export and import real exchange-rate coefficients, respectively.

4. In terms of the Dornbusch-Fischer notation, the dynamic aggregate demand function can be written as:

$$\pi_t = \frac{1}{\phi + \varphi} \left[\phi m + \varphi\rho - (y_t - y_{t-1}) + \gamma f + \eta \, \Delta\pi^e\right] + \sigma f, \tag{2}$$

where m and ρ are the rates of change of nominal balances and of the nominal rate of exchange; ϕ is a combination of γ, b and h of equation (1), and the predetermined initial level of real balances; η is a combination of γ and b; φ—a combination of γ, the export supply and the import demand coefficients of the real exchange rate and of the predetermined previous rate of exchange, σ is the ratio of γ and the sum of ϕ and φ, and f is ΔA—the current period change in the combination of fiscal variables. These coefficients thus represent the same factors as in the parent equation (1) in note 3 above. A similar formulation, which, however, refers to a closed economy and therefore excludes trade coefficients and the exchange rate, thus allowing for a simpler expression, appears in Dornbusch and Fischer (1990), p. 540.

5. The latter consideration is one factor contributing to the significant price dispersion of quite identical items between retail outlets; see Lach and Tsidon (1992), pp. 349–89. These authors use Israeli price data to spell out the properties of this relationship.

6. In Dornbusch-Fischer notation, the AS function for the price level is:

$$P_t = P_{t-1}[1 + \lambda(Y_t - Y^*)], \tag{3}$$

where Y^* is full-employment output, reflecting labor productivity, and λ is a combination of Y^* and the speed of adjustment coefficient of the original Phillips Curve generalization. It is thus, in practice, a combination of the speed-of-adjustment coefficient and of labor productivity (Dornbusch and Fischer, 1990, p. 490).

7. The dynamic aggregate supply function (AS) is $\pi = \pi^e + \lambda(Y_t - y^*)$, where π^e is expected inflation (see Dornbusch and Fischer, 1990, p. 515).

8. In terms of the Dornbusch-Fischer notation (1990, p. 248), the Lucas supply curve is specified as $y = \phi (P/P^e)$, where P^e is the expected price level.

___ 2 ___

The Revving-Up Phase

The study of the 45–48 months of the take-off period is significantly facilitated by breaking this interval down into several phases. The first of these phases, which we will call the "revving-up" phase, starts, by definition, with the take-off itself. The evidence of the three major domestic price indicators—the GDP deflator, the consumer price index (CPI), and the wholesale price index (WPI) of manufactured goods—is conclusive. Though somewhat different in their exact timing, these three upward leaps to annual rates of 6–7 percent in the two quarters which cover the end of 1969 and the beginning of 1970 can be identified as the months in which the great inflation began to rev up.

This phase came to an end in the third quarter of 1970; in the following quarter prices took another leap. With an annual rate of increase of about 20 percent in the cost of living and the implicit GDP deflator, and close to 25 percent for wholesale prices in the fourth quarter of 1970, inflation had quite definitely moved into the two-digit stage. A 20 percent import surtax and a corresponding rise in the rate of the export subsidy, both imposed late in August 1970 as substitutes for devaluation, were the apparent causes of this upward turn of the price spiral. As such, they serve as a qualitative indicator of the end of the revving-up stage toward the end of 1970/III.

THE INSIGNIFICANCE OF INERTIAL FACTORS

Inertial forces did not seem relevant in the revving-up stage. With inflation effectively dormant for over three years (since 1966), price expectations were not geared to a rapidly rising pattern. Economic agents on either side of the market were therefore not inclined to adjust demand and supply prices upward in the course of 1968 and part of 1969 in response to a non-existent rising price pattern.

Lingering structural price linkages might, of course, have provided the "lubricant" required to help turn even an accidental push along the slippery price path into a substantial move up on the ladder of inflation. The financial system did, indeed, have a built-in inertial feature that could affect the supply of money: the foreign exchange linkage of a specific and restricted type of deposit owned by recipients of German personal restitution payments (known as NATAD accounts). The potential impact of these deposits on the liquidity of the system and thus on the supply of money could, however, only be triggered by a formal devaluation of the Israeli currency. Such a devaluation was made in November 1967, but its expansionary monetary effect was spent long before the end of 1969 (without affecting prices). The decline of the NATAD rate in 1970 indicates that the exchange-rate mechanism related to these accounts had only a slight negative impact on the supply of money during the revving-up stage.[1] Furthermore, although the ratio of exchange-rate-linked deposits to money (M_1) was relatively high, "restitution deposits" were not only formally but also effectively long-term deposits in those days.[2] Thus, although the devaluation generated a wealth effect, its immediate impact on liquidity was not at all in proportion to the volume of these deposits. The two devaluations of the 1960s—in 1962 and 1967—showed that the expansionary effect of this potential source of liquidity was far smaller than expected. The stability of the formal exchange rate from November 1967 through July 1971 means that no inertial forces were exerted, either on the monetary dimension of the economy or on aggregate demand during the recovery stage.

Such inertial forces did, however, surface in the labor market, that is, on the cost side of the system. The revival of the mechanism linking wages to the CPI in January 1970 should be understood in these terms. The 4 percent cost-of-living allowance (COLA) paid at that time (in January), after four years in which the wage-price linkage had effectively (though never formally) been held in abeyance, could hardly be considered as a cost-raising move. It was part of an overall tripartite wage-price-tax package deal negotiated by the Histadrut (the federation of labor unions), the employers' associations, and the government. This package deal involved a 3.2 percent rise in real wages in 1970. The direct cost-push implications of this agreement require reference to labor productivity, too. Since productivity gains in 1968–69 clearly warranted that rise in real wages (see below) this wage hike could hardly have had a cost-push effect.

Although reference to similar real-wage increases in 1968 and 1969 could support the argument that the first package deal of 1970 could not awaken the dormant inertial (wage) cost-push mechanism, the mere reappearance of the COLA as a component of the wage contract may have created a different impression by contributing to the revival of "traditional" price expectations. If impressions do count, the fact that a component of the wage hike was presented as a COLA move—although, in fact, it was warranted by rising productivity—

may have been a public relations error. As such, it could have had a significant albeit latent inertial cost effect, given the circumstances prevailing in the first two quarters of 1970.

COST PUSH?

Wages

A general rise in wages, whether imposed by the clout of the unions or engineered by political considerations in a public-sector-dominated economy such as Israel's, offers a clear case of wage push. However, with the general elections out of the way by October 1969 (the composition of the Knesset remained basically unchanged), the January 1970 package deal could not have been substantially influenced by short-run politics, nor can it be described as a cost-push factor imposed by union power. Wage and productivity data for the period support this reading of the events. At about 2.5 percent, the post–package deal real wage rise in 1970 was not significantly higher than the average annual rise in 1968 and 1969 (about 2 percent), although labor cost per employee rose more than that (Kleiman, 1986, table 15-1, p. 309).

Approximations can be made only for the business sector, but the comparative patterns of wages and productivity in this sector are of even greater significance for a judgment on this matter. A comparison of wage and productivity data for 1968 and 1969 suggests a substantial lag of wages behind productivity gains: product per man-hour rose about 13 percent in these two years, and product per employed person rose even more than that. Nominal wages rose too, by 8.6 percent, but labor costs per unit of product were more than 11 percent lower than in 1967 when unemployment levels were high. Indeed, they were almost all the way back to the 1965 level (Tables 11 and 12).

The cumulative lag of wages behind (average) labor productivity was smaller in the longer run, 1966–70. The series of labor costs per unit of product (Table 11) suggest the existence of a reserve of productivity gains in 1970, which could warrant a wage increase of the size implemented in 1970, while leaving unit costs lower than in 1966. Table 11 shows that in 1970 the rise in nominal wages did outrun average labor productivity gains by about 7 percent, but, with an accumulated gain of about 14 percent of productivity over nominal wages, the system had ample reserves with which to absorb the 1970 wage hike, by squeezing profit margins, without necessarily pushing up prices. The significantly lower rate of change of factor productivity in the business sector (Table 11, column 8) suggests that profit margins were indeed somewhat squeezed in this year. The reason is obvious—they had to absorb the lagged wage adjustment. A rate of return estimate for the business sector, the mean for 1967–72, supports this reading of the state of affairs (Bruno, 1986, table 14-2, p. 284).

All this means that the 1970 package deal, which did raise wages and other labor costs, did not have a meaningful cost-push effect. The rapid productivity rises of 1967–69, and even the lower gains of 8.1 percent in average labor productivity and 5.6 percent in total factor productivity in 1970 (Table 11), signified a steep rise in the demand price for labor.[3] This suggests that market forces were pulling real wages up without necessarily driving up unit costs. But the *image* of the package deal, with the COLA a highly publicized component of the wage settlement, made a different impression.

Import Prices

Consider now the other main candidates for the role of an exogenous or endogenous cost-push factor: foreign-currency-denominated import prices and the effective exchange rate. The Vietnam War inflation, peaking toward the end of the 1960s, was pushing prices upward all over the industrialized world. Germany's annual inflation rate, in terms of its GDP deflator, rose to 9 percent in 1970, after having been fairly stable in 1967 and 1968 (Table 19). An inspection of the commodity and petroleum price series, the most relevant proxies for Israel's import costs, shows that the former rose 3 percent between 1969 and 1970, and then declined to the 1969 level in 1971, while the cost of crude petroleum in 1970 was the lowest in a decade.[4]

The import price series in Table 1 shows a 1 percent rise in dollar import prices in 1970 and a 4.5 percent increase in the sheqel prices of imports, which are more relevant in this context. Table 2, which presents quarterly data, clearly identifies the time when sheqel import prices jumped upward—the third quarter (actually, September) of 1970, in the wake of the 20 percent import surcharge imposed late in August of that year. This, however, goes beyond the revving-up phase, which is the subject of the present discussion. In the first two quarters of 1970, sheqel import prices were stable. Indeed, the quarterly data in Table 2 clearly show that 1969 sheqel (and dollar) import prices rose 1.9 percent in each of the two last quarters of that year, and declined in the two first quarters of 1970.[5]

The cumulative change in import prices in the course of these two years (1968–69)—about 20 percent—offers prima facie evidence in support of the cost-push explanation of the revving-up period. However, the suggested effect of previous import price rises, going all the way back to the November 1967 devaluation, assumes a substantial lag between the impact of rising import prices and rising domestic prices. This presumed lag and the strength of the impact of import prices on domestic prices has been tested by means of a single-equation regression model. The model (not constrained by an aggregate demand equation) implicitly assumes accommodation, and is estimated on the basis of the quarterly import price and domestic price data. Domestic prices—the CPI and, alternatively, the GDP deflator—were regressed on a proxy for import prices allowing for various time lags. The estimates for price lags of more than one quarter had small and statistically insignificant coefficients. Yet both the rate of change of the GDP deflator and the CPI exhibit a highly statistically significant relation with both current import prices and import prices lagged by one quarter. This implies domestic-price/import-price elasticities ranging from 0.76 to 0.64 for the more comprehensive basket represented by the GDP deflator.[6]

These estimates suggest that the price level during the revving-up period and through the first half of 1970 was subject to the cost-push effect of import prices from, say, the fourth quarter of 1969 at the earliest. With sheqel import prices rising at a quarterly rate of about 2 percent in the last quarter of 1969 and then declining (though more slowly) in 1970/I and 1970/II (Table 2), and with elasticity coefficients smaller than unity, the cost-push effect of import prices in the first two quarters of 1970 was, at most, 1 percent in the last quarter of 1969, at which time the stable price environment turned into one of substantial inflation. However, in the first two quarters of 1970, inflation was already running at average quarterly rates of 4.5 percent (equivalent to 19 percent annually) in terms of the GDP deflator and at about 1.5 percent in terms of the (partly administered) CPI (Table 2). This clearly suggests that the contribution of import prices to the inflationary process during the revving-up period was minor, or even negligible.

With wages accounting for some 50–60 percent of cost for the business sector as a whole, the post–package deal rise in labor costs over and above the rise in productivity in 1970 could generate at most a quarterly cost-push effect of, say, 0.6–0.7 percent on total business sector supply prices, assuming no squeeze on profit margins. Adding the negligible import-price cost push (a fraction of 1 percent), the cost-push hypothesis contributes very little, if anything, to an explanation of the emergence of a very substantial inflationary process in the first three quarters of 1970, when inflation was already running at two-digit rates in terms of the GDP deflator (the CPI implied annual rate through July 1970 was close to 6 percent).

THE IMPACT OF HOUSEHOLD AND BUSINESS DEMAND

Private Consumption and Booming Investment Demand

The rapid expansion of the aggregates, with average annual GNP growth rates exceeding 10 percent in the three years ending in 1970 and disposable income rising at annual rates above 8 percent, suggest strong and sustained aggregate demand for private consumption and investment (Table 7). The rates of increase of the aggregate's components were not similar over time. Real disposable income per capita (from all sources) grew at an annual average rate of 7 percent in 1967–69 and consumption expenditures were a robust component of the rising pattern of aggregate demand.[7] Thus, private consumption was at an all-time high in 1970, sustaining the level of activity. The growth rate of real disposable per capita income from all sources declined to only 3 percent in 1970, but its level, which by that time was more than 25 percent higher than the peak reached in 1965, still supported a 3 percent increase in total private consumption expenditure at this juncture, and the economy was already operating at full employment (Table 7). Though lower than the 10 percent (and more) growth rate in the two previous years, the lower growth rate of the main component of aggregate demand thus did not sufficiently reduce the pressure on capacity at this critical stage.

Investment demand was still booming in 1970, increasing annually at about 13 percent. The growth rate of investment in the production sector did decline significantly, but the housing sector was expanding rapidly. The acceleration of investment in this sector in 1970 is underlined by the quarterly entries for new housing starts in Table 8. Toward the end of the revving-up period (the second and third quarters of 1970), public housing starts were more than 40 percent higher than the already very high level of 1969. A similar upward trend can be seen in the private housing sector (Table 7).[8] The strong expansion of activity in the housing sector reflected an all-out government effort to cope with the tide of immigration and was encouraged by the very low real cost of investment funds for both business investment and housing (Table 13).

Exports

Finally, the rising Vietnam War inflation sellers' market at the end of the decade sustained strong demand for Israeli exports.[9] These rose by about 8 percent in 1970, a higher rate of increase than that of GNP for the same year, although the relative price pattern was not conducive to exports before the August 1970 increase in export subsidies. Thus, the three components of demand that were geared to the decisions of individual agents—households, business, and foreign consumers—were expanding rapidly during the revving-up period and pushing the system vigorously toward the limits of its capacity.

THE STANCE OF THE PUBLIC SECTOR

The stance of the public sector had more than the usual significance for the forthcoming events. It was the size of government and its claims on resources that put it into this strategic position in the first place. These claims rose from 24.5 percent of a depressed 1966 GNP to almost 29 percent of a GNP that was higher by more than 30 percent in 1969, a proportion that was considered economically "reasonable" at the time. This strategy can be visualized as pump priming; it was fully warranted in the wake of the 1965–67 slowdown and was designed to drive economic activity to its ceiling of capacity. But at close to 29 percent of a booming GNP in 1969, and with an economy already operating very close to full capacity, it was hardly reasonable to push for any further increase in real government domestic demand. In any case, an 11 percent increase in real government expenditure at this time, which brought its claims on resources close to 30 percent of GNP, was preposterous in the prevailing macroeconomic circumstances.[10] At this specific juncture, though, things might have looked different from the perspective of defense and foreign policy requirements.[11]

This does not imply that government pushed ahead with this increase in expenditure on goods and services without any reference to macroeconomic constraints. Table 3 also shows a major increase in taxation: the gross public sector tax bill rose from 33 percent of GNP in 1969 to 40 percent in 1970, and the *net* tax ratio—macroeconomically more relevant—rose by almost 4 percentage points in 1970. This attempt at fiscal rectitude involved a substantial rise in direct taxation; it was reinforced by a compulsory saving scheme imposed on businesses and households as part of the January 1970 package deal. Indeed, despite the massive increase in defense imports (by 4 percentage points, to 11.8 percent of GNP), these measures contained the total budget deficit within a one percentage point increase, to 15.7 percent of GNP, and reduced the more significant factor in this context—domestic excess demand—from 6.6 percent to 3.9 percent.

The difference between these two measures of the deficit is equal to the value of net defense imports (both in terms of GDP) and represents the direct pressure exerted by the public sector on the current account of the balance of payments. The domestic excess demand figure is an underestimate of the pressure brought to bear by the government on the flow of resources at the disposal of the economy. Its obverse, the gap in the government's domestic cash flow, represents the size of the potential monetary impact of the government deficit. Resorting to the capital market could, indeed, reduce the immediate (though not the long-run) monetary effect of a domestic deficit. Similarly, foreign aid could offset either the potential (negative) monetary effect of a loss of reserves and/or an increase in the foreign debt.

Foreign aid, United Jewish Appeal funds, and the net inflow of funds from the Bonds Drive—over 12 percent of GNP in 1970—were somewhat higher than the value of defense imports: 11.8 percent of GNP in 1970, a year in which defense imports rose sharply.[12] This suggests that the potential negative monetary effect of government expenditures abroad was effectively neutralized by the inflow of these funds. However, since a sizable fraction of these funds (U.S. government aid and funds from the Israel Bonds Drive) were long-term credits rather than grants, their direct effect on foreign indebtedness, hence on the long-run stability of the balance of payments, was obviously far from neutral.

The direct, short-run balance-of-payments effect of the tremendous total budget deficit (almost 16 percent of GNP, after having been only 7 percent in 1966; see Table 3) was indeed neutralized during the revving-up phase, through August 1970. This, however, could hardly be maintained with respect to the domestic excess demand, which was running at about 4 percent of GNP for the whole year, and undoubtedly at a higher rate in the year's first three quarters.[13]

The political community considered the reduction of domestic excess demand from 6.6 percent of GNP in 1969 to 3.9 percent in 1970 a master stroke. Such a claim, though probably reasonable in terms of immediate political feasibility, was hardly warranted in the prevailing macroeconomic environment. It was one thing to run an 8.8 percent of GNP (domestic) budget deficit in 1968, and even a 6.6 percent deficit in 1969, when unemployment rates were about 5–6 percent and an untapped reserve labor supply was available from the West Bank and Gaza (Tables 3, 4). It was another thing to maintain a domestic budget deficit of even 4 percent of GNP in the full employment environment of late 1969, while moving rapidly into overemployment in the beginning of 1970 (Table 7). The forces emanating from this expansionary fiscal policy inevitably had a direct bearing on the booming markets for commodities, for production factors, and for imports. The financial counterpart of excess domestic demand simultaneously generated expansionary forces in the money and capital markets (see below).

It was not only the direct fiscal impact on markets that pushed for expansion in an overheated economy. Government policy in the capital market, where it played a dominant role both as an agent acquiring funds and as a source of medium- and long-term credit, was highly conducive to expansion. Its monopoly, imposed by fiat on the flow of contractual savings and supported by discriminating tax concessions favoring government bonds in the capital market, put most private savings at the disposal of the treasury. These funds were used to finance investment in manufacturing, agriculture, and housing. With nominal debitory interest rates (set during the 1965–67 slowdown) ranging between 6 and 9 percent, the implied real rates still averaged 4–5 percent in 1969 at a time when prices were rising at 2–3 percent annually.[14] With (GDP) prices rising at double-digit annual rates in the second quarter of 1970 (Table 2), such an interest rate on medium- and long-term housing and development credits implied at most zero (and in some cases even negative) real rates of interest. The 1 percent negative real interest rate for "development" credit in 1970 (Table 13) clearly shows that the investment boom of 1970 (Tables 7 and 8) was undoubtedly the product, by commission or omission, of government policy. The government did indeed make an effort to reduce private consumption expenditures by means of taxation, but at the same time it offered increasingly attractive incentives for investment by sticking adamantly to a policy of stable nominal interest rates on "development" and "housing" credits that were subject to its direct or indirect control.[15]

Fiscal measures did, indeed, restrain disposable income toward the end of the revving-up phase, but this attempt to restrain private consumption was not supported by a reduction in public sector demand for goods and services. True, the overall fiscal stance was, as noted, less expansionary than in 1967–69, but it was not neutral; it grew by 10 percent in 1970 (Table 7)—still expansionary, even in terms of its ratio to GNP. Simultaneously, and in part by omission (given the explicit and implicit investment subsidies), fiscal policy was fuelling private sector demand, even though the economy was already running at full throttle by that time.

THE ROLE OF MONEY AND MONETARY POLICY

Monetary Developments

Monetary developments were, of course, highly relevant as inflation was phas-
ing in at the end of 1969; the money series (Table 16) for the entire take-off
period and for the revving-up phase, through August 1970, suggests that this
was apparently the case. But quantitative data alone are an inadequate gauge of
the stance of money and financial markets, since they do not properly represent
the impact of the demand dimension of the market. As rising economic activity
requires more liquidity at a given price level, the rapidly rising GNP (by almost
30 percent in the three years ending in 1969) could absorb a substantial increase
in liquidity without generating significant upward pressure on prices. Likewise,
the corresponding upsurge in financial activity, as indicated both by a leap of
almost 2.5 times in the volume of business in the stock exchange and by a 25
percent rise in share prices, required more liquidity—hence it increased the
demand for real balances.[16]

M_1 grew by 45 percent in 1967 and 1968, but prices, which were simultaneously hit by a cost shock in the wake of the November 1967 devaluation,
hardly budged until the third quarter of 1969. The growth of M_1 in 1969 was
small, its 13 percent or so growth rate in 1970 (Table 15) still meant an average
annual rate which was not greater than the corresponding growth in GDP for
the two years. The take-off of prices in 1970 could thus reflect a decline in the
demand for money, say, an expectations-induced reduction in the demand for
real balances as income levels were still rising at about 9 percent annually.

The velocity data presented in Table 13 offer a rough test of the above hypothesis. The entries in column (3) indeed show an 8 percent jump in bank
deposit velocity in 1970. The implied income velocity data—the reciprocal of
the M_1 and M_2 ratios to GNP series, presented in columns (1) and (2)—exhibit
a similar rise.[17] The 1965 and 1966 velocity data—both deposits and the corresponding income velocities—indicate that the 1970 rise in the bank deposits
and M_1 velocities merely brought them back to their levels during the previous
peak of economic activity in 1965. The fact that a 10 percent movement in
velocities could indicate stability in the demand for money is underlined by
reference to subsequent entries in these series. Bank deposit velocity in 1977
(about 39) was twice as high as the corresponding figure in 1969–70, and the
income velocity of M_1 (8.2) was 40 percent higher. By 1980 the corresponding
figures were 104 and 22 for bank deposit velocity and M_1 income velocity,
respectively.[18]

The judgment that demand for money was more or less stable during the
revving-up interval—indeed during the whole take-off period, 1970–73—as
suggested by the velocity data, is upheld by a series of more sophisticated attempts to derive a demand function for money for the Israeli economy. Four

empirical studies on demand for money, by the Bank of Israel's Research Department, conclude that a structural change, a steep decrease in demand for money, occurred after the October 1977 liberalization of financial markets—namely early in 1978. Two of these papers identify a similar change toward the end of 1973.[19] All four estimates agree that the demand-for-money function in Israel was stable throughout 1970–73/III, that is, during the whole take-off period. This suggests that the impact of money on prices during the entire period can be discussed by reference to both the rising income-induced demand for money and the supply of liquidity. These involve the supply of money, the relevant proxies for which in this period are still M_1 and M_2 and the expansion of less liquid monetary assets which add up with money supply to form M_3 (Table 15).

M_1 (and the corresponding outstanding bank credit) in Table 16 rose rapidly in the first two quarters of 1970. With M_1 growing at an annual rate of about 11 percent in the first seven months of 1970, and bank credit growing at an even higher rate, the supply of money clearly outpaced GNP growth (about 9 percent, see Table 9). The much smaller than unity short-run income elasticity of demand for money suggested by the econometric estimates means that both M_1 and bank credit (increasing at an annual rate of about 15 percent) were growing much more rapidly than income-induced demand for real balances.[20] The well-known inherent lags in the transmission mechanism suggest that monetary expansion should not immediately generate pressure on output and/or prices. Note, however, the high (20 percent) growth rate of bank credit in 1969, whose effect on aggregate demand was presumably infiltrating into the system more rapidly than that of money (Table 16). This means that the lag might have been quite short. The findings of Leiderman and Marom ("average lag in the adjustment of real balances was of two months only"), though based on data for a later period, point to the same conclusion.[21]

An obvious objection to the claim of an extraordinary monetary expansion during the revving-up phase would cite the low—2.5 percent—growth rate of M_1 through 1969, reflecting, among other things, a substantial decline in the fourth quarter of 1969. One might therefore argue that the 10–11 percent annualized rate of change of M_1 in the first half of 1970 was merely a lagged response to its substantial decline in the last quarter of 1969. But this argument assumes a very narrow definition of liquidity. The development of bank credit, which grew at rates above 20 percent both in 1969 and in 1970 as well as in 1969/IV, yields an altogether different impression of the state of liquidity. The pattern of aggregate demand was undoubtedly affected by the whole range of liquid assets, including (though to a smaller extent) those financial assets not included in the narrowly defined M_1 concept of money. M_3 (presented in Table 15), which includes non-linked and foreign-exchange-linked financial assets, grew 11 percent in the first two quarters of 1970—at a significantly higher annual rate than M_1—pushing financial wealth upward.

We may therefore conclude that the increase in the supply of money during the first two quarters of 1970 represents a substantial monetary expansion that exceeded the growth of full employment output across the whole range of financial assets and, even more so, the (short-run) income-induced increase in demand for real balances.

With demand for money growing at a rate commensurate (at best) with the growth of GNP (at an annual rate of close to 9 percent), and due to the short-run low income elasticity coefficients, actually growing at an even lower rate (no more than 5 percent in the first half of 1970), monetary policy was obviously expansionary throughout this interval, too, as it indeed had been since 1967. This should have made for ease in the money markets. The proposition that the monetary stance was not restrictive during the three quarters of the revving-up period can thus be put to the test using interest-rate data.

A once-and-for-all structural change in the financial market—the abolition of the legal interest-rate ceiling on short-term (bank) credit—implemented in the first quarter of 1970 makes the comparison with 1969 and earlier years somewhat tricky.[22] The "free" rate after abolition of the formal interest-rate ceiling could be expected to rise. Tables 13 and 14 show a slight shift upward in the nominal interest rate on short-term funds, from an annual rate of about 16.5 percent in the last quarter of 1969 to 17.9 percent in the first quarter of 1970. The remarkable consequence of the abolition of the ceiling is thus not the rise in the nominal rate, but its *small* rise, which virtually signifies stability rather than a rising trend.

The significant feature in this context is thus the stability of this nominal rate throughout the revving-up period. In an economy operating at its capacity constraint—in its third year of vigorous growth, in boom conditions and with strong demand for bank credit, and after the abolition of the ceiling on interest rates—nominal interest rates should have been moving up significantly. Yet with bank credit growing at twice the rate of growth of product, the quarterly nominal short-run interest-rate series shows no sign of an upturn. Rather, it moved slightly downward (Table 14). This is clear indication of comparative ease in the financial market, reflecting a monetary policy that fully accommodated demand pressures from "other" sources.

Monetary Policy

Monetary policy during the revving-up period was, in fact, more than merely accommodating. The real interest series in Table 13 and the quarterly series in Table 14 reflect the marginal cost of commercial bank credit and support this reading of the state of money markets. The interest series show a substantial decline in the real rate in the transition from 1969/IV to the first quarter of 1970. Even if this comparison of these two consecutive quarters exaggerates the change in the state of financial markets, a comparison of the three first quarters of 1970 (the revving-up quarters) with the three last quarters of 1969, which reduces the effect of seasonal and irregular factors on the quarterly averages, tells the same story: the implied real annual rates of interest in the last three quarters of 1969 were about 13 percent and 12 percent in terms of the GDP and wholesale price deflators, respectively; they declined in the first three quarters of 1970 to about 4 and 6 percent, respectively. A comparison of the annual real rates on "free" bank credit in terms of the CPI in 1969 and 1970 also shows a substantial decline. This significant reduction in the marginal cost of short-term credit clearly indicates that monetary policy was, on the whole, highly expansionary during that interval. But these rates, which seem high by conventional standards, applied only to a fraction of bank credit—the non-directed, "free" credit component of total bank credit. Rates charged for most outstanding bank credit—"directed credit"—were much lower. Indeed, by the first half of 1970 the average real cost of bank credit was close to nil.[23]

The impression gleaned from the interest-rate series that monetary policy was, on the whole, expansionary, is supported by the available information on the instruments and intermediate targets of monetary policy. The monetary base, which declined about 7 percent in the last two quarters of 1969, made an abrupt about-turn. During the revving-up quarters of 1970, it grew at an annual rate of 20 percent (Table 15). The turnaround in the foreign reserve position in 1970— the 1969 substantial loss in reserves turned into a small gain—generated an expansion of the monetary base; in any case, it could no longer compensate for the expansion of Bank of Israel credit to the government and to the public as the worsening of the reserve position did in 1969. Thus, the expansionary effect of even a 4 percent of GNP (domestic) fiscal deficit on that base was no longer neutralized by the countervailing effect on domestic liquidity of a growing deficit in the current account.

The sale on the open market of treasury bills amounting to 0.5 percent of GNP in the interval under review could not compensate for the far greater (over eightfold) central bank advances to government. Furthermore, a more vigorous open market policy was, of course, inconsistent with the policy of maintaining the price of government bonds within a narrow band. The treasury insisted on this constraint on the central bank's freedom of action although it did not formally impose it. In view of its growing needs, the treasury needed free access to money and capital markets and simultaneously requested the maintenance of low nominal rates on government paper.

The only other instrument left to the central bank with which to restrict the growth of the money supply was the required liquidity ratio. A rise in this ratio, with banks "borrowed-up" to the hilt, could reduce the size of the money multiplier and thus its multiplicand—the quantity of money. Yet with an overall formal legal liquidity requirement of 63 percent (and a corresponding effective ratio of 38 percent) the central bank was reluctant to wield this instrument to restrain money creation. In any case, an attempt made in the first half of 1970 to raise this ratio was reversed in the second half of that year (Table 16). This might have been due to the reshuffling of the types of deposits (to which different reserve requirement ratios applied). At any rate, even this feeble attempt at restraint was hardly a signal of restrictive monetary policy.

AGGREGATE DEMAND, QUANTITIES, AND PRICES

The reduction in the real cost of short-run credit during the revving-up period had an obvious expansionary effect. Even more significant was the declining real cost of medium- and long-term funds, which moved into the negative range in this period (see Table 13).[24] While expansionary monetary policy induced demand for inventories by reducing the cost of working capital, treasury policy, which allowed a reduction in the real cost of long-term funds by maintaining stable, long-term nominal rates of interest through 1970, offered a major incentive for long-term investment in fixed capital and in housing. These expansionary policies, pursued simultaneously, could not but generate pressure on quantities and on prices. The relevant quantities are output and the import surplus. If these were not responsive, the clout of the expansionary forces unleashed by reducing the real cost of long-term finance and of bank credit, in an economy already hovering at full employment, could not but generate immediate pressure on prices.

An inspection of the trade account figures (Table 10), which also reflect export performance, shows a slight improvement, although imports in the first two quarters of 1970 were slightly higher than in the closing quarter of 1969. Thus, in contrast to 1967–69, when the rapid increase in imports and in the trade account deficit were absorbing part of the pressure exerted by the growth in aggregate demand, the slight reduction in the import surplus during the revving-up phase suggests that it could no longer offset the upward pressures on the price level (as it had done before, directly and indirectly, via the loss of reserves). This was, of course, not accidental. The rapidly rising deficits on the current account in 1968, and particularly in 1969, and the net loss of reserves in 1967–69, led to a first attempt to curb imports implemented in January 1970.[25]

The absence of depressant support from the trade account meant that the ongoing surge of domestic demand—private consumption, gross investment, and government demand for goods and services—had to be met by rising production. But GNP growth was slowing down, owing to supply constraints. The substantial decline in unemployment (to 3.7 percent in the first half of 1970) meant that by that time the economy was definitely operating at the full employment ceiling. This reading of the signals is supported by the employment series: a 9.2 percent annual rate of increase in employment in 1968 was followed by a low 2.1 percent in 1969 (Table 7); by mid-1970 employment was less than 1 percent higher than in June 1969. The spare capacity in manufacturing in 1968, which allowed a major upsurge of industrial output through 1969, had disappeared. Early in 1970 further increases in output were already crucially dependent on increases in manufacturing capacity, that is, on the growth of industry's capital stock.[26] A significant increase in the capital stock, 8.3 percent in 1970 (compared to 7.9 percent in 1969), supported by an almost 2 percent growth in employment, still provided for a robust 9 percent growth rate of GNP.[27] Yet the sustained growth of investment, especially in housing, at an annual rate of over 14 percent, and of government demand at an annual rate of about 11 percent, were not fully compensated for by the lower (3 percent) growth rate of private consumption in the first two quarters of 1970. Aggregate demand was still pushing ahead of production.

Part of the demand pressure which was not absorbed by the foreign account was therefore inevitably transmitted to prices. The resultant annual price rise of 7–8 percent in terms of the CPI and WPI measures (and significantly more in terms of the more comprehensive GDP deflator) in the seven months through July 1970 implies that by the end of the revving-up period, and before the August cost-push effect of the 20 percent (partial) import imposition, inflation was already rising at rates that were two or three times higher than during the "stable" price interval of 1967–69. The public image of this turnaround in prices, which became a characteristic feature of the economic scene *before* the implementation of the August 1970 (cost-push) measures, was probably even worse than reality.[28]

NOTES

1. The *price* of NATAD was actually a rate of exchange for a specific kind of monetary asset—a "bond" denominated in terms of foreign exchange. The bond could be bought by Israeli residents for local currency. The source of the foreign currency required to make the first purchase of these instruments was funds from German restitution payments, whose recipients were allowed to sell a small fraction of their annual receipts in this market, which offered them a premium on the official exchange rate. The size of this premium was determined by the market; higher rates induced conversions into local currency; but this was not the case in 1970, when the rate did not move up.

2. The ratio of the foreign-exchange-linked deposits (restitution funds) to M_1 was about 0.75 in 1969 (*Report 1970,* tables XIV-5 and XIV-6, pp. 263–64). If, indeed, a devaluation had induced an immediate conversion of a substantial fraction of these funds, it would have generated a monetary explosion. Hence the repeated reference from the early 1960s onward to the monetary "time bomb" which could be set off by devaluation. In practice, the "bomb" never exploded. No major devaluation-induced conversions of funds occurred either in the 1960s or in the early 1970s.

3. Data on cost-of-living allowances (COLA) and on changes in nominal and real wages are from Liviatan (1987), tables 1 and 2, pp. 5 and 12, respectively. The productivity and wage data for 1964–70 are from *Report 1970,* table IX-5, p. 151, and Diagram IX-4, pp. 157–58. Details of the "wage price tax settlement" of January 1970—the first package deal—appear in *Report 1970,* pp. 158–59. Note that the rapid rise in output which, among other things, allowed for more intensive use of fixed capital equipment, allowed a rise in the total profit even of firms that, by absorbing the over-and-above, productivity-warranted wage rise, were forced to have lower profit margins.

4. For oil price data see Barkai (1976, 1977).

5. The difference between the changes in shekel and dollar prices reflects changes

in the effective exchange rates for imports. In years when the formal exchange rate was not changed, the average of the latter could move because of changes in the composition of imports (due to the differential customs rates), because of changes in specific customs duties, or due to a general levy on imports (as in August 1970).

6. The higher coefficient refers to the current quarterly price relation; the lower one to the one-period lagged GDP price deflator–import price relationship. With R^2 values of 0.35 and 0.29 respectively, the current price relation performs "better" and suggests a stronger immediate effect of import prices on the price level. The 24 and 23 observations, respectively, used for the estimate allow for high t-statistics and also for an estimate passing the Durbin–Watson serial correlation test.

A similar estimate, in which the CPI figures as the domestic price proxy, yields import price coefficients of 0.6 and 0.84 for the current and one-period lag relations, respectively (the corresponding R^2 values are 0.33 and 0.54). Both the value of the coefficients and the R^2 values suggest a stronger *lagged* than current, import-price–CPI relationship. This feature is fully consistent with the policy pursued by all governments, Israel's included, which usually attempts to delay the effect of devaluation and/or price changes in world markets on the cost of living. In Israel this was carried out by the direct control of the government over the supply prices of essential goods, whose weights in the basket of the CPI in the early 1970s was approximately 25–30 percent (*Report 1970,* table VI-3, p. 101). The partial indirect control of the government over current CPI readings, as well as more general considerations related to the much more representative (implicit GDP deflator) basket, suggest, of course, that the GDP deflator is a better gauge of overall price developments.

7. See Tables 7 and 8. The disposable income figure in the text refers to disposable income from all sources; source: *Report 1970,* table II-12.

8. For the pattern of aggregate investment and by industry, see *Reports 1970* and *1973,* table V-1, pp. 83 and 129, respectively.

9. *Report 1970,* table II-1, p. 11, and table III-1, p. 25.

10. The 10 percent increase in claims on resources refers to government consumption expenditure including (domestic) defense expenditures and direct government investment. It thus excludes a substantial fraction of government-sponsored, non-budget-financed investment in housing (Table 3, cols. 3 and 5; and Table 7, col. 5).

11. The extraordinary increase in government domestic consumption expenditure reflected a major buildup of the Suez Canal defense line before (and especially in the immediate aftermath of) the ceasefire in the War of Attrition (August 1970). Significant resources were also being poured into defense works along the Jordan river, where skirmishes and artillery duels were reaching a climax at that time.

12. Source: *Report 1972,* table III-24, p. 70, table III-25, p. 73, and table II-1, p. 12.

13. The 20 percent import tax and export subsidy imposed in August improved the budgetary position in the latter part of the year, *after* the revving-up stage. The well-known seasonal lag of tax revenues and the delay in the implementation of the compulsory loan (generating an inflow of 2.9 percent of GNP in 1970 and 4.5 percent in 1971) also suggest that treasury revenues improved in the second half of 1970. The 4 percent domestic budget gap, which is the average for the year, thus understates the size of this gap, and hence its monetary implications in the first half of 1970, when inflation was revving up. Because of differing marginal propensities to spend, the equal treatment of tax revenues and the inflow from the compulsory loan implied by the domestic excess

demand and the budget deficit series of Table 3, these two understate the expansionary impact of the fiscal stance on aggregate demand at this critical nexus.

14. For the interest rate set for medium- and long-term credit, see Table 13, and *Report 1970*, p. 299.

15. Indirect control was implemented through government control over the investment portfolio of contractual saving agents and by discriminatory tax concessions for funds flowing into saving schemes.

16. See Ben-Shahar et al. (1972), table 1.2, p. 67, and "Index of Share Prices" in *Reports 1970, 1972*, and *1974*.

17. Income velocity of M_1 was 5.55 in 1969/III and rose to 5.88 in 1970/I—a rate maintained through 1970. Yet income velocity of M_2, which throughout the first three quarters of 1969 was 3.57, declined to 3.33 in the last quarter of this year and in the first two quarters of 1970, moving back to the level of late 1969.

18. See *Report 1977*, table XVIII-2, and *Report 1981*, table VIII-5.

19. See Leiderman and Marom (1988), Melnick (1988), Ben-Bassat and Marom (1988), and Piterman (1988).

20. The statement on the relative increase in the supply of and demand for money holds in the long run, too, although to a lesser extent. The Leiderman–Marom estimate for the period from April 1973 to December 1981 yields a short-run (monthly!) elasticity of 0.357, which implies a long-run income elasticity "somewhat greater than unity" as the authors put it (Leiderman and Marom, 1988, p. 18, table 2, p. 24, and table 3, p. 26). The Ben-Bassat–Marom estimate for 1965/I-73/IV yields a short-run (quarterly) income elasticity of 0.276, which implies a long-run income elasticity of 1.17 (Ben-Bassat–Marom, 1988, table 3, p. 63). Note that this estimate of the demand function for money relies on data for the revving-up phase. Melnick's estimate for 1970–1981 has a low 0.19 short-run (quarterly) elasticity, which implies a long-run elasticity of unity; the income coefficients of this estimate are, however, not statistically significant (Melnick, 1988, table 1, p. 38).

21. Leiderman and Marom (1988), p. 18.

22. The Minzli series of interest rates (Table 14) represents two spliced series. The entry for 1970/I belongs to a new interest-rate series on bank credit; the entries for 1969/IV and previous entries are the rates for "arbitraged bills," a legal device used to evade the legal interest-rate ceiling abolished in January 1970.

23. On the composition of bank credit and interest charged for such credit see *Report 1970*, p. 277.

24. Detailed data on the cost of "development" credit appear in *Report 1970*, p. 299. The volume of medium- and long-term outstanding "development" credit balances was 1.6 times larger than total outstanding bank credit. See *Report 1970*, table XVI-2, p. 302, and table XIV-10, p. 275; see also this volume, Table 13, column (6).

25. A non-interest-bearing compulsory "import deposit" was the device used for this purpose (*Report 1970*, p. 32). Its purpose was to raise the cost of imports at the pegged formal exchange rate and simultaneously to reduce the liquidity of the non-government sector. Import and trade deficit data appear in *Report 1972*, table III-3, p. 39, and similar tables in previous reports. Data on international reserves appear in *Report 1972*, table III-29, p. 80, and in Table 10 in this volume.

26. The spare capacity of 1968 and the tightening of the capacity constraint thereafter (especially in 1970) are underlined by Gaathon's estimates of the determinants of growth of industrial production (*Report 1970*, table XI-3, p. 198; *Report 1971*, table XI-3, and

the same table in later *Reports*). While the increase in number of employees "explained" 31 percent of the increase in production in 1968 and only 2 percent were "explained" by the rise in capital stock, the corresponding ratios were 39 to 19 in 1969 and 35 to 35 percent, that is, *equal,* in 1970. These findings are supported by the productivity data—the increase in total productivity in manufacturing explained 67 percent of the increase in output in 1968, 42 percent in 1969, and only 30 percent in 1970. The excess capacity feature in 1968 is also implied by the comparative rates of increase of employment and the capital stock in manufacturing. Beenstock's estimates of business sector actual and equilibrium output 1961–89 are fully consistent with this reading of the relation between capacity and actual output data (Beenstock, 1991, figure 3; see also Metzer, 1983, table A-5, p. 80).

27. Data on non-housing capital stock are from *Report 1973,* table II-8, p. 205.

28. The inclusion of a COLA in wages in the "package deal" presumably contributed to the public image of a change in the price trend. Note that the entire (or close to the entire) wage hike agreed upon was warranted in terms of previous productivity gains. See above, pp. 27–28.

— 3 —

Breaking the Single-Digit Barrier
and the Following Lull

THE CONTEMPORARY VIEW OF THE NEW INFLATION

The clear-cut signal of the end of the revving-up period, after the seasonal July-August 1970 price lull featuring a slight slowdown in the upward trend of prices, was the 20 percent surtax levied on imports and a corresponding rise in the export subsidy. Behind this move lay both balance-of-payments considerations related to a substantial loss of reserves (Table 10) and an attempt at fiscal discipline. By the fourth quarter of 1970, annual inflation was well beyond the single-digit threshold in terms of the price measures presented in Tables 1 and 2.

This was undoubtedly a new point of departure. The cost-of-living index had not come close to the two-digit threshold for 10 years, and the wholesale price index for over 15 years. Once beyond the single-digit threshold, the rising price pattern showed no sign of abating. The semiannual price data from 1970/IV onward imply double-digit annual inflation rates in terms of the comprehensive basket of the GDP deflator and the cost-of-living basket for all the six-month periods from 1971 on. The same applies approximately to the wholesale price basket. According to our implied price criteria, the fourth quarter of 1970 is thus the beginning of the second phase of the take-off—which we call "the lull." This phase ended just over two years later, as the inflation level took another upward turn early in 1973, pushing annual inflation to 20 percent and beyond.

The new, two-digit price environment proved resilient in terms of the rate of change of prices, though not, of course, in terms of the absolute price level. An inspection of the annual data underlines an interesting feature for the eight quarters through the end of 1972: the annual inflation rate hovered around the lower teens, a relative stability that was maintained in spite of a 20 percent official devaluation of the currency in September 1971, which administered a second, substantial cost shock to the system within one year.

The full significance of the price developments, which within a single year pushed the economy from relative price stability to inflation in the low two-digit range, was not immediately apparent. Among other things, this reflected the fact that the new inflationary environment was not unique to Israel, being not altogether out of line with contemporary price patterns in other industrial countries—all of which were subject to the pull of the U.S. (Vietnam war) inflation. With the German inflation rate over 9 percent in 1970 and an annual average inflation rate of 6 percent for the industrialized countries (Table 19), the Israeli 6–7 percent rate of CPI inflation during the revving-up period and through the summer of 1970 did not seem unusual (inflation in terms of the GDP deflation was twice as high, but at that date this information was not available). Inflation in the United Kingdom was close to the top of the single-digit rates through 1972, the German inflation slowed to 7–8 percent in 1971, and the United States, at 5.4 percent, was not far behind; thus, Israel's 12–13 percent inflation, which became public knowledge early in 1971, was not re-garded as a disaster, either by the treasury or by the monetary authorities.

Phillips Curve trade-off notions, still in vogue at the time, implied that Israeli inflation, although 5–6 percent higher than that of its main trading partners, did not differ much from what it had been in the late 1950s and the mid-1960s. Consequently, it was not considered catastrophic by the political community, by business, by labor, or by households. On the contrary, boom conditions and major capital gains could hardly generate an unfavorable public opinion during the take-off of inflation.

THE TWIN EXCHANGE-RATE COST SHOCKS

The quarterly cost indicators (Table 12) reveal the source and size of two cost shocks that occurred in the third quarter of 1970 and exactly one year later, in the third quarter of 1971. These twin shocks can be attributed squarely to the strain on the current account of the balance of payments: they reflected the substantial effective devaluations of the currency that were designed to relieve this strain, though only the second shock (August 1971) also involved a formal devaluation (Tables 1, 2, 11, and 12). The simultaneous rise in the price of essentials, due to a cut in subsidies and higher purchase tax rates, had a similar cost-push effect. These two measures (formal devaluation and a reduction of subsidies) were directly linked and were implemented together with the rise in the formal exchange rate (in 1971) but were avoided when the August 1970 effective devaluation was implemented.

An inspection of the quarterly data in Table 12 indicates that dollar import prices were almost at the same level in the first quarter of 1971 as they were a year earlier. They did move up, by about 2 percent, in the last three quarters of

1971, but at this rate of change they had only minor significance. Even assuming a full pass-through, the import/GDP ratio implies that their cost-push effect was only around 0.5–1 percent. The 1970 and 1971 cost shocks could therefore hardly be attributed to exogenous foreign price patterns.

The substantial rise in shekel import prices from the third quarter of 1970 onward, in response to an unofficial effective devaluation, and through 1971 when the upward trend gained significantly greater momentum due to the (formal) devaluation of August 1971, was thus of Israel's own making. The two upward adjustments of the exchange rate reflected a policy decision dictated by balance-of-payments considerations. The significant deterioration in reserves, from 4.3 months' worth of imports at the end of 1968 (5.8 at the end of 1967) to 2.5 months' worth at the end of 1969, with a further decline in the first two quarters of 1970, forced the hand of a reluctant minister of finance (Table 9). The even lower (1.8 months) reserve ratio in the last quarter of 1970 and the strain on the foreign payments position in the first quarter of 1971 finally led to an official 20 percent devaluation which, unlike the 1970 measure, affected import prices across the board. "Essentials," which were exempt from the 20 percent import surcharge imposed in August 1970, were not excluded this time. The significantly greater increase in shekel import prices in 1971/III–IV, compared with the same quarters one year earlier (Table 2), was due to the universal effect of the formal 1971 devaluation, in contrast to the policy-constrained, partial effect of the August 1970 move.

THE PACKAGE DEAL AND IMPORT COST EFFECTS

The argument that attributes the cost shock of the latter halves of 1970 and 1971 solely to the rising cost of imports (by 8 and 22 percent respectively) is prima facie inconsistent with the wage data. The package deal on wages, prices, and taxes concluded between the Histadrut, the employers associations, and the government, and implemented in January 1970 (eight months before the first effective devaluation), included an immediate substantial wage hike at the very beginning of the revving-up period. The annual average rise in the business sector's labor cost per employee, 15 percent in nominal terms (7.5 percent in real terms) in 1970, and the further 16 percent nominal rise (5.4 percent in real terms) in 1971, were therefore inevitable. Similarly, the quarterly cost data (Table 12) show that the 7 percent hike in nominal labor costs (an annual rate of over 14 percent) in the revving-up period subsided somewhat in the second half of 1970. Yet another major turn of the wage screw occurred early in 1971 with an 8.5 percent rise due, among other things, to the payment of a COLA—the second since January 1970. The rate of wage inflation fell again in the following quarters (Table 12). But an annual rise in nominal wages of about 16 percent in 1971 (14 percent in 1972) suggests that the claim that the economy was subjected to a wage cost-push during the lull—the period between, say, 1970/IV and 1972/III—is not entirely unfounded.

The above scenario, however, reflects the *perception* of the effect of labor costs on prices, not the reality. Even in an environment of institutionalized wage setting, the cost of labor is not exclusively determined by its supply price. Demand, too, affects the setting of prices, or, if the former is exogenously constrained, the effect of demand is expressed in terms of quantity. The pattern of productivity, or, more specifically, the product at the margin, is obviously one determinant of demand, specifically of the demand price for labor. The macroeconomic stance (the level of activity and the employment situation) is clearly another factor that can boost or restrain the demand for labor.

The rapid rise in factor productivity, at annual rates of 5 percent and more, from 1967 through 1972, suggesting a corresponding rise in marginal labor productivity, indicates that the rise in real wages over this interval largely reflected the rising real demand price for labor (Table 11). The average labor productivity data for 1967–72 and, more specifically, for 1971 and 1972, which show annual rates of increase of about 6.5 percent, suggest that after allowing for the contribution of non-labor inputs, *real* wages could have been raised by some 4–5 percent in these years without affecting unit costs. These labor productivity figures refer only to the business sector, and reflect average (not marginal) product. They thus exaggerate the contribution of labor to production. To compensate for that, and as suggested above, the annual average increase in labor productivity (about 6.5 percent in 1971 and 1972) warranted a rise in the demand price for labor by, say, 4–5 percent. Note, further, that the annual data on productivity and wages in the business sector (Table 11) clearly suggest that the substantial productivity gains made in 1967–69 did not generate a corresponding rise in nominal or real wages in this period. High initial unemployment rates followed by major inflows into the labor market (reflecting the rise in immigration and a massive inflow of labor from Gaza and the West Bank) offer an obvious explanation for this lag of wages behind productivity.

Even if the 15–16 percent rise in labor costs (in the private sector) in 1970 and 1971 was not fully matched by a contemporaneous rise in marginal labor productivity, the sizable gains in productivity over and above the rise in labor costs in 1968 and 1969 provided a cushion in terms of profit margins. Furthermore, the quarterly data in Table 12 (for manufacturing only) clearly show that in the calendar year 1971, unit wage costs were declining after a 5.5 percent rise in 1970. During the lull, 1970/IV–72/IV, nominal wages in manufacturing did not increase significantly more than productivity gains, which means that cost-push forces in the labor market were either completely absent or miniscule (Tables 11 and 12). Thus, although the unit wage cost in manufacturing did rise during the revving-up period, it declined in 1971, turning up again in the first quarter of 1972.[1]

Another reversal in the two following quarters put the unit wage cost in manufacturing back to where it had been at the beginning of the lull, in the fourth quarter of 1970. The wage and productivity data for manufacturing (Table 12) clearly suggest that the substantial rises in productivity pulled the *demand* price for labor upward throughout most of the lull. These, rather than push factors, explain the rising trend of wages.[2] The annual wage and productivity series and the cost of labor per unit of product series in the business sector for 1971–89, presented in two diagrams in recent *Reports,* offer the same verdict—it was demand pull rather than cost push that led to the rise of wages and prices, the former following the latter, during the lull.[3]

The argument that labor cost push was absent during the lull or, at most, miniscule, and that even the 5 percent rise in unit labor costs during the revving-up period (from 1970/I to 1970/III) could rely on a cushion of accumulated productivity gains over and above wage rises in 1967–69 to soften its impact on prices, could be supported by reference to a relevant quantity variable. The macroeconomic context of the problem suggests that the most relevant indicator for this purpose is the state of the labor market. A wage-push hypothesis would not be rejected if, in response to a significant rise in nominal wages and/or nominal labor costs, measures showing slack in the labor market surfaced after some lag. A rise in unemployment, or at least a significantly lower growth rate of employment, would indicate a weakening labor market.

An inspection of the employment and unemployment series in Table 7 and of the quarterly employment series in Table 8 reveals no such slack in the Israeli labor market between 1969/III and 1973/III. In spite of the rapid growth of Israel's labor force and the full employment level reached in the closing quarter of 1969, unemployment rates did not rise through 1973. With unemployment declining to 3.5 percent in 1970 and to 2.7 percent in 1972, signifying a level of employment that was 16 percent higher than in 1969, the system had in fact been moving into an overfull employment environment. These figures clearly indicate that the Israeli labor market was booming in the revving-up phase (through August 1970) and the following lull (through the closing quarter of 1972). This, of course, supports the argument made above, that the wage-push hypothesis cannot be upheld, suggesting that the wage hike resulting from the 1970 package deal and the January 1971 COLA reflected the booming demand for labor in this period.

The cost effect, whatever its size, should therefore be ascribed mainly, perhaps even exclusively, to the impact of the rise in the cost of imports in the wake of the two devaluations: effective in 1970, and effective and formal in 1971. Assuming a full pass-through (which presumes monetary accommodation), the 7.2 rise in the sheqel cost of imports in 1970/III–IV and 1971/I explains a rise of the rate of inflation by no more than 2–2.5 percent during the fourth quarter of 1970 and the first quarter of 1971, over and above the approximately 6 percent at which it was already running in terms of CPI (about 12 percent in terms of GDP) in the first quarter of 1970.[4] Yet in the first two quarters of the lull (1970/IV and 1971/I) inflation jumped to an annual rate above 15 percent in terms of the CPI measure and about 24 percent in terms of the GDP measure. This rise is three to four times greater than the 2.5 percent rise which can be attributed to the devaluation-induced rise in import prices at the end of the revving-up phase. The contrast between the inflation rate in terms of the WPI and the import cost-push effect is similar to that at the CPI measure.

An analogous calculation for the post-1971 devaluation period suggests a similar, even shorter-lived, import cost-push effect. By that time inflation was already marking time at 13 percent in terms of CPI and 17 percent in terms of the GDP deflator, yet its impact did not increase at all in the following five to six quarters through the end of 1972. The cost-push hypothesis, in terms of its import cost component, thus cannot explain either the substantial rise in the inflation rate in the second half of 1970 or the jump to an annual rate beyond the single digit, more than twice as high as in the first two quarters of the revving-up phase. Nor is it consistent with the relative stability of that rate through the end of 1972, although the import cost effect of the 1971 devaluation was three times greater than that imparted by the 1970 (effective) devaluation.

This means, of course, that cost push in its two variants, the wage and devaluation variants, was at best of minor consequence on this score. Other factors, which do not come under the umbrella of the cost hypothesis, were at work, whose impact on the take-off of inflation dominated the scene during the lull, too.

FISCAL INDULGENCE AND AGGREGATE DEMAND

Direct Government Demand and Absorption

Consider now the demand pull on prices during the lull: roughly from 1970/IV to 1972/III–IV. Thanks to its sheer size—public sector domestic demand at almost 30 percent of GNP and gross taxes at an even higher ratio—fiscal policy was inevitably a major determinant of aggregate demand. The latter, as noted, was affecting activity in the full employment environment which the economy reached toward the end of 1969 and which, by that time, had moved into an overfull employment situation.

A conventional gauge of the macroeconomic effect of public sector operations on the level of activity is the size of the budget deficit. However, in view of the enormous defense imports—averaging about 8–9 percent of GNP in 1968–72 and financed largely by U.S. aid—the more relevant measure in the Israeli context is excess domestic demand, or the domestic budget deficit, in effect: the net demand of the public sector for accommodation by the capital market and by the central bank (including government shekel receipts for the sale of foreign currency).

Table 3 shows that after a single year, 1970, in which domestic excess demand went down to about 4 percent of GNP, the government deficit bounced back. In the first full year of the lull, 1971, the deficit was once again running at 6.6 percent (as it had in 1969), although the economic environment, with 3.5 percent unemployment, was already clearly beyond the full employment level (Table 7).[5] The further climb of the deficit to over 10 percent of GNP in 1972 suggests that from 1971/III onward the fiscal stance also had highly expansionary monetary effects.

Of much greater immediate significance in this context was the direct effect on the level of activity of government demand for goods and services. A continuous increase in the ratio of domestic government demand to GNP after the 1968–69 plateau of 27.6 percent is a constant feature. In 1970 and 1971 the growth of public sector demand was outrunning production in spite of the latter's rapid growth (Tables 3, 7, and 9). The comparative growth abated slightly in 1972, but at average annual rates of growth exceeding 11 percent between 1970 and 1972, government was constantly increasing its real pressure on resources at an extremely high rate (Table 5). As long as unemployment stood at 10, 6, or even 4.5 percent, with correspondingly substantial excess capacity in manufacturing and farming, this pressure was tolerable from 1967 through, say, the first two (perhaps even three) quarters of 1969. With virtual full employment in 1970 and an employment level almost 16 percent higher than in 1967, the rapidly rising trend in total public sector demand was clearly unwarranted from the macroeconomic point of view. Yet this was the persistent pattern of government policy through 1972, when an unemployment rate of 2.7 percent meant that the economy was already running beyond the full employment ceiling.

These domestic demand figures actually understate the impact of the public sector on economic activity. They do not reflect a major determinant of aggregate demand promoted by government: investment (especially investment in housing). This policy was set in motion by non-budgetary devices and is therefore not captured by the budgetary data.[6] The previous peak in public housing starts, in 1970 (close to 60 percent higher than in 1969), was overshadowed by a further acceleration during the two years of the lull (Table 8). The gross domestic investment figure shows the pull of growing investment promoted by government subsidies (see Chapter 4). Annual growth rates of investment in manufacturing—10 percent in 1971 and 1972, while the 1970 level was already more than 80 percent above the 1966 level—is an obvious case in point.[7]

All this is not to say that fiscal policy did not also feature in attempts at restraint. An attempt to rein in defense expenditures was clearly made in 1972; for the first time defense outlays dropped 3 percent in real terms (Table 5). But the effect of this decline on total direct government demand was canceled out by a 55 percent increase in government investment. The only kind of fiscal restraint attempted from 1970 onward is clearly visible in the tax column of Table 3. The 1970 package deal implemented in January, and the imposition of a 20 percent import duty (in August 1970) as a substitute for devaluation, abruptly increased the gross tax burden from 34 to a record 41 percent of GNP. An increase in export and other subsidies meant that only part of the increase in gross taxes ended up in the government coffers. But the increase in net domestic absorption, from 21 percent to 25 percent of GNP, which had a negative effect on disposable income, undoubtedly reflects an attempt at restraint of a specific type—it was designed to restrain household demand.

The series in Table 3 indicate that net absorption reached an all-time high in 1970 (actually, in the 1970/71 fiscal year). At the same time, the expansionary effect on liquidity, expressed by domestic excess demand, reached its trough which, at about 4 percent of GNP (Table 4, column 9'), was still substantial. According to this series, the fiscal restraint was relaxed with the advent of the lull. With a domestic excess government demand of 10.6 percent of GNP in 1972 (the 1972/3 fiscal year), the attempt at restraint collapsed altogether. In other words, the fiscal stance from, say, 1970/IV through 1972/IV was expansionary throughout and grew in intensity over time.

This does not seem to have been the way in which the pattern of absorption (and the fiscal stance) was grasped by those in charge of economic policy. The kind of data they were probably using to evaluate the impact of the public sector on demand and on liquidity is presented in columns (7'), (8'), and (9') of Table 4, which should be juxtaposed with columns (7), (8), and (9) of Table 3. Note, first, that from 1970 onward the net absorption rate according to column (8') is far greater than that suggested by the entries in column (8). It even rose in 1971, and though it declined slightly in 1972, it was still close to the peak reached in 1970. Only in 1973 was absorption, according to this series, substantially reduced, though according to the corresponding series in column (8) it had actually collapsed already in 1972. The domestic excess demand series, column (9'), declined all the way through 1972. The deficit levels of 1.5–3 percent of GNP appearing in column (9') must have suggested fiscal fortitude to policymakers. They visualized only a minor expansionary impact, if any, on liquidity throughout the lull.

The reason for the difference between these two sets of series describing the level and pattern of absorption and domestic excess demand is made clear by reference to the corresponding subsidies and transfers, columns (7) and (7') in Table 4. These, we note, show a drastic increase by a factor of 2.3 in real terms between 1969 and 1972, and by 84 percent in terms of GNP according to the first series, which includes an imputation of the implicit credit subsidies to households and to firms (Tables 4 and 9). The credit subsidy rose strongly and rapidly in response to the rise in and acceleration of inflation from 2–3 percent annually in 1967–69 to 10 percent and more in 1970–72 (calendar years). It did not surface, however, in the government accounts, which present a cash-flow record. It is this latter record that underlies the column (7') series, which shows a similar (indeed lower) ratio to GNP of total subsidies, transfers, and domestic interest (payments and receipts!) in 1970 than shown by the column (7) series. Yet in 1971 the gap between the two series, 22 versus 18 percent, is quite significant, and keeps growing steadily in 1972 and later.

Note that the "subsidy component," involving actual (and not merely imputed) transfer payments, also grew substantially, as clearly indicated by the rise in its GNP share from 15.3 to 18 percent, and entailed a corresponding 33 percent increase in real transfer payments between 1970 and 1972 (Table 4). This reflects a deliberate policy of boosting transfer payments, put into effect in 1970, and substantially expanded from 1972 onward.[8] This boost in recorded transfers from 1972 onward dissipated the entire increase in gross taxes, so that by 1973, net domestic absorption (boosted by the 1970 tax hike to 25 percent of GNP) was back at square one, the level of recorded (net) absorption in fiscal 1969/70 (Table 3, column 8').

Consider now the economic significance of the widening difference, from 1970 onward, between the recorded cash flow series (column 7') of subsidies and transfers and the corresponding series (columns 8' and 9') describing the fiscal stance, on the one hand, and those of (columns 7, 8, and 9), which reflect an imputation for ex post inflation-generated real credit subsidies. The first set, which measures actual net absorption and thus current "domestic excess demand," is obviously an indicator of the government's net cash requirements. It measures the impact of the public sector budget on the liquidity of the system, that is, on monetary expansion and/or on the expansion of the debt overhang. Thus the "decrease" in domestic excess demand (column 9') from (fiscal) 1970 through (fiscal) 1972 implies that public sector infusion of liquidity into the economy declined considerably throughout the lull, 1970/IV–72/III.

However, this overall excess demand measure alone does not show how much of the cash-flow shortage was covered by central bank accommodation and what fraction of it was covered by selling interest-bearing debt in the capital market (see the next section). The "well-behaved" fiscal behavior that these figures might have suggested to the policymakers refers only to the liquidity dimension, subject to the proviso on access to the capital market. The figures thus reflect the short-run monetary effect of the budget deficit. In the long run, the size of the national debt, which is a liquid financial asset whose size is affected by the sale of interest-bearing debt, counts too.

A Negative Inflation Tax and Disposable Income

These series significantly understate the boost given to demand in real markets generated by the implicit credit subsidies to firms and households. The data in Table 4, column (7'), and in the corresponding series do not fully describe the immediate impact of the fiscal stance on aggregate demand at one remove— through the effect of the latter on the business sector's and households' financial wealth and thus on permanent disposable income. This is so because these series, derived from government cash-flow data, exclude by definition the effect of prices on financial wealth. This would not make much difference in a stable price environment, as a comparison between columns (7) and (7') for 1967–70 clearly suggests, but it is an altogether different proposition in an economy with accelerating inflation, particularly during its take-off and before financial markets (and hence nominal interest rates) adapt to the rising trends of prices.

The inflation tax concept was designed to deal with this phenomenon, on the presumption that government debt, which includes the monetary base and interest-bearing bonds, is a nominal liability. But this was not at all the case in the Israeli economy of the early 1970s. Although currency and commercial bank reserves were, indeed, nominal public sector liabilities, all the other debt instruments were price-linked. The government's dominant position as an intermediary agent in the capital market and its activity as the ultimate source of housing and development credit involved holding a huge financial asset portfolio, most of which was not linked at all or, at best, only partly linked. Inflationary developments therefore generated a negative inflation tax. The swift move, within one year, from a negligible rate of price change to the upper range of a single-digit inflation rate and beyond soon generated huge capital gains to government debtors: households, as beneficiaries of unlinked or partly linked mortgages, and firms, which relied on government or government-controlled credits for capital investment. The Tanzi effect—the erosion of the real value of government revenues in systems subject to rapid inflation—added another component to the negative inflation tax feature.

These developments naturally had an immediate effect on the current and permanent real disposable income of households and on the profits and net worth of businesses. With inflation rising at 11 percent annually, the real value of installment payments made by households and business on unlinked debt was being eroded, creating a corresponding increase in real disposable income and profits. By early 1971, that is, with the advent of the lull, economic agents could not but take note of this effect. By early 1972, with a 25 percent or so erosion of the value of repayments on debt incurred before 1970, the increase in real disposable income was there for all to see.

The quantitative significance of the inflation-driven rise in real disposable income is visible from the difference between the entries in Table 4, columns (7) and (7'); the former series includes an imputation for implicit, price-driven credit subsidies. Whereas in 1966–70 the gap between these two series was around 1–1.2 percent of GNP, it rose to 4.4 percent of GNP in 1971 and to 6.3 percent in 1972. The full increase in credit subsidies, calculated on an accrual basis, did not materialize immediately. Its immediate effect was felt in the declining real value of monthly mortgage payments by households and debt repayments by firms. This, of course, boosted profits and equity values.

Most of the surge in private consumption expenditures in 1971 and 1972 can be explained in terms of the high rates of growth of disposable income, both current and permanent, which, due to the implicit credit subsidies, actually grew at rates over and above those suggested by the national accounts (Table 9). With investment sustained by a housing boom in 1972 and rising exports (induced by the 1970 and 1971 devaluations), the level of aggregate demand clearly outran the supply of available resources. An unemployment rate of only 2.7 percent in 1972 is an obvious case in point.

This tremendous demand pressure, resulting from the highly expansionary fiscal stance, could not but push inflation beyond the single-digit level. It would have generated an even higher inflation rate if, in spite of two effective devaluations (1970 and 1971), the safety valve of rising imports had not been available to stem the tide (Tables 7 and 9).[9]

MONETARY OVERACCOMMODATION AND INERTIAL FACTORS

The impact of an expansionary fiscal policy on real markets in a full employment milieu could be countervailed, temporarily, and probably not fully, by an appropriate monetary policy. The same applies to upward pressures on prices due to cost-push factors, though the effect of a restrictive monetary policy on the level of activity would be different if the latter rather than the former factor was the cause of the upward pressure on prices.

The monetary sector could, conceivably, generate pressures on its own on prices. Although conventionally associated with a rapid growth of the money supply, such pressures might also emanate from the demand side. A decrease in the demand for money (real balances), quite conceivable in an inflationary situation, would undoubtedly have an expansionary effect. This possibility, usually associated with high inflation rates, is quite feasible and requires an analysis of the demand for money during the lull period.

The Demand Dimension

We have already noted (Chapter 2) that the velocity series in Table 13 offers a first approximation of, and probably the most important piece of evidence on, developments in the demand sphere. An inspection of the velocity of the M_1 series, the most important monetary aggregate at that time, shows a small variance ($\sigma = 0.4$, $\sigma/\mu = 0.07$) for the whole decade ending in September 1973 (or at the end of that year). It shows hardly any variance for the most relevant interval, 1970–72. Indeed, at the end of this period velocity was slightly lower than it was at the beginning of the period. The shorter M_2 series has an even lower variance ($\sigma = 0.1$, $\sigma/\mu = 0.04$). Similarly, the best statistical measure of money velocity—bank deposit velocity ($\sigma = 2.5$, $\sigma/\mu = 0.12$)—shows a very small variance for the whole decade and an even smaller one for 1970–72. This suggests that the demand for money did not budge in the two crucial years in which the system was in a lull, just beyond the single-digit level of inflation. In other words, there is no evidence whatsoever of even the beginning of a flight from money during this period, in spite of persistent inflation at an annual rate beyond the single-digit level, which could only have added fuel to the inflationary process. The figures clearly show that this also holds for the last phase of the take-off from, say, 1972/IV to 1973/III.

The evidence derived from the velocity data receives clear-cut confirmation from several studies on the demand for money, cited above, and from Yashiv's more recent study, in which a novel econometric technique is applied to the data for the 1970s and the 1980s.[10] Yashiv, too, finds that following the ''1977 liberalization plan there occurred a shift in the demand function'' of money (Yashiv, 1990, p. 39).

This means that all the studies mentioned did not reveal a shift in the demand function for money throughout the whole take-off period under investigation. But these findings convey a more general, and highly significant, message on the role of money. They underline the very high value (hence the significant consumer surplus) of the services of money to economic agents, both firms and households. If inflation rates in excess of 10 percent in 1970–72 did not induce a flight from money, it means that the benefits to economic agents from money balances are greater than the annual cost of 12–13 percent entailed in holding such balances. Indeed, even the 1973 rate of 20 percent did not send these agents scurrying for cover. It was only when the economy crossed the threshold of a 50 percent annual inflation rate that the demand-for-money function shifted and a flight from money occurred. But this happened several years later, in 1977, and was not relevant throughout the take-off period.

The Supply Dimension

The contribution of monetary developments to the inflationary process in the second phase of the take-off can thus be attributed exclusively to the supply of money and its determinants. Consider now the impact of the money supply and of liquidity in general. A growth rate of about 13 percent in 1970 (Table 15) in the annual M_1 series might not warrant the identification of such a rate of monetary expansion as unusual. The high growth rate of the economy in those years and past performance suggest that such a growth rate of money supply is not beyond reason. The miniscule growth rate in 1969 (2.5 percent for M_1 and 1.9 percent for M_2), and the fact that the 1970 rate was lower than that of 1967 or 1968 (which did not generate inflationary pressures at the time) lend apparent support to what was in those days a cavalier attitude to the pace of monetary expansion.[11]

However, this line of reasoning ignores the differences in economic environment. It is one thing to allow a rapid expansion of credit and of the money supply when the level of unemployment and spare capacity are exceptionally high as they were in 1967 and 1968; it is an altogether different proposition to allow monetary expansion at a rate much higher than the potential growth of production in an economy operating at (and even beyond) its ceiling capacity, which was definitely the case early in 1971 (Tables 7 and 8). Note, too, that in the second half of 1970, that is, at the very beginning of the lull, monetary growth jumped from a ''reasonable'' annual rate of about 10 percent to an annual rate of 18 percent and accelerated further in the first half of 1971 to an annual rate of 32 percent (Table 16). Indeed, with average annual rates of about 30 percent in 1971 and 1972, one may conclude that the economy was clearly in the throes of a tremendous monetary expansion. This could not but pull prices upward. Were it not for the countervailing quantity effect of imports (non-defense imports in 1972 were 25 percent higher than in 1970), this exploding money supply might have pushed price inflation far beyond the single-digit threshold actually reached by the end of the revving-up period.

The timing of the monetary forces unleashed in 1970 is, however, not properly described by the M_1 series. The M_2 and bank credit series offer supporting evidence on its force and timing. These two series clearly predate the timing of the rapid growth of money up to 1970 (Tables 15 and 16). Note, too, the rapid rise of outstanding treasury bills, a short-run instrument, which in those years was a substitute for the CDs that appeared later. Their growth was one of the factors contributing to the spurt of M_2, predating the lower acceleration of M_1 by two quarters.[12] The 40 percent rate of increase in M_2 in 1970, and the 30 percent rates for 1971 and 1972 (Tables 15 and 16) suggest that the system was inundated with liquidity from the very beginning of the revving-up period and that the process, which by 1971 was showing in M_1 figures, was proceeding along a strong upward trend during the lull (1971–72) phase. The outstanding bank credit series, reflecting the financing of business, with an annual growth of about 20 percent from 1969 onward, offer further support to the suggestion that liquidity was inflated far beyond the potential expansion of capacity and the actual growth of real product.

Interest Rates

The above data on monetary aggregates, indicating monetary ease, suggest a corresponding pattern of interest rates and yields of financial instruments, offering instantaneous signals on the state of the financial markets. Some insight is offered by the interest rate and the rate of return to treasury bills presented in Tables 13 and 14. The quarterly nominal rates on "non-directed" bank credit suggest a one-time tightening at the advent of the revving-up period (the first quarter of 1970). Yet even this reflects a mere technicality, related to the new interest-rate series due to the abolishment of the legal ceiling on the interest rate. From that time on nominal rates hardly budged until the second quarter of 1971. The slight upward movement from an annual rate of about 18 percent to an annual rate closer to 19 percent, effectively maintained from 1971/II to 1972/III, can hardly indicate an attempt at effective monetary restraint, both during the revving-up phase and in the lull phase.

At first glance, this statement seems inconsistent with the facts of the level and pattern of interest rates. A nominal annual rate of close to 18 percent, up 2.5 percentage points from the 1969 level, suggests a forceful attempt at monetary restraint and a restrictive monetary stance, at least by international standards. With the prime rate in the United States at 7.9 percent in 1970, declining to 5–6 percent in 1971 and 1972, with German interest rates under 10 percent in 1970 and declining to 6–7 percent in the following two years, and with similar patterns of rates in the United Kingdom, the Israeli figures seem inordinately high.

So much for appearances; the reality is another matter. Note, first, that the Israeli inflation rate, even in 1970, was significantly higher than the 6 percent average for the industrialized countries (Table 19). Toward the end of 1970 and then in 1971 and 1972, Israeli inflation was already running at double the annual rates of the group of industrialized countries; it was 1.5 times higher than in Germany, which in 1970 had an unusually high rate by its own standards.

The acceleration of inflation had a lagged effect on financial markets, reflected in *expected* real interest rates. Reference to the proxy for these, the implied ex post real rates (Tables 13 and 14), reveals an effective relaxation rather than a tightening of the monetary stance in 1970. The real interest-rate series (Table 14) reveal a feeble attempt at restraint after the first quarter of 1970 and again after the first quarter of 1971, as real interest rates on short-term "free" bank credits moved back into the positive range.[13] This attempt came to nothing, as seen in the annual average real interest-rate series: these declined abruptly in 1970, and although they turned up again in 1972 (Tables 13 and 14), they were only 50 percent of the effective levels in the 1960s through 1973. At 5–6 percent according to the CPI deflated series, 4–5 percent in the GDP deflated series, and about 9 percent in the series derived by applying wholesale prices as the deflator, these real rates seem, however, formidable by the standards of the main international financial centers.

Yet in contrast to the information on the state of the money and capital markets conveyed by series such as the U.K. lending rate, the German Lombard rate, and the U.S. prime rate, the information to be gleaned from Israeli interest rate series (Tables 13 and 14) reflects the cost of only a small fraction of outstanding bank credit. It does not show the pattern of average costs of the whole range of short-term funds at the disposal of business in those days, although it does adequately describe the cost of "marginal" funds. In and around 1970 the latter accounted for only about 20 percent of total outstanding bank credit; by 1973 the ratio might have risen to 25–30 percent of the total.[14]

The nominal cost of the so-called "directed" credits—about 45 percent of total outstanding bank credit throughout the entire take-off period (1970–73)— was about 9 percent; it was as low as 6 percent for the "export credit" component. The former was raised in May 1972 to 11 percent, although inflation was higher than that and had been so for two years.[15] The interest on export credit was not changed at that time.

The segmentation of Israel's bank credit market into "free" and "directed" components (with the latter further broken down into several groups), inevitably involving some "leakages," explains why the perception of a "high" level of real interest rates and the 2.5 percentage point rise of the nominal rate in 1970 (Table 13), which seemed to suggest a drastic tightening of credit, was so misleading. It is the *trend* of real interest rates rather than their level that tells the true story, and this trend, on the whole, moved downward both in annual and in quarterly terms (Tables 13 and 14). These trends clearly support the impression gleaned from the quantity of money and volume of credit series, which reveal the impact of the monetary momentum to which the system had been subjected as it moved from the revving-up phase through the lull phase, terminating somewhere toward the end of 1972. Whatever the *intentions* of the monetary authorities, neither Governor Horowitz, who completed his 17 years of service in November 1971, nor his successor, Sanbar, persisted in the feeble attempts at restraint. Both the monetary aggregates and the effective marginal interest cost series suggest, as do the relevant quantity of money series, a highly expansionary monetary policy.

THE STRAITJACKET AND THE FAILURE OF MONETARY POLICY

The monetary policy responsible for the developments described above surfaces quite clearly from the data in Tables 15 and 16. The tools available to the monetary authorities usually include reserve ratios and discount rates, supported by open-market operations. The latter would affect the size of the monetary base and, indirectly (by means of its effect on interest rates), the monetary multiplier. The central bank can also attempt to manipulate the size of the multiplier directly, by changing reserve ratios and discount rates and by using rationing devices such as credit ceilings.

The Bank of Israel Law, enacted in 1954, created the legal framework for these conventional central bank instruments. Yet the shallow money market, the small size of the government-dominated capital market, and the currency controls (wielded by the treasury), meant, in effect, that the economic and political environment severely circumscribed the freedom of the monetary authorities to run a restrictive monetary policy as required by the full employment (in fact, overfull employment) conditions prevailing from 1970 onward.

The Money Multiplier

Consider this policy with reference to the money multiplier and the monetary base—the direct determinants of the money supply. The size of the multiplier (m) depends, among other things, on the public's choice between currency and deposits. An inspection of the currency/deposits ratio and the currency/M_1 ratio in Table 15 suggests that these two ratios were fairly stable in 1969–73. Indeed, with a somewhat greater variance, this stability can be observed in the entire 1967–74 interval.[16] Thus, changes in the money multiplier, if any, were the result of changes in the effective reserve ratio of commercial banks. Since banks had no excess reserves in most of that period (1969–73), changes in legal reserve requirements were an effective way of forcing them to toe the line.[17] Reserve requirements were thus a handy instrument at the disposal of the central bank with which to control the size of the money multiplier.

An inspection of the reserve ratios reveals no tightening up to the end of 1970. But this is not the whole story, as the figures in Table 15 give end-of-year data. More detailed monthly data show a rise in this ratio through the revving-up period ending in July 1970 (Table 16). In the second half of 1970 the effective ratios began to decline, a pattern followed through 1971/I. Thus, the slight increase in the money multiplier (from 1.60 in December 1969 to 1.61 in December 1970) properly conveys the trend of this determinant of the money supply at a crucial juncture—the beginning of the lull. Although the effective devaluation of August 1970 and the reduction of subsidies to "essentials" undoubtedly required a restrictive monetary stance, the monthly effective reserve ratio figures definitely show that for almost nine months (until April 1971) no attempt was made to implement such a policy by means of a higher reserve ratio.

Since the effective reserve ratio (given the public's choice of the corresponding currency deposit ratio) determines the size of the money multiplier, the authorities attempted initially to induce banks to increase their effective reserve ratios by means of an interest-rate instrument. This device was a so-called "penalty rate" charged on the outstanding balance of "not recognized" reserve deficiencies. The latter was the difference between the volume of the formal reserve requirement *minus* the volume of "directed" credits, and the actual reserves of a commercial bank. The penalty rate was designed to reduce the profitability of expanding marginal credit lines. To reduce the expansion of bank lending and the corresponding increase in the money supply, the penalty rate was increased from the first quarter of 1970 onward, peaking in the middle of 1972 (Beenstock, 1991). Yet, the continuous hiking up of that rate, highly resented by the banking community, did not succeed in reducing its propensity to lend in an exploding market for bank credit. The Bank of Israel was therefore finally forced to support its attempt to control the size of the money multiplier by means of an interest-rate instrument, by wielding the axe of higher reserve ratios.

The entries giving the end-of-year multipliers for 1971 and 1972 do reveal such an attempt.[18] A first minor attempt to reduce the size of the money multiplier was made at the beginning of the revving-up phase, early in the first half of 1970. It was abandoned in the second half of that year, although the monetary avalanche, which can be clearly dated from the middle of 1970 onward, in terms of M_1, and from 1969 in terms of bank credit, was common knowledge (Table 16). The next, more substantial attempt to curb the money multiplier was made a year later, early in 1971. This was done by substantially raising the reserve ratio from 38 percent at the end of 1970 to 48 percent at the end of 1971, and to almost 58 percent at the end of 1972. The next attempt to further reduce the size of the money multiplier was made only in May 1972 and shows up in the entry for 1972 (Table 15) as a low money multiplier (1.37), signifying a two-step, 18 percent decrease from about 1.6 at the end of 1969 (*Report 1972,* table XIII-6).

This means that, although the monetary base had been expanding rapidly since the beginning of 1970 (Tables 15 and 16), the monetary authorities, who must have been aware of the force of that monetary expansion from its very beginning, failed to respond immediately by wielding the weapon at their disposal. The two-staged attempt to reduce the size of the money multiplier lagged far behind the events. The 20 percent increase in the monetary base in 1970 and the 48 percent leap in 1971 made imperative the very action that was required far earlier, before April 1971 and May 1972, respectively. The money supply series provides clear evidence that the attempt at restraint by manipulating the money multiplier was too little and came too late. Annual rates of increase of M_1 and M_2 (25 percent and 30–35 percent, respectively) from mid-1970 through the end of 1972 are obvious cases in point.

A reasonable excuse for the reluctance of the monetary authorities to wield the reserve ratio instrument to stem the monetary tide was, in the first place, the absolute level of this ratio. Effective reserve ratios of even 40 percent are very high by international standards and require a very wide margin between creditory and debitory interest rates. An inevitable outgrowth of this state of affairs is the evolution of a "grey" non-banking money market in which both borrowers and lenders get better terms (at a risk!) than by using the intermediation services of banks. The growing relative size of these grey markets, a well-known feature in every system which uses high and rising reserve ratios, increases risks and uncertainty in financial markets and erodes the power of controls used by the monetary authorities.

In view of the technique employed in Israel, of providing bank credit to priority sectors (exports, farming, etc.), which allowed counting these balances as "reserves" for the purpose of calculating "effective required reserve ratios," reserve ratios which were to be maintained for non-privileged credits were much higher. Thus, the "low" 38 percent effective reserve ratio for the end of 1970 implied a formal (in practice, marginal) reserve ratio of 63 percent. This, of course, led to an all-out effort by the banks to prevent a further tightening of the screw, and it explains the hesitant and lagging application of this restraining device by the Bank of Israel, although it was clearly called for by monetary developments from mid-1970 onward.

The Determinants of the Monetary Base

An attempt to apply the brakes to the explosive growth of the monetary aggregates should have entailed a two-pronged attack that also attempted to curb the expansion of base money. Success on the latter front would have reduced the burden imposed on the money multiplier (actually, on the reserve ratio), which had been overstrained in the first place. One might therefore dispute the apparent equanimity with which the authorities accepted the rapid and accelerating expansion of base money during the lull phase of the take-off. Even if the rate of increase of base money to an annual rate of 20 percent in the revving-up period could be rationalized away (in view of the actual decline of all the monetary aggregates in the second half of 1969, with growth, though lower than previously, quite vigorous), the sustaining of that pattern later on in 1970 and its rapid acceleration in 1971 were hardly warranted. The emergence of boom conditions in the wake of the effective August 1970 devaluation certainly called for monetary restraint. In any case, an increase of the monetary base at an annual rate of 70 percent, as in the first two quarters of 1971, and the repeat performance one year later during the same interval, suggest that the central bank had by that time—the beginning of the lull (1970/IV)—lost control over the monetary sphere (Tables 15 and 16).

Open-Market Operations

Tables 17 and 18, which describe the level and flow of the monetary base (a liability of the central bank) and its determinants, offer some important insights. Consider first treasury bills, the only instrument with which the central bank could engage in open-market operations. The data clearly show that intervention by selling treasury bills to the public, even at its 1971 peak, when the public holdings increased by almost 30 percent, was comparatively modest: it amounted to about 6 percent of the liquidity-boosting rise in net international reserves *plus* public sector accommodation by the central bank. This, of course, suggests that the open-market operations of the central bank were strictly circumscribed.

This was true even on the purely technical level. Although the domestic national debt was by that time already substantial, most of it was denominated in long-term, non-marketable bonds available to institutional investors only (pension funds, the insurance sector, etc.). Thus, most of it could not be traded, and the bonds market was therefore narrow in the first place. Furthermore, even the traded component of the debt did not allow significant degrees of freedom to pursue open-market operations. To maintain an "orderly" market the central bank had to exercise extreme delicacy in its intervention on either side of the fence; and even if it were not committed to a policy designed to *assure* a floor to bond prices (see note 12), its power to conduct open-market operations was constrained by the size of its bond portfolio. With a total bond portfolio of less than 2 percent of the monetary base in the early 1970s and less than 5 percent of the (positive) *change* in this base in 1972, sale of its entire portfolio would hardly have made a dent in the 48 (41) percent annual rate of increase in that base in 1971 (1972).[19]

Open-market operations were therefore conducted mainly with treasury bills, issued "on tap" at a price agreed upon with the treasury, involving a commitment by the latter not to use the net proceeds, if any, to finance government expenditures. Of course, this technique did not allow the central bank to pursue a policy designed to manipulate short-term interest rates. With treasury bill prices given within a very narrow range, operators in the market could decide what *quantities* to hold by comparing alternative yields. In other words, with these instruments' yields preset, it was the market that determined the quantity of treasury bills it held. With the range of predetermined prices strictly constrained, the central bank obviously could not determine the volume of its open-market operations.

In consequence, open-market operations were on the whole a very feeble instrument with which to accomplish the main mission—draining excess liquidity from the system. Indeed, the yield on treasury bills was raised only twice—in November 1969 and in August 1971—and the response was quite visible (Table 18). These effects rapidly wore off, however, as inflation in the second half of 1970 accelerated toward the 10 percent rate and beyond and yields on competitive financial instruments (large time deposits, for example) in 1971 blunted the edge even of the 8.5 percent nominal yields on treasury bills (Table 13).[20] The upturn in 1973—the relatively small increase in outstanding treasury bills in the first three quarters of that year (Table 18)—reflects the "moral suasion" of the central bank, which, by means of self-terminating "underwriting agreements," forced commercial banks to distribute to the public (or absorb) given quotas of these bills.[21]

An equivalent technique of reducing liquidity would have been to *reduce* the volume of outstanding directed credit to privileged sectors and activities. An inspection of Tables 17 and 18 shows that, except for 1972, this component of the Bank of Israel's assets increased rather than drained liquidity. And although the effects of the 1971 monetary avalanche were manifest, the Bank of Israel waited until April 1972 to make an official recommendation designed to reduce the monetary effect of directed credit: the governor's MPR suggested a sweeping increase in the interest rates charged on such credit. This recommendation, which meant that the Bank was not at liberty to set its own discount rate, was later approved by the Cabinet Committee on Economic Affairs, although the rates set were lower than those proposed by the Bank.[22]

Although "technical," these constraints on the central bank's freedom of action in the very sphere in which it was supposed to exercise its own discretion—short-term interest rates—indicates that these constraints were a matter of policy. The political community, represented in this case by the minister of finance and the Cabinet Committee on Economic Affairs, were unwilling to relinquish their hold over the level and structure of short-term interest rates. The tardy proposal by the governor to raise interest rates on some components of directed credit came after approximately two years in which inflation was running at a somewhat *higher* rate than the interest rates which he dared propose. And even this slight restrictive measure was not fully approved.

The half-hearted effort to stem the tide of liquidity using open-market instruments can be explained in terms of the political realities, some of which were rooted in the Bank of Israel Law. Yet attitudes also count: with inflation running at 12–13 percent and after an explosive growth in the monetary base in the first two quarters of 1971, the governor's statement that "the increase of Bank of Israel credit to the public is almost exclusively due to the financing of exports" should have raised some eyebrows.[23] This statement would have seemed quite odd in any case, but particularly when made in an official report, whose very purpose was to warn about the excessive rise of liquidity.

The Fiscal Stance

The Bank's impotence in handling the liquidity problem was not due only to its inability to engage in substantial open-market sales.[24] An inspection of the government net debt underlines the role of the fiscal stance in the explosive rise of the monetary base in 1971 and its major contribution to its earlier expansion. The central bank's government credit series in Tables 17 and 18 is the obverse image of the public sector's (domestic) fiscal deficit, net of borrowing in the domestic capital market. The Bank of Israel obviously had no control over the size and structure of the budget. The special legal twist in the Israeli case, which had far-reaching monetary implications (in fact, until 1985), was the fact that the central bank had no control over the volume of its *own* credit to government. The maximum (annual) volume of central bank credit to government was legally prescribed at a percentage of the budget as approved by parliament. The approval of the political establishment (in practice, the approval of the Finance Committee of the Knesset) was all that was needed for that purpose.

Unlike major industrial countries, where a government deficit would force the treasury to resort to the capital market (and generate upward pressure on the yields of government paper and on the structure of interest rates, thereby leaving the decision on how much to monetize the deficit to the central bank), in Israel these decisions, made by politicians, applied not only to the size of the deficit. In view of the government's direct access to central bank credit, a decision on the size of the budget gave full discretion to the treasury to decide on the (potential) size of accommodation by the central bank, actually on the printing of (base) money. The Bank's automatic financing of the huge budget deficits of 1970 and 1971 (some 6 percent of GNP) was one of the two main determinants of the explosive increase in the monetary base and of overall liquidity in the system. The fact that this need not have been so is clearly demonstrated in Table 18 by the negative entry for 1972—the monetary effect of the fiscal stance in that year was slightly restrictive (equivalent to sales in the open market).

A great deal of the monetary momentum generated by the rapid increase in the monetary base during the revving-up phase and in the first half of the lull can be ascribed to the effective (though not formal) money-printing powers which the Bank of Israel Law ceded to the Finance Committee of the Knesset. Furthermore, political control over the size and pattern of the monetary base was not restricted to financing the budget deficit by direct access to central bank accommodation. At one remove, it affected the potential printing of base money by its substantial influence on the net foreign asset position (i.e., the level of international reserves).

Currency Control and Short-Term Financial Movements

Our analysis also calls for reference to the series presented in column (4) of Tables 17 and 18—commercial bank foreign currency balances with the central bank. This liability item of the central bank reflected mainly the balances that commercial banks were obliged to maintain as an almost 100 percent backing for foreign currency deposits by recipients of German restitution payments and other depositors entitled to hold foreign currency balances. The Israeli pound value of these balances, and also their change in a given year, depended on the exogenously determined annual inflow of such foreign currency payments, on the portion thereof converted into Israeli currency, on the exchange rate of the DM vis-à-vis the dollar and, of course, on the Israeli currency/dollar rate of exchange.

The extraordinary expansion of these balances and the rise in their rate of exchange in 1971 resulted from a significant revaluation of the DM vis-à-vis the dollar, and from a 20 percent devaluation versus the dollar of the Israeli currency. Note, too, that the entries for every year in the series increased, indicating that these balances, which enter with a negative sign into the set of determinants of the monetary base, had a restraining effect on the latter's size. Indeed, the impact of this restraining influence was six to ten times greater than that of sales of treasury bills. This was, however, a voluntary decision by the owners of these balances, who could easily, at some interest cost, convert them to finance purchases of goods and services, or use them to acquire financial shekel assets.

The ever-increasing overhang of foreign-currency-linked deposits in those years was described as a "monetary time bomb," in view of its potential ability to generate a huge increase in the supply of money. The series show that during the entire take-off interval, from the beginning of 1970 to the Yom Kippur War, this bomb never exploded. In terms of its effect on the monetary base, it was undoubtedly restrictive; but this does not mean that it had no positive impact on aggregate demand, transmitted by means of the wealth effect. The devaluation-cum-DM revaluation of 1971, that is, the higher shekel value of the foreign-currency-denominated deposits, induced owners of these balances to increase real demand. This was equivalent to a reduction in these persons' saving rate from shekel-denominated income.

This is not to suggest that a rise in the annual inflow of receipts from German restitution payments, pensions, and immigrants' transfers did not affect the size of net foreign assets in the central bank's balance sheet, which more than doubled between 1969 and 1972 and helped pay for the huge (and growing) import surplus, with an inevitable expansionary effect on the monetary dimension of the economy.[25] But the overall monetary impact of Israel's reserve position depended on a medley of factors: the size of the import surplus, the volume of transfer payments, and the flows on capital account, both long-run and short-run.

Tables 17 and 18 underline the restraining monetary influence of the balance of payments in 1968 and 1969. The huge increase in imports and in the import surplus after the post–Six Day War jump in the level of economic activity was responsible for these increases. The corresponding rapid loss of reserves pushed them, early in 1970, below the threshold of two months of imports (Table 9). This restraining monetary effect disappeared at the beginning of the revving-up stage in 1970, although the import surplus position did not improve at that stage (Table 10). The data clearly show that it was a major improvement in the long-term capital account, supported by a relatively novel item in the short-term capital account—PATACH deposits[26]—which turned the tables and led to a slight increase in net foreign balances by 1970. While the substantial rise in long-term capital inflows was due mainly to a political decision (most of the increase reflected a major stepping-up of U.S. aid), this was not the case with short-term capital flows, which had a similar impact on the monetary dimension of the system. These short-term flows were directly linked to developments in the economy and to the workings of the exchange-rate regime.

The major inflow of short-term funds after the 1967 devaluation undoubtedly reflects the workings of forces outlined by the Mundell–Fleming hypothesis for the case of a fixed exchange rate regime. This model suggests that, with full capital mobility, a small country cannot conduct an autonomous monetary policy, which means that its nominal interest rates cannot differ from those set in the major financial centers. Israeli nominal marginal interest rates were, of course, significantly higher than comparable rates in financial centers (Table 14). But after two devaluations in the 1960s (1962 and 1967) its exchange-rate regime was evidently conceived as an "adjustable fixed rate regime," that is, expectations about the date and the size of a future devaluation would substantially affect the flow of short-term funds across exchanges. Furthermore, exchange control, which at that time was formally fully applicable to transactions on capital account, allowed the existence of interest rate differentials, which thus offered a standing temptation to move in if and when inflationary expectations subsided, and move out as they increased. The implementation of such moves required the explicit or tacit approval of the currency-control authorities.[27] In view of the direct impact of such flows on international reserves (and hence possibly on the monetary base as well), the policy of the exchange-control authorities had an immediate effect on the supply of money. At that time currency control was run by a department at the treasury and not by the central bank. This means that the treasury had another lever to use on the monetary and liquidity dimension of the economy at its discretion.

A juxtaposition of the data on the current account of the balance of payments, the net long-term capital flows and series of PATACH deposits (Table 10), and the monetary series in Table 15 offers more insight on the forces that set the strongly rising and accelerating pattern of the monetary base between 1970 and 1973. The very rapid (stable price) growth in 1967–69 led to a major deficit in the current account, in spite of the 1967 devaluation vis-à-vis the dollar and some European currencies. With long-run capital flows dormant, this caused a severe loss of reserves: by late 1969 they were below the "red line" of two months of imports (Table 9).

The situation would have been worse had Mundell-Fleming-type stabilizafjtion forces (relying on the increased credibility of the Israeli economy) not come to the rescue. That tacit relaxation of currency controls, whose main vehicle was PATACH deposits, offered a technical opening for the inflow of short-term funds. The increase of these deposits from close to nil in 1967 to $115 million in 1969 is an obvious case in point. This increase offered immediate support to the rapidly dwindling international reserves and at the same time prevented a further significant deflation of the monetary base and the money supply (Table 18).

With nominal interest rates around 15–16 percent (significantly higher than those in the main financial centers), the temptation to borrow abroad was strong as long as expectations of devaluation were low, as they were between 1967 and 1969. This was not the case in the first two quarters of 1970, in view of the continuing loss of reserves, but the situation changed abruptly after the August measures. These measures included, first and foremost, an effective (though not a formal) devaluation. The subsiding expectations of a formal devaluation thereafter paved the way for the inflow of funds with the tacit approval of the currency-control authorities. The almost threefold jump in the level of PATACH deposits within two years, to an annual inflow of over $300 million in 1971, is clear indication of the strength of the Mundell–Fleming forces and of the benign attitude, if not more than that, of the currency-control authorities toward the inflow of short-term funds.

The rise in unilateral transfers and long-term capital inflows from 1970 on, and the stabilization of the import surplus in 1971 (at a higher level than in 1969), meant that from the last quarter of 1970 until 1972 the balance of payments no longer functioned as a mechanism draining liquidity from the system. Although the import surplus had reached an all-time high, by 1970, long-term capital inflows were already almost equal to the deficit in the current account. From 1971 to September 1973 the basic balance (the difference between long-term capital and the current account) was positive. This meant that any net inflow on the short-term capital account contributed directly to the reserves and—unless sterilized by open-market sales and/or lower government accommodation by the central bank—to the rise of the monetary base (Tables 10 and 18). The explosive rise in the monetary base during the lull (1970/IV–72/IV) was therefore an inevitable result of the inability of the Bank of Israel to control another determinant of the monetary base—the flow of short-term capital. This was not just a matter of technique. An attempt to run a restrictive monetary policy, with inflation already beyond the single-digit rate, required pushing nominal interest rates to levels about twice as high as the effective LIBOR rates. This could be accomplished either under a flexible exchange rate regime, or with an adjustable-peg regime, by running tight currency controls geared to a monetary target (defined either in quantitative or interest-rate terms).[28]

As authority over currency control was vested in the treasury, the effective influence of the central bank on this link in the monetary setup of the economy was minute. The effective relaxation of currency controls toward the end of the 1960s also reflected the treasury's reluctance to go along with a sizable increase in nominal interest rates, in spite of accelerating inflation. The treasury used its authority to formally (and, in the case of PATACH deposits, tacitly) approve short-term capital imports as a device to circumvent attempts at monetary restraint agreed upon with the Bank of Israel. This agreement involved an attempt to pay higher interest rates due to the expected tightening of the domestic money market. The "loosening" of controls on short- and long-term capital account operations dulled the edge of a more restrictive policy[29] to force restraint on "non-privileged" borrowers (households and trade) and non-privileged activities.

The Failure of Monetary Policy

The failure of monetary policy from the beginning of the lull is seen in terms of its own public opinion instrument—the number of governor's Reports on the Means of Payment (MPRs).[30] After an interval of three years in which no MPR was published, two MPRs were presented in 1971 by the outgoing governor of the Bank. The next three MPRs (two in 1972 and one in July 1973) were submitted by the new governor. In view of the Bank's negligible control over the size of foreign reserves, its statutory automatic credit accommodation to government, its inability to set the quantity of sales in the open market and, finally, the constraint agreed upon with the treasury on the discount rate of financial instruments, the Bank could hardly attempt to manipulate the level of the monetary base. Monetary policy therefore amounted to nibbling away at the already high reserve ratios and/or setting temporary credit ceilings, both of which affected the monetary multiplier. The only support offered to these weak instruments was the statutory requirement to publish another in a series of MPRs. These did make the proper sounds about the need for monetary restraint involving a hike in interest rates, but it took two years, with inflation accelerating from 2–3 percent to 12–13 percent, before the new governor's MPR of April 1972 proposed to raise interest rates for the whole range of "privileged" credit. Although the real rates proposed for these privileged credits were still negative at the going inflation rates, they were not fully approved by the cabinet economic committee and were only partially implemented after a long delay.

The inevitable result of the delay in implementing these modest recommendations and their partial adoption gave another nudge to the monetary wheel. The 60 percent annual growth rate of the monetary base in the first two quarters of 1972, which forced the new governor to publish his second MPR within five months of the first, was an inevitable result of this delay. Two facts speak for themselves: (a) nominal interest rates on free credit did not rise at all, in spite of the high inflation rate, and (b) strong demand for credit. The stability of these nominal rates (Tables 13 and 14) and the extremely high inflation rate for over two years offer clear evidence that the Bank's attempts at restraint were too small and usually also too late. This, of course, is a reflection of the reluctance of the political community, supported by businesses and households, to allow a meaningful and effective rise in nominal short-term interest rates.

Such a feat would have been difficult to implement in any case, without a flexible exchange-rate regime, and in view of the institutionalized leaking of currency controls. It was also inconsistent with the policy of maintaining effective negative interest rates on development credits (Table 13) to which the government adhered steadfastly—even the minor key recommendation of the Bank (in the *Report* of April 1972) to raise interest rates on development credit by 2 percent was not accepted.[31] The "public outcry against a rise in interest rates" is referred to in *Report 1972* as a factor that forced the Bank to avoid the use of the price of credit as a rationing device.[32] This outspoken admission of the political constraints on interest rates offers the best explanation of the futility of a policy that attempted to stage "The Tempest" without Prospero.

NOTES

1. The nominal cost series was deflated by the annual average rate of change of the manufacturing products price index to derive the entries of Table 11, column 4, and the labor cost per unit of product series (column 7). As the 1970 package deal involved non-wage benefits, wages rose less than did total labor costs in 1970 and 1971. Note also that the quarterly series in Table 12 refer to manufacturing only, while the wage data in Table 11 refer to the economy as a whole. This, of course, means that the cost per unit of product series in Tables 11 and 12 are not fully compatible in terms of level and sometimes even in terms of the direction (sign) of change.

2. See Bruno (1986), p. 291, and table 14.2, p. 284. According to Bruno's series of "product wage" and his comments (p. 291), wages in 1969–72 and even later did not generate an upward shift of the AS curve. See also *Report 1974*, table XIV-1, p. 283.

3. See, e.g., *Report 1987*, Diagram IV-1, p. 68. The base year for the data in this diagram, which represents annual labor cost and labor productivity in the business sector, begins in 1971. The entries in Table 11, col. (7), are derived from these series, and those for 1965–71 are derived from cols. (5) and (7) of the same table. Since col. (5) gives wages in the economy as a whole and col. (6) gives a productivity series for the business sector only, the annual unit-cost data for 1965–71 in col. (7) are only rough approximations of the information on the pattern of this variable conveyed by the Bank of Israel's 1971–89 series. Furthermore, somewhat higher wage rises in the public sector than in the business sector (*Report 1971*, table IX-9, p. 171) entered in the wage and cost of labor series—cols. (4) and (5) of Table 11—"explain" the high entries for unit costs in 1971, seemingly inconsistent with the corresponding quarterly data for manufacturing in Table 12.

4. The conceivable 2–2.5 percent impact of sheqel import prices on the price level

was calculated using the ratio of the value of imports to resources as weights. This was, in those years, about 36 percent; see *Report 1972,* table B-2, p. 15.

5. The annual data in Tables 3, 7, and 9 represent changes between mid-calendar years. Since the lull begins toward the end of 1970/III, the annual average for 1971 approximates developments in the first year of this interval, the 1972 figures refer to the second year, etc.

6. Extra-budgetary devices used to promote public housing included widespread use of government guarantees for price-linked mortgage credit and for purchases of housing units if promoters failed to sell them at a preset price. These long-run commitments did not appear in current budget estimates—they surfaced as an expenditure item much later, if and when they came into effect. This indicates that domestic government demand (Table 3) understates the impact of government policy on aggregate demand. The same applies to the tax credit technique of investment promotion applied mainly to encourage investment in the production and services sectors. Since only future tax receipts were offered as an investment subsidy, current data (such as tax receipts) do not reflect the effect of these concessions. By offering a higher rate of expected return, the higher levels of investment had an immediate impact on aggregate demand.

7. The figures for real investment in manufacturing are from *Report 1972,* table XI-1, p. 233.

8. This policy was implemented mainly by expanding the scope of income mainte-nance to include a major expansion of the child allowances program. The annual rate of increase of income-maintenance payments between 1970 and 1972 was almost 14 per-cent. Another major boost occurred in 1973, when these allowances grew by about 28 percent (source: Kop, 1989).

9. The non-defense import series in Table 9 is a better gauge than total imports of the price-depressing effects of imports, since the latter includes and the former excludes "direct defense imports."

10. See Chapter 2, and notes 19–21 there.

11. This was, presumably, the attitude of policymakers, if not in the Bank of Israel then undoubtedly in the treasury. The submission, in March 1971, of the governor's *Report on the Increase in the Means of Payment,* instigated by the increase of M_1 at an annual rate of over 15 percent in 1970—the first such report after an interval of three years—is revealing. It is implicitly critical of the expansionary fiscal policy in a full employment context, and recommends "measures to reduce the rapid growth of means of payment." Yet its description of the monetary policy of 1970, as "highly restrictive," while allowing such an increase in the supply of money and a significantly greater in-crease in the more significant monetary aggregate for the short run—bank credit (Table 15)—in a full employment environment, sounds quite off the mark (*Review,* No. 38, p. 84).

12. The high liquidity of these instruments, hence their virtual function as CDs, was effectively (though not formally) guaranteed by the practice of the central bank of main-taining their stable yield over long durations. The yield, set at 7.75 percent in November 1969, was maintained for 21 months. The higher 8.5 percent yield set in August 1971 was maintained through October 1974. The latter nominal yields imply, of course, neg-ative real yields from, say, 1970/III onward. Hence the rapid decline of the outstanding balances from 1972/II on. The lagged response was due mainly to "special" devices used by the Bank of Israel to compensate commercial banks for the inflation-generated real cost of holding these nominal assets.

13. Although the annual and quarterly real interest rates follow a similar declining pattern through the entire take-off period, 1969/IV–73/IV, the pattern is not identical, either for the quarterly series of real interest rates derived by applying the GDP deflator as the measure of the price level, or for the quarterly series derived by applying the index of wholesale prices of manufacturing output (Table 14, cols, 2' and 3'). The latter is the more relevant gauge for the (ex post) real rate relevant to manufacturing enterprises; the former, based on the much more comprehensive GDP basket, is a better representative of effective ex post rates for business enterprise as a whole. The annual series (Table 13), derived by applying CPI as the measure of the price level, better represents the point of view of households. However, in view of the greater power of government to influence (temporarily!) the prices of a significant fraction of the CPI basket (say, 20–25 percent of its value), quarterly real-interest series derived by applying this measure might be misleading. These considerations also suggest that the implied annual rates derived by the GDP deflator (Table 14) offer a better approximation of the real ex post interest-rate concept. On the other hand, GDP-deflated data are not available to the public until the end of the year, while both the CPI and wholesale price indices are published monthly, with a two-week lag. This means that they are much more effective in the formation of price expectations, and are therefore better indicators of real interest rates in "real time."

14. The only available nominal interest-rate series for this period, presented in Tables 13 and 14, reflects the average effective interest rate on brokered and discounted bills. This type of bank lending was designed to circumvent the legal ceiling on the nominal interest rate (11 percent in the 1960s) and thus reflects the free credit market component through 1969. The abolition of the legal ceiling interest rate in March 1970 immediately eliminated this type of commercial bank lending, which was absorbed into the larger pool of "non-directed" credit. From 1970 through 1973 the series represents the interest cost of a growing component of the funds, described in bank credit statistics as "free credit denominated in Israel currency." (From 1974 onward, this interest-rate series describes the cost of credit for overdraft facilities.) In 1969, just before its disappearance, "bill brokered" credit balances were 33 percent of outstanding free credit and 19 percent of total bank credit. However, the market-determined higher interest cost of the "free" credit was only gradually imposed on the whole spectrum of "free credits." The process was not completed by the end of 1973. On this issue see, for example, *Report 1970*, p. 277, and note 1.

15. See *Report 1972*, p. 320, and the *Reports on the Means of Payment*, April 16, 1972, and September 1972 (*Review*, Nos. 39, 40). In spite of the monetary avalanche stressed in these Reports, the Cabinet Committee on Economic Affairs did not accept the governor's recommendation (made in the first Report) to raise the subsidized interest rate on directed "domestic credits" by 3 percentage points, to 12 percent. It was raised by only 2 percent, and the governor's recommendation to raise the cost of export credits from 6 to 9 percent was rejected.

16. This squares fully with the stability of the demand function for money discussed above. See Chapter 2.

17. In 36 of these 60 months, the actual reserve ratio was lower than the legal minimum. Excess reserves in 7 of the remaining 24 months were negligible. See *Reports 1969–1973*, tables XIV-5, XIV-4 and XIV-6.

18. Actual reserve ratios were declining through March 1971. Only the May figures show a rise to the December level shown in Table 15 (*Report 1971*, table XIV-4, p. 281). This move was initiated by the new governor, who took over at the end of 1971.

19. Bond portfolio data are from Bank of Israel, Balance Sheet, December 31, 1972, *Report 1972.*

20. The significant rise in the net sale of treasury bills in 1970 (Table 18) occurred in the first half of that year. Similarly, the significant rise in the sale of treasury bills in 1971 occurred in the last quarter of 1971, in the wake of the decision forced on the treasury to raise the yield to 8.5 percent. See *Report 1970,* p. 257, and table XIV-6, p. 265; *Report 1971,* p. 282, table XIV-6, p. 287; *Report 1972,* pp. 300–310.

21. The agreement, reached in November 1972, was to come into force on January 15, 1973. The termination of that agreement, which did not reflect financial market realities at that time, and the Yom Kippur War's impact on inflation, can be seen in the rapid disappearance from the scene of these bills, as the 1973/IV figures clearly show (Table 18). See *Report 1972,* p. 310.

22. In his recommendations of April 16, 1972, the new governor of the central bank proposed to raise the annual interest rate on credits from the shekel-denominated "circulating capital" funds from 9 to 12 percent, and the rate on funds for export finance from 6 to 9 percent. The recommendation to raise the export credit rate was rejected by the Cabinet Committee on Economic Affairs, and the rise on "circulating capital" credits was scaled down to 11 percent. See *Review,* No. 40, p. 119, and *Report 1972,* p. 320.

23. *Report on the Increase in the Means of Payment, Review,* No. 39.

24. The Bank of Israel Law, 1954, allowed issuing Bank of Israel Bonds; hence, the technical constraint mentioned above could have been overcome. In practice, the issue was one of policy, expressed in the all-out opposition of the treasury to allow this degree of freedom to the central bank.

25. For data on the inflow of pensions, restitutions and immigrant accounts, see *Report 1973,* table III-27, and *Report 1970,* table III-23.

26. PATACH (a Hebrew acronym) deposits are foreign currency, effectively dollar-denominated term deposits of non-residents, and thus are not subject to exchange-rate risk. The only risk is the risk of default—Israel's inability to redeem foreign currency commitments upon demand. Credibility was accordingly a sine qua non of tapping these funds, which, to some extent, represented an outflow (or flight) of capital from the unstable political and economic environment of several South American countries. These deposits may also have been used as a vehicle for "laundering" Israeli "black capital." The Six Day War, the 1967 devaluation of the Israeli pound, relative price stability through 1967–69, and the high growth rates maintained between the two wars greatly enhanced Israel's economic credibility. This gain in credibility, and the wide gap between Israeli nominal interest rates and those in the main financial centers, allowed operators to offer interest rates on funds denominated in foreign currency that were substantially higher than the alternatives available to investors in North American or European financial centers. This gap and events in the Israeli economy explain the sudden emergence and growth of PATACH deposits (Table 10) and their monetary implications.

27. For obvious reasons, the PATACH account system was operated as a sieve through which funds could flow in and out of Israel without too much interference by the currency-control authorities.

28. A monetary target—say, the growth of relevant monetary aggregates at rates adjusted to potential growth of real product—might be inconsistent with a balance-of-payments target such as an improvement in the reserve position. This was, however, not the case from 1970/III to 1973/III. The two devaluations (the 1970 effective and the 1971 formal devaluation) did stabilize the level of the import surplus and the increase

in unilateral transfers, and the long-term capital inflow provided a protective shield for the level of reserves.

29. A rare critical public expression on the treasury's policy of approving capital imports, designed for this very purpose, was made in a governor's Means of Payment Report (MPR) in 1968. Without referring explicitly to the treasury, it says: "Some of the licenses required for borrowing abroad were given to institutions and entities . . . for financing domestic activities in Israeli pounds. In this way constraints on monetary expansion are circumvented" (*Review*, No. 34, p. 97).

This statement referred to the workings of exchange control in 1968, when both the incentive to borrow abroad and the monetary implications of these activities were significantly smaller than from the 1970s onward. Though direct proof of the scope of such borrowing is unavailable, the practice apparently did not disappear in the 1970s. On the contrary, with greater temptation, the pressure on the exchange control for permits for foreign borrowing at the subsidized insurance premiums for exchange-rate risk, was undoubtedly much stronger. The data, particularly those on PATACH deposits, which were a major device for access to the foreign short-term finance, offers convincing proof that this was clearly the case, at the juncture at which restriction of monetary expansion should have been the order of the day (Table 17).

30. *Review*, No. 40, p. 133.

31. This proposal (which would have left the real rate negative) is supported by the highly illuminating statement that "very rapid expansion of development credits [in 1971], offered at very lenient terms, contradicts the attempts to restrain monetary expansion by means of a restrictive policy." See *Review*, No. 40, p. 119.

32. *Report 1972*, p. 301. This is not an unusual statement. Many others can be found in the "Reports on the Means of Payment" (in various *Reviews*) and in the relevant chapters in the [*Reports*].

— 4 —

The Brakes Are Off:
1972/IV–1973/III

THE LEAP OF INFLATION

The lull, with inflation hovering just beyond the single-digit level for two years, came to an end in the last quarter of 1972. This is clearly visible from Figure 2 and especially from the quarterly price data in Figure 3. These show that the rate of inflation nearly doubled at one go. The quarterly price data in Table 2 show this abrupt acceleration of the price trend and reveal the contours of the price explosion.

The three domestic price measures show annual inflation rates of well above 20 percent already in the first half of 1973, with the most comprehensive price index—the implicit GDP deflator—ranging above the 40 percent threshold. In the first nine months of 1973, before the Yom Kippur War, the economy moved onto an inflation rate just beyond 20 percent in terms of the CPI and the whole-sale price index (of domestically manufactured products), and just beyond 30 percent in terms of the more comprehensive (and less subject to indirect government interference) basket—the GDP implicit price deflator.[1]

The acceleration of Israeli inflation was out of line with the trend in the industrial world.[2] True, inflation was still high by the accepted standards of these countries, but it was, on the whole, subsiding. Before the onslaught of OPEC I in October 1973, it had been on a downward trend for several quarters. The move of Israeli inflation from an annual rate of just above 10 percent in 1970–72 to 20–30 percent was not merely a change in quantity: it reflected a pervasive change in the modus operandi of economic agents, who could not have been immediately or fully aware of the leap in price inflation.[3] Thus, when the oil price shock of 1973–74 hit the world economic system, Israel was already in the throes of galloping inflation. These contrasting developments—price accelerations in Israel while the rate of price increases was decelerating in the economies of its major trading partners—call for an explanation.

In the spring of 1973 the issue was the subject of a heated debate in the context of an argument on wage policy. In view of the rise of the annual rate of price inflation, in CPI terms, to about 20 percent in the first quarter of 1973 due to an unexpected high "reading" for March (which became public knowledge after April 15), the Histadrut made a bid to change the timing of COL allowances (COLA). From 1970 onward, these allowances were added to wage packets each January. The Histadrut did not propose a revision of the union–employers wage contract, which among other things spelled out the timing and rates of COLA; it simply sought to advance the date of the next COLA payment from January 1974 to July 1973. The acceleration of price inflation at that time, still conceived as temporary, was cited as the grounds for this claim. Although the claim was specific, it was obvious that, if granted, it would amount to a change in substance, namely, more frequent (semiannual, instead of annual) COLA adjustments.

The Manufacturers' Federation, supported by the treasury, initially rejected the Histadrut's claim. Both argued that the recent increase in the rate of inflation reflected exogenous, temporary cost-push factors. Thus, bringing forward the date of the COLA payment scheduled for the end of the year would only add to the upward cost-push pressure on prices. By the middle of the year the two parties to the wage agreement no doubt believed that inflation was zooming upward from the "stable" 12–13 percent in the lull phase. The employers and the treasury naturally attributed the new turn of the inflationary wheel to cost factors. The Histadrut did not reject this diagnosis, although if it were indeed costs that generated the jump in prices, particularly if these reflected either worsening terms of trade or the imposition of sales taxes, its call to advance the date of the COLA was unwarranted.

A MINOR COST SHOCK

Was the surge in prices really a cost shock? The quarterly price series in Table 2 shows a rise in the dollar prices of imports from the last quarter of 1972 through the third quarter of 1973. With the effective exchange rates for imports kept stable (Table 12), these dollar prices, reflecting an upturn in commodity prices worldwide, were passed through to the Israeli pound (IL) prices of imports. It was this development that gave a semblance of authenticity to the attribution of the 1973 acceleration of inflation to exogenous cost-push factors.

Note, however, that the cost-push effect of the August 1971 devaluation on IL-denominated import prices in the last two quarters of 1971 and first quarter of 1972 was three times greater than that generated by the world commodity prices in the same three quarters one year later. But the rate of price changes in the first three quarters of 1972 stayed put just beyond the single-digit threshold. In any case, assuming a *full* pass-through, the cumulative two quarters' increase in import prices (1972/IV and 1973/I) of about 8 percent would warrant, say, a 3 percent hike (at most) in the rate of change of the GDP price deflator in the first quarter of 1973; this rate, however, leaped by about 7 percent, to a quarterly rate of 9.9 percent. A similar estimate for the first half of 1973 would put the hike at 4 percent.[4] With inflation at a 9.5 quarterly rate (in terms of the GDP deflator) in the first half of 1973 (equivalent to an annual rate of over 40 percent) the exogenous cost hypothesis explains at best only a minor fraction of the leap in the inflation rate.

One other obstacle which the import-cost hypothesis has to surmount, at least as a major explanation of the abrupt upturn of price inflation in the 3–4 quarters preceding the Yom Kippur War, is the trend of prices in the major industrial countries. The significant rise in world commodity (and pre–OPEC I) oil prices should have had the same cost-push effect worldwide (Table 20). Yet the trend of domestic prices in the United States, the United Kingdom, Germany, and effectively all the industrial countries in the first three quarters of 1973 was downward, not upward.

This leaves a domestic cost shock as a possible explanation of the acceleration in inflation. The formal and effective import exchange rate was practically stable from 1972/I through 1973/III, so that the exchange rate could not have induced a rise in the inflation rate. Wages, however, were another story: the nominal wage shocks of 1970/I–II and 1973/I–II, in which COLAs and basic rates were adjusted, are definitely visible in the nominal quarterly wage series. The 11 percent rise in nominal wages in 1973/I, followed by more than 8 percent rises in each of the two following quarters, give credence to the treasury's and Manufacturer's Federation's argument, made as early as April and May of that year, that wage inflation was tantamount to "Hannibal at the gates."

The Histadrut, like every labor union, naturally rejected the wage inflation argument out of hand; it maintained that nominal wages lagged behind rather than led inflation. The political climate (see Chapter 5) helped the Histadrut to have its way on the predating, and a 5.5 percent COLA was paid in July. The extraordinary 8 percent rise in nominal wages in 1973/III can undoubtedly be attributed to this Histadrut victory.

Yet this does not justify the attribution of the move of the rate of inflation beyond the 20 percent threshold exclusively to the wage push, nor even exclusively to the cost push, which reflects both the wage and import price rises described above. The cost effect of a rise in wages obviously depends on the pattern of productivity, too. After subsiding somewhat in 1972 (to a still significant annual rate of 5.3 percent), productivity turned up again in 1973 (Table 12). The immediate cost-push effect of wages on prices was thus significantly reduced, to 5.5 percent in terms of a unit-cost proxy (wage per unit of product) in 1973/I after a low 1.2 percent rise in 1972/IV and to even less than that in 1973/II. Note that this cost increase in 1973/I was the same as in 1972/I and that the latter did not affect the rate of inflation in the next two quarters (Table 12). The Bank of Israel's estimate for labor cost per unit of product in the business sector supports this reading of the pattern of unit costs: it shows a rise in 1973 from a very low level in 1972, though the 1973 level is still lower than the unit labor cost of 1972, in which inflation was marking time.[5]

Thus, the unit-cost proxies for the period do not warrant an all-out rejection of the wage-cost argument of the treasury and the Manufacturers' Federation. Nor do the import price data presented above justify rejecting the claim that the rise in import prices contributed to price acceleration in 1973/II. Yet an attempt to attribute the acceleration of inflation *exclusively* to these cost-push factors is clearly untenable, since this hypothesis fails the level of macroeconomic activity test. A hypothesis attributing the leap of inflation to a cost-push effect implies a leftward shift of the aggregate macroeconomic supply curve (in terms of any of the alternatives of the two-dimensional setup—price level output or inflation output). The attributed cost push should thus show some trace of an effect on the relevant quantity measures—output and employment. Yet instead of some decrease in the quarterly employment data (Table 8) in the three prewar quarters, as implied by the cost hypothesis, the data show vigorous growth of employment at a rate greater than in 1970 and similar to the rapidly expanding employment in 1971 and 1972. The unemployment data for the first three quarters of 1973, with an unemployment rate of 2.6 percent (slightly lower than in 1972), indicate that the overfull employment of 1971 and 1972 was still dominating the scene at this juncture. The Beenstock series for the business sector actual and equilibrium output identify the three years 1971–73 as the interval in which the business sector was clearly operating beyond capacity, with a peak gap in 1972 (Beenstock, 1991, figure 3).

The continuing rapid rise in GDP clearly supports the reading, suggested by the labor market data, that in these quarters the economy was operating at full capacity and probably beyond it. This labor market situation suggests a different interpretation of the substantial wage increases of 1973 (until September of that year). Appearances—clad in terms of the predating of the COLA—notwithstanding, the strongly rising wage pattern of 1973 was (labor-market) demand determined. This, of course, means that although cost-push features were undoubtedly present, as they are in any inflationary situation, they did not set the economic tune as manifested, among other things, in a major acceleration of price inflation.

AN INVESTMENT AND CONSUMPTION BOOM

The situation in the real markets in the third and fourth quarters before the Yom Kippur War reveals a very strong thrust by the investment sector—housing as well as investment in the production and service branches of the economy (Tables 7, 8). Although in its sixth year of rapid growth, this investment shows no sign of slowing down, though at that time it was already almost double the 1969 level. On the contrary, in 1973/III it was 25 percent higher than a year before, and 20 percent above the level of 1973/I. The entries for new housing starts (Table 8) show that this was the case in the housing industry, which at that time was running flat out. Some shortage of cement, which generated an inevitable accumulation of stocks and a corresponding pressure on prices, offers clear-cut evidence of the strain on resources in these activities.

With very strong demand by households (underlined by a phenomenal 12 percent leap in private consumption expenditure) and reasonable export markets, the manufacturing industry catering mainly to these markets maintained the momentum of investment in real capital stock.[6] Another manufacturing sector—the rapidly growing defense industry—was making the heaviest capital investment in this very period; these were the years in which this sector made a breakthrough, growing rapidly at annual rates of over 20 percent in terms of employment. The move into the production of highly sophisticated weapon systems (the Kfir fighter plane is a case in point) required a corresponding rapid buildup of the sector's capital stock.[7]

Facing booming demand, which allowed entrepreneurs and firms to maintain and raise their profit margins, and very low and rapidly declining negative real interest rates, the impact of investment spending is fully explicable in behavioral terms. Note, in particular, that once the abrupt upturn of inflation became public knowledge, early in 1973/II, the temptation to increase capacity by firms eligible for "development credit" at negative real rates of interest (-10 percent at that time) might have been overwhelming. Moreover, with real interest rates on "free" bank credit approaching zero and sinking into the negative zone from early 1973 onward, firms had a major incentive to increase inventories, which they proceeded to do.[8] The very low rates of interest on bank credit encouraged entrepreneurs to start implementing capital investment projects even before the long-term "development credit" line to finance it was approved. They financed investment activity temporarily by means of cheap, zero real interest cost, short-term bank credit (Tables 13 and 14). The same rationale guided the behavior of contractors in the housing industry and the attitude of households.

The negative "development credit" rates applied, mutatis mutandis, to mortgage credit as well. Strong investment demand coincided with a boom in consumer expenditure. After marking time (at 9 percent or so higher than in 1971) in the second half of 1972, its rate of change accelerated steadily in each of the three prewar quarters of 1973, reaching an almost unheard-of annual growth rate of over 12 percent, corresponding to a 9 percent per capita growth of consumption expenditure. An inspection of disposable income and consumption data offers the main (although not the exclusive) clue to the major upturn in this *rate* of growth of consumption. The rise in the growth rate of consumption and of consumption per capita began in mid-1971 (Table 8). Its further rise in 1973, hence the strain it imposed on resources, exceeded that of 1972. The implementation of a wide range of social policy measures, focusing on income maintenance (children's allowances and old-age pensions) made a major contribution to the jump in the growth of real disposable income in 1971, and again in 1972, when it grew by 19 percent (GDP grew by 12 percent).

This leap of real disposable income over and above the growth of GDP and national income was not due only to the liberal income-maintenance policy implemented at that time;[9] it also reflected the major capital gains of households and of firms from the once-off leap of inflation to rates beyond the single-digit level in 1970 and 1971. The decline in the real value of payments on mortgage debt soon made a major difference; by 1972 it became an established fact of life affecting consumer behavior.[10]

Application of the permanent income hypothesis, which assumes a lagged adjustment of consumption to changes in *actual* income, to the almost 10 percent rise in per capita consumption expenditure in 1973/I–III following a 15 percent rise (in 1972) in per capita disposable income, makes perfect sense. So does the 6.4 percent increase in per capita consumption in the wake of a 7.5 percent increase (in 1971) in disposable income (Tables 7 and 9). Furthermore, the rapid increase in transfer payments to households belonging to lower income brackets worked in the same direction. These households, of course, have high (approaching unity) propensities to consume.

All this suggests that the outstanding leap of consumption expenditure in the nine months preceding the Yom Kippur War had its roots in developments that occurred a year or so earlier. The data at our disposal do not preclude the contribution of a contiguous factor to this dramatic upsurge in consumption. Quite possibly an abrupt change of expectations occurred in the specific circumstances of the prewar quarters of 1973. Thus, by the second quarter of that year, when the dry facts of the upturn of price inflation became available and the debate on the timing of the COLA brought it to the attention of all and sundry, an upward revision of price expectations may have been inevitable. Rational behavior in such circumstances, in an economy flush with liquidity (see below) induces a more rapid move into real markets by firms implementing ongoing investment projects and by consumers. With an election campaign on the way, an ongoing economic boom and overfull employment, a tremendous pull on aggregate demand, implemented by household consumption expenditures and by real capital formation by firms, was a foregone conclusion.

FISCAL LAXITY

In the period under review, Israel's economic leadership was effectively vested in the Ministry of Finance, which was quite aware of the rapidly rising trend of consumption in 1972 caused by the rapid rise in disposable income. This was clearly stated on the opening page of the National Budget for 1973, the annual document submitted for public perusal as the background for the budget legislation process.[11] The overfull employment situation and boom conditions, which were the official reading of the omens clearly spelled out in this document, required a highly restrictive fiscal policy. An inspection of Tables 3 and 5 does not reveal even a glimmer of an attempt at such a policy. Nor do the data show a reduction in government demand for domestic resources or an increase in absorption. The separate entries for the nine prewar months of 1973 indicate that public sector demand for goods and services did not grow at a significantly higher rate than GDP. But the annual rate of growth of over 8 percent, similar to that of GDP, does not reveal an attempt to reduce the public sector's claims on real resources.

The comparative restraint on the public sector's demand for goods and services was the more reasonable dimension of the budget's macroeconomic effect on developments in 1973. The other side of the coin—absorption—is quite another matter. Note, first, that although gross taxes grew at the same rate as GDP for the whole year, inclusive of the war quarter (Table 3, column 6), this was not at all the case in the three prewar quarters.[12] What made the major difference was the leap in the size of subsidies and transfers. Data on this component for the prewar quarters are unavailable, but since direct transfers were not increased during the war months (they were actually reduced), the full year entry probably does not exaggerate the rise in transfers and subsidies for the prewar interval. Given the much lower gross taxation rate (36 percent of GNP in the three prewar quarters as compared to 42 percent for 1972), the collapse of net government absorption from 18 percent in 1972 to about 11 percent in all of 1973 might rather understate the figures for the prewar quarters.

The expansionary impact of this development was inevitably transmitted through a considerable effective rise in disposable income, discussed in the previous section. The latter is obviously the mirror image of the former. As a matter of fact, the collapse of government absorption was not due to the increase in direct transfers (income maintenance payments and subsidies to "essentials"). They reflect mainly the imputed effect of inflation which, even at 12–13 percent annually, was rapidly eroding business and household debt to the government. The significant short-run effect of this phenomenon was the rapid erosion of the real value of installment payments on mortgages and development credit, an ongoing process which increased the permanent and actual disposable income, hence the real demand, of economic agents.

The available figures on government absorption at that time present a different picture. The subsidy and transfer figures at the disposal of policymakers (and public opinion) at that time were based on cash-flow data. These, of course, did not include inflation-generated imputations, so that the figures for transfers were lower, and net public sector absorption appeared significantly higher. The two alternative subsidy and transfer series—the corresponding alternative net absorption series and the domestic series of excess demand presented in Table 4— reveal the considerable differences between these series for the three prewar quarters of 1973. The cash-flow net absorption series, which was the information used by policymakers, shows a reduction in net absorption from 24 percent in 1972 to about 21 percent of GNP in 1973. An absorption rate lower by 3 percent only must have seemed quite virtuous to policymakers in a preelection year.

The real situation was, of course, quite different. Although neither policymakers nor public opinion and economic agents were aware of the magnitude of these inflation-generated capital gains, by early 1973 they undoubtedly felt the pocketbook effects of what had been going on for three years. The data on exploding consumption expenditure and on capital formation are an obvious case in point. The interesting and significant message of this argument is the fact that fiscal policy was highly expansionary, indeed, much more so than the information available to the political leadership might have suggested. This, then, was the policy implemented in an environment where overfull employment was clearly manifest, in the sixth year of rapid growth. With "big government" a fact of life, and a formidable domestic deficit (domestic excess demand) of over 10 percent of GNP in 1972, which had to be financed by the sale of bonds and by base money creation, the implementation of a countervailing monetary policy was an unenviable task. The lower gross tax revenues (as a share of GNP) in the prewar quarters of 1973 (Table 3) and the continuous rise in the size of transfers suggest that the financing of government during this interval required even greater creation of liquidity—creation of funded debt *plus* creation of base money—than in 1972.[13]

UNCONTROLLED MONETARY EXPANSION

A domestic deficit of over 10 percent and overfull employment would be a major monetary policy problem in any economic system. The statutory arrangements in Israel, whereby the central bank had no control (excluding "moral suasion") over the level of its short-term credit accommodation to the government, made the task an even more difficult one.[14] The relatively easy access of the Israeli government to foreign borrowing imposed another constraint on the management of monetary policy.

The standing orders for monetary policy are well known. On the whole, it should lean against the wind. In a full employment, inflationary environment such as existed in the early 1970s and in the third year in which the price level had been rising at more than single-digit rates, *restraint,* indeed a highly restrictive monetary stance, was undoubtedly necessary. However, an inspection of the monetary aggregates and the relevant interest rates reveal no such constraint. An (annualized) rate of growth of M_1 (at that time still the most relevant "money") of 26 percent in the prewar months of 1973 indicates no all-out attempt at restraint. Although somewhat lower than the 32 percent rate in 1972, the monetary avalanche was not brought under control. The 32 percent rise in outstanding bank credit (Table 15) suggests that both businesses and households were awash in liquidity in the three prewar quarters of 1973, even in the context of, say, the 1972 economic environment—a 10 percent real growth rate and inflation just over that rate (as in 1970–72). These data clearly indicate that the monetary sector did nothing to offset the expansionary forces generated by the fiscal sector. Indeed, the monetary aggregates in 1973/I–III only fanned the conflagration. They generated upward pressure on prices with some slightly reduced clout, at most, as they had done continuously from 1970 onward.

The official line on monetary policy, constantly reiterated in the governor's MPRs, stressed the absolute necessity of monetary restraint.[15] But the data for the prewar quarters clearly indicate that the central bank, which had lost effective control over the money supply early in 1971, failed to regain it during this interval. The dismal failure of monetary policy was not due to a misreading of the omens: the message which the Bank had been attempting to convey to the government and the public for over two years was that monetary restraint was imperative. However, in 1973 (as in the previous two years) the supply of money *more* than accommodated the 1972 rate of change of the price level and the growth-induced real income quest for liquidity.[16] Greater insight on this policy failure can be gained from the background factors underlying the development of the monetary base and of the multiplier.

The Money Multiplier

The size of the money multiplier is set by the currency/deposits ratio and the effective reserve ratios of the commercial banks. The latter is controlled by the central bank, particularly when banks are "loaned up." The currency/deposit ratios, however, are determined by the public, whose choice regarding the composition of its monetary assets can either drain or expand bank reserves. Table 15 shows that this ratio was stable in 1972 and 1973. Thus, it is in contrast to the 1970–72 interval, when the currency/deposits ratio decline contributed to monetary expansion.

The trend of the reserve ratio is, however, another story. The series indicates that this determinant of the size of the multiplier fell substantially from an admittedly high level of 57 percent for the so-called effective liquidity ratio to 52 percent. Thus, the money multiplier increased by 6 percent at this crucial juncture. This undoubtedly reflected the continuous reduction of the penalty rate on reserve deficiencies (Beenstock, 1991). Since control of the multiplier by manipulating the effective reserve ratio was, at that time, the main instrument for the implementation of monetary policy, this might raise some eyebrows. Lowering the effective reserve ratio generated the very opposite results from those of the monetary restraint policy which the Bank had been preaching.

Reference to the data on the formal reserve ratios—which differ from effective ratios—offers another clue to this upward move of the M_1 multiplier. The formal ratio, which was raised to 72 percent early in 1972, remained stable through December 1973. This was an outstandingly high ratio, and it contributed to the expansion of a non-bank (grey) credit market, a familiar feature in economies subject to prolonged bouts of high inflation.[17] The commercial banks, a powerful lobby in those days, were clamoring for relief and the monetary authorities were, of course, aware that in microeconomic and structural terms the banks did have a case. Although the Bank of Israel did not alter the formal ratio (in effect, the *marginal* reserve ratio), in practice it gave in to the combined pressure of the business sector, the commercial banks, and the treasury, which resulted in an increase of the credit tranche excluded from the reserve ratio rule. The quotas of the so-called "directed credit" formally allocated to privileged sectors (exports and the two "producing" sectors—farming and manufacturing) were increased.

The inevitable result of this retreat under pressure was a reduction in the average *effective* reserve ratio, affording greater leeway to banks to grant more credit (Table 15), albeit only to privileged sectors. But this restriction had no effect on the money supply—the increased credit inevitably boosted it. Outwardly, maintaining the formal reserve ratio projected an image of a staunch defense of the restrictive monetary stance; in practice, however, the central bank was yielding under pressure. The effective, not the formal reserve ratio was what really counted. Its substantial downward trend which, by definition, involves an increase in the money multiplier, was therefore a significant factor contributing to monetary expansion.

The Monetary Base

The second variable determining the trend of monetary aggregates—the monetary base—was highly expansionary. True, its growth rate was significantly lower in 1973/I–73/III than the incredible 40 percent and more of 1971 and 1972, but at 21 percent in the prewar quarters of 1973 it clearly paved the way for a highly inflationary monetary expansion. Although the components of this base are liabilities of the central bank, the Bank of Israel did not have full control over the creation (or destruction) of such liabilities. The effect of the balance of payments (current and capital account transactions) on the flow of international reserves (hence on the monetary base) is an obvious example. If currency controls had been run by the central bank, it could have wielded another monetary control lever, but although currency controls on capital account transactions were in force at the time, they were run by the controller of currency at the treasury. Currency controls could therefore not be used as an instrument of monetary control without the treasury's consent.

The direct access of the treasury to Bank of Israel accommodation was another factor that reduced the Bank's discretion in attempting to control the monetary base. Tables 17 and 18, which describe the level and flows of main Bank of Israel balance sheet items, indicate that it was not the expansion of government credit which called the tune in prewar 1973. In contrast to 1972, when government significantly reduced its debt to the Bank, its outstanding credit was increased. Yet the IL84 million increase in short-term government debt to the central bank accounted for only 11 percent of the increase in the monetary base. If this government accommodation were the only reason for the increase in the volume of base money, its expansion would have been miniscule, contributing to a restrictive monetary stance.[18]

The 1973(9) figure for Bank of Israel credit accommodation to the public, which represents the "directed" credit component of its assets, shows that this component's contribution to the expansion of the monetary base, although lower than that of foreign reserves, was still significant. Thus, while preaching restraint, the Bank actually accommodated monetary expansion. After a long delay the Bank proposed measures to reduce the growth of this "privileged" credit tranche, a proposal that was only partly approved by the cabinet's economic committee (headed by the minister of finance).[19] The delay in discussing the Bank's proposals and their partial acceptance in spite of the leap of inflation beyond 20 percent stresses the fact that the Central Bank was not a master in its own house. It could neither set the terms on which it accommodated the public nor attempt to control the volume of one of its main assets, if and when such control was warranted by considerations of monetary policy.

The main factor fueling the expansion of the monetary base was the hefty expansion of foreign reserves. These grew 40 percent in the three prewar 1973 quarters, after a formidable 100 percent expansion in 1972 (Table 10). It is well known that central banks have only remote control, and that only after a substantial lag, over the current account of the balance of payments, and this applies, of course, to the Bank of Israel, too. But in 1973 it was not the current account that caused reserves to expand. On the contrary, booming aggregate demand and inflationary expectations led to a major increase in the deficit on the current account, by about $500 million (Table 10). It was the capital account that moved into surplus, both for long-term capital inflows (as in 1972) and in the short-term interbank account. The latter development—the credit accommodations to Israeli banks by their foreign correspondents—took on outstanding proportions. Whereas such accommodation had been negligible as far back as 1965 (Table 10), in 1973(9) it surged to $360 million. The surplus on the long- and short-term capital accounts thus covered the $500 million current account deficit and also allowed a $400 million increase in reserves. This boosted the volume of base money.

With free capital mobility and a fixed exchange rate, central banks usually try to reduce the inflow by manipulating domestic interest rates downward. But the momentum of inflation was pressing for higher interest rates. Marginal nominal interest rates were thus much higher in Israel than in the world financial centers. A reduction of nominal rates was not a viable option, owing to Israel's comparative rate of inflation; hence the all-out effort by Israeli banks to borrow abroad on short-term account, and by Israeli businesses to increase this outstanding foreign trade credit. But these moves made sense only if the exchange risk was deemed small. The elections set for October 1973 suggested that in spite of the worsening of the current account and the rapid loss of competitiveness of Israel's export and import substitution industries, no devaluation would be likely before a new government was sworn in. This, of course, reduced the exchange risk. The nominal interest rate differential therefore offered a major lure for those seeking short-term foreign credit accommodation.

Capital account controls, still in place at that time, could have been used to reduce this inflow of funds, which was obviously inconsistent with the restrictive stance professed by the Bank of Israel. Yet currency control was vested in the treasury, which had other priorities: its policy of promoting investment by non-budgetary devices was implemented by a liberal capital-import licensing policy made attractive by low-cost (subsidized) exchange-rate guarantees. Data on medium- and long-term capital import licensing are unavailable. PATACH deposits, though designed as an instrument to attract short-term funds, offer a clue on this score. This instrument, devised by the treasury, was designed to attract foreign (mainly Jewish) funds from residents of politically unstable countries. After the Six Day War, which boosted the credibility of the Israeli economy, these deposits became a significant source of funds: massive inflows began in 1971 and reached an all-time high in the three prewar quarters of 1973 (Table 10).

The absolute levels of this inflow were at that time quite significant in terms of the relevant monetary aggregates. The inflow of over $400 million in 1973/ I–III contributed a great deal to the growth of the monetary base. The permissive policy of the treasury, which actually promoted the inflow of foreign funds, was obviously at cross purposes with a restrictive monetary stance. The governor of the Bank was finally forced to go public with his objection to this policy. Though delicately phrased in a short passage in the MPR of July 1973, the message the Bank sought to convey on this subject was quite clear.[20]

In view of the "division of labor" between the Bank and the treasury, with currency control in the hands of the latter, the central bank was powerless to stem the tide of medium- and long-term capital imports encouraged by the treasury. It could only attempt to convince the political leadership (in which task it failed), or appeal to public opinion (as it did). Even though its regulatory power gave the Bank substantial leverage over the commercial banking system, it nevertheless failed even to prevent the clearly speculative 1973 onslaught of short-term foreign borrowing by these banks, which, in terms of sheer volume, was clearly a new departure (Table 10). Indeed, the $360 million short-term borrowing from foreign correspondents contributed almost as much to the expansion of the monetary base in 1973 as did the inflow of PATACH deposits.

Modest open-market operations, which raised the outstanding volume of treasury bills by about IL80 million, could sterilize only a fraction of the "hot" money imported by the banks (Table 10). And even this volume of open-market sales barely made a dent in the rising tide of base money through September 1973. Even that level of sales was achieved by applying "moral suasion" (supported by some material rewards). The banks agreed, in return for some privileges, to sell (or purchase on their own account) a quota of these securities.[21]

The data reveal the dismal failure of monetary policy during the last stage of the take-off of the Great Inflation, in the nine months ending with the outbreak of the Yom Kippur War. As in the previous stages—the revving-up phase and particularly the lull phase—the monetary stance was more than accommodating. This is indicated not only by the quantitative data; it is clearly demonstrated by the nominal interest-rate series on "free" bank credit (Table 14). Although inflation was already well beyond 20 percent in the first quarter of 1973, commercial bank interest rates hardly budged through September. In the third quarter of 1973 these rates were about 20 percent annually, signifying a negative real rate for most outstanding bank loans. Monetary policy, such as it was, was quite loose during that explosive boom. Rather than attempting to apply the brakes, this policy was, in practice, adding to the conflagration.

THE CAPACITY CEILING AND GROWING INERTIAL FORCES

Although both fiscal and monetary policy were flashing "go" rather than "stop" signals throughout this crucial interval, one might still look for other factors which contributed to the sudden upsurge of inflation.[22] Monetary ease in 1971 and 1972, and fiscal policy in 1972, were as expansionary as in 1973, but inflation was still marking time throughout most of 1972. Household demand did increase significantly in 1973 and investment demand was still growing by leaps and bounds. While these upsurges no doubt contributed to the price explosion, their very existence (Table 2) defines the dilemma.

The supply side, represented by productive capacity, offers one highly significant clue to a tentative explanation. GDP figures indicate a much lower growth rate in the nine prewar months of 1973. It was down from 12 percent annually to about 6.5 percent (Table 9), still formidable, but significantly lower than the 1972 figures, and only about half the 11.7 percent average growth rate from 1968 through 1972. This decline occurred while the demand for goods and services was bursting at the seams—the upsurge of imports at double the rate of 1972, in real terms, clearly supports this reading of the state of the markets.[23]

All this clearly means that the slowdown was a production phenomenon, a familiar event in economies subject to the ups and downs of the business cycle. At its peak, as the system operates close to its (Hicksian) capacity ceiling, a halt in the rate of growth of output is inevitable. By 1973, the Israeli economy was already in its sixth year of roaring expansion. It was operating well beyond its capacity since late 1971 or early 1972. With a much smaller expansion of real supply and an all-out expansion in aggregate demand (only partly offset by growing imports), another turn of the inflation wheel seemed, at least in retrospect, inevitable.

The impact of real demand in these circumstances is another issue. Indeed, the business cycle theories invoked above to explain faltering supply also cite weakening demand factors at and around the peak interval of the cycle. Yet though the classical theories of the cycle take account of some inertial factors, the economic system to which these theories apply was presumed to be subject to constraints by several "anchors" such as the nominal supply of money (liquidity), nominal wages, and a fixed nominal exchange rate. The Israeli economy in 1973—in its fourth year of two-digit inflation—had by that time totally eliminated (or at least partly impaired) the effectiveness of nominal anchors. Price and exchange-rate linkages were by that time undermining the power of the nominal anchors, thus opening the floodgates to the "entry" of inertial forces. While these forces were probably weak at the revving-up stage of the inflation take-off, they had acquired substantial momentum by 1972 and were finally unleashed in 1973.

The price-wage linkage is, perhaps, the most famous of these inertial factors. The surge in its momentum was revealed by the claim made by the Histadrut (and granted) for a mid-year COLA in 1973, boosting both price expectations and expectations of rising disposable income. Yet the indirect linkage of money by means of the highly liquid price-linked government bonds, price-pegged within a narrow range by the Bank of Israel, was perhaps of no smaller significance in this context. The price linkage of monetary assets thus rendered the major nominal anchor of the system—money—impotent. With inflation continuously eroding the non-linked business sector and household debt to the government (and thereby increasing the net wealth of the private sector), the persistent inflation-generated rise in permanent income added another expansionary inertial factor to the equation.

What undoubtedly gave a strong upward push to aggregate demand—household consumption demand and business investment demand—in the feverish 1973 economic environment was the temporary stability of one nominal anchor: the exchange rate. It was clearly expected that the impending devaluation would not be implemented before the end of the year, that is, only after the elections.[24] Rational behavior in a full employment environment, with real disposable income growing more rapidly than GNP, could be expected to induce an immediate movement into real markets. The exploding aggregate demand of 1973 was thus not only sustained by the inertial factors at work, it was also induced by the expectations of an inevitable change in a temporarily stable factor—the exchange rate.

This, of course, underlines the relevance of politics and its impact on the workings of the economy during the almost four years of the take-off of the "great inflation," an issue we address in the next chapter.

NOTES

1. Government involvement in price setting was implemented in several ways. One of these was to set the date on which price changes of "essentials" were implemented. This had a significant effect on the time pattern of the CPI, as essentials at that time accounted for 20–30 percent of the value of the CPI basket. These manipulations could be easily implemented, since a significant fraction of the items defined as essentials (bread, grains, meat, milk) were either imported by government purchasing agencies or, if produced domestically, used inputs imported by these agencies (e.g., animal feed). Another technique employed was "moral suasion." This was used usually after devaluations, by "advising" the trading sector to sell existing stocks of commodities at pre-devaluation prices. A case in point is the August 1971 devaluation (*Report 1972*, p. 127).

2. Table 19, which refers to calendar years, indicates that in Germany and the United Kingdom, effectively, in the EEC, inflation was definitely down in spite of the major

(OPEC-induced) cost-push effect in the fourth quarter of the year. Quarterly price data for the United States (IMF, *Financial Statistics Annual,* 1974) show that this was the case through October 1973 in the United States, too.

3. An interesting example is an illustration used by Don Patinkin in a column dated April 6, 1973, in the *Ma'ariv Economic Panel.* He discusses the demand of the Histadrut to advance payment (to June 1973, instead of at the end of the year) of a COL allowance. Patinkin refers to a "13 percent expected rate of increase in prices in 1973" (Barkai et al., 1975, p. 155). At that time, before the publication of the March 1973 price index, Patinkin could not have known that the economy had already been subject to an annual rate of price inflation above 20 percent in terms of CPI and GDP for two quarters, and close to that rate in terms of the wholesale price deflator. The official forecast of the 1973 expected inflation, published earlier in the 1973 National Budget, referred to "a 1973 inflation in terms of the GDP deflator similar to that of 1972" (*Review,* No. 41, p. 104).

4. The cost-push effect of import prices was estimated by applying the import price/GDP price deflator coefficients derived from the same equation described in Chapter 2, and note 6 in this chapter. It was weighted by the ratio of the value of imports to GNP, which was about 0.55 in the early 1970s.

5. See *Report 1990,* Diagram IV-1, p. 133. This annual series, which refers to labor cost *in the business sector,* is qualitatively superior to and more reliable than our estimates in Tables 11 and 12, which refer only to wages. Although this is an annual series, it nonetheless lends credence to our estimated quarterly (Table 12) and annual (Table 11) series, though they refer to manufacturing and to the whole economy, respectively, and not to the business sector only.

6. The booming demand and the case for expansion is underlined by the intermittent shortages of cement in 1973. This shortage was not only due to strong demand, it was also the result of protection designed to exclude imports and maintain the monopoly power of the only domestic producer. See *Report 1973,* p. 130.

7. For data on the defense industries, see Barkai (1987), tables 1 and 2.

8. The real value of inventories in 1973 grew three times more rapidly than in 1972; this rate was some 1.5 higher than the growth rate in 1971 (*Report 1973,* table V-1, p. 129).

9. The decision to give social policy high priority in the 1973 budget was spelled out in the National Budget, published in January: "The budget for 1973 is designed . . . to contribute, first and foremost, to the progress of the weaker social groups" (*Review,* No. 41, p. 88). Income maintenance expenditure rose at an average annual rate of about 15 percent in 1971 and 1972 and at an annual rate of 18 percent in 1971–73. Children's allowances grew 24 percent during these three years. See Kop (1989), pp. 52–53, and the 1970–80 database of the Center for Research on Social Policy, Jerusalem.

10. The capital gain to debtor households and firms and the capital loss of the lender—the government—is reflected in the 1970 and 1972 jump of the negative inflation tax series presented in Sokoler (1987), tables 8 and 9. Early in 1973 the real cost of an installment payment by a household that had taken a mortgage in 1969 was about 70 percent of its value before 1970. By the middle of the year it was down to 66 percent.

11. Sokoler (1987), p. 77.

12. The substantial difference in the tax columns for the full year and for the prewar period of 1973 (Tables 3, 4, and 5) reflect the raising of tax rates in October and November 1973 to finance part of the war expenditures (*Report 1973,* pp. 169–70).

13. Specific data on transfers and subsidies for the first three quarters of 1973 are unavailable. The figures for the full year show an enormous leap in these budgetary (actual and imputed) expenditures. But these were undoubtedly affected by the war; the leap in National Insurance Institute (NII) payments to reserve soldiers who were called up is a case in point. The full year figure therefore overstates the rise in transfers in the prewar quarters of the year. Yet the acceleration of inflation to 20–30 percent and the corresponding private sector capital gains pushed this imputed item—transfer payments—upward. Although no specific figures are available, the subsidies-cum-transfers entry for 1973/I–II was higher than in 1972, but lower than the 31 percent entry for the whole year. The implications for the size of the government deficit in this interval are obvious.

14. The only formal constraint on government access to Bank of Israel short-term credit was the approval of the Knesset Finance Committee (see Chapter 2).

15. In his covering letter, included in the July 1973 *Report,* the governor refers to his proposals to restrain the inflation process "submitted with the two Means of Payment Reports of April and August 1972 and the proposal submitted to the joint government, unions, and employers committee for the restraint of inflation" (*Review,* No. 42, December 1974, p. 121).

16. This refers, of course, to price inflation somewhat beyond the single-digit level, prevailing since 1971. Monetary accommodation in 1971 and 1972, given the 10 or so percent growth rates of GNP, would mean an expansion of M by, say, 20 percent. This figure is significantly lower than the actual figures of the expansion in M_1 and M_2 in 1971 and 1972 and also for that of M_1 in 1973—the subject of our discussion.

17. In the first place, it increases the risk, hence real costs in the credit market; it also reduces the effectiveness of monetary policy. The nominal reserve ratio figures are taken from *Report 1973,* table XIII-6, p. 304.

18. This is inconsistent with the substantial increase in government deficit (domestic excess demand), which was running at over 10 percent of GNP in that interval. The reason for the small Bank of Israel credit accommodation was a booming demand for government paper—"the very substantial increase in demand of price-linked government bonds by households, firms and financial intermediaries" (*Report 1973,* p. 351). These provided the government with most of the funds needed to cover its cash requirements. Since linked government medium-term bonds, effectively pegged within a narrow range of prices, were highly liquid instruments, the liquidity creation due to the huge deficits did not surface as a money supply issue at that stage. The seemingly small accommodation by the central bank was considered by the political community as a sign of commendable government retrenchment. That it was nothing of the sort is clearly indicated by the rush of households and businesses into (price-linked) bonds—a clear indication of rising inflationary expectations from the last quarter of 1972 onward.

19 .*Review,* No. 42, p. 136. The date of the report suggests that the Bank's specific proposals came far too late. In less specific terms, the proposal called for tightening the terms under which these credits were granted, raised in the two 1972 MPRs and in the numerous formal and informal discussions between the Bank and the treasury. But all this was to no avail until the summer of 1973. See also *Review,* No. 40, pp. 119, 142.

20. "The data show that the number of licenses for foreign borrowing granted recently has been slowing down, but in spite of this the inflow of credit from abroad is not sufficiently lower; more action on this score is required." This is how the Bank of Israel chose to phrase its objection to the treasury's promotion of capital inflows in an infla-

tionary environment, attributed in the same document to "excess aggregate demand over an extended period" (*Review,* No. 42, pp. 134, 139). The reference to the inflow of cash is followed by specific proposals to restrict foreign borrowing by imposing "a maximum interest rate," and target requirements.

21. The arrangements concerning this open-market sale were codified in an "under-writing contract" between the Bank of Israel and the commercial banks. The banks' attempts to unload these securities involved highly discriminatory treatment in favor of big investors in these treasury bills, who were offered significantly higher yields; the cost was borne by the banks, partially reimbursed by the Bank of Israel (*Report 1973,* pp. 368–70).

22. The leap to an inflation rate beyond 20 percent was unexpected until late April 1973, and even after that. The National Budget proposal, published in January 1973 (*Review,* No. 41, p. 104), predicted a similar rate of inflation in 1973 as in the previous two years. A case in point, reflecting professional opinion which had for two years been highly critical of government policies, is Patinkin's reference, made early in April 1973, to a similar figure (see note 3 to this chapter).

23. The figure relates to non-defense imports (in constant prices) excluding ships, airplanes, and raw diamonds, which are the most relevant gauge in this context (*Report 1973,* tables III-2 and III-3, pp. 43–47). Non-defense imports inclusive of these items grew at an even higher rate.

24. A clear indication of these expectations is the banking system's plunge into foreign short-term borrowing, referred to above. The outstanding foreign bank credit to Israeli banks grew from $24 million at the end of 1972 to $262 million in September 1973 (Table 10). Statistics of the NATAD rate and of the black-market exchange rate support this view of expectations concerning the exchange rate in 1973. See *Report 1973,* p. 47.

—5—

The Political Economy
of the Take-Off

THE ECONOMY: PERCEPTION AND REALITY

The outbreak of the Yom Kippur War was a major political debacle and, ultimately, the undoing of a whole generation of political leaders. The ensuing economic fiasco, showing up immediately in terms of an outstanding leap in inflation and then in a major slowdown of economic growth, is usually wrapped up in the same package with the unfortunate results of the political disaster.

While the army chief of intelligence and the minister of defense were sticking adamantly to their preconceptions, causing them to be caught by surprise by the outbreak of hostilities, the political leadership, misled by the advice of Moshe Dayan, could not make a similar claim about inflation. There was no Yom Kippur surprise on this score. At the outbreak of the war, inflation had already been running at over 20 percent annually for about four quarters; and it had crossed the single-digit threshold four years earlier. Its leap from somewhat above the single-digit rate to 20 percent and beyond had, by the outbreak of the war, been common knowledge for almost six months.

Whether the outbreak of the war was a tactical or strategic surprise is a moot point. But this is obviously not the case with respect to inflation, which did not materialize like a bolt out of the blue. The very high rates, even by Israeli standards, for four years in succession signalled the advent of economic failure long before the unexpected onslaught on Yom Kippur, 1973.[1] However, neither public opinion nor the political community perceived the state of the economy in such terms at that time, that is, in the early 1970s and until October 1973. On the contrary, in the public perception and in public lore, these years, going all the way back to the postwar quarters of 1967, were and are imprinted as the ''seven good years'' of the Israeli economy.

A retrospective view gained by inspection of the price curves (see especially Figures 1 and 2) suggest that inflation was indeed a minor affair if compared with what happened from 1974 onward, and especially after 1977. By the standards of the late 1980s and early 1990s, with inflation marking time at an annual 17–20 percent for some seven years, the price trend of the early 1970s seems quite reasonable. Furthermore, the data on production show that on the eve of the Yom Kippur War the Israeli economy was twice as large, in terms of private sector GDP, as at the previous all-time high in 1965 and more than 50 percent larger in terms of that year's GDP per capita, in spite of a hefty 27 percent increase in the size of population (Table 9). In the aggregate, and also in its structure, due to a major expansion of manufacturing industries in general and a high-tech defense industry, the Israeli economy in 1973 was an altogether different entity than the one emerging from the 1966–67 slowdown. In terms of its real aggregates it was undoubtedly a success story.

The inevitable result of all these developments was a substantial improvement in living standards. This rapid growth, supported by the net inflow of resources from abroad, meant that per capita consumption levels were 35 percent higher than in 1966 (Tables 7, 8, and 9). Housing standards, in terms of stock per capita, rose at a similar rate.[2]

Benefiting from the inflation-induced major capital gains,[3] most Israelis in those years (and more so in 1972–73) felt that they had never had it so good.[4] Euphoria spread immediately after the Six Day War and again after the August 1970 ceasefire along the Suez Canal, Nasser's death, and the almost simultaneous defeat and expulsion of the PLO forces from Jordan (in September 1970). With quiet along Israel's vulnerable frontier in the northern Jordan valley and a strictly enforced ceasefire both in the Suez Canal zone and on the Golan Heights, the political leadership tended to rest on its laurels. The ongoing six-year economic boom and a welcome new wave of immigration supported a similar reading of the omens.[5] Neither the economic leadership in the treasury nor the political leadership, which had absolute confidence in and gave all-out support to Pinhas Sapir, the minister of finance, were ready to admit that a 20 percent rate of inflation could be a sign of economic failure. It was considered a minor blemish on an otherwise outstanding record of performance.

THE BENIGN NEGLECT OF INFLATION

To people at the economic helm the leap of annual inflation beyond 20 percent was regarded as an unfortunate happenstance. They did, however, feel quite comfortable for several years with inflation just beyond the single-digit level, undoubtedly believing that it could be contained at that level; and they did admit that inflation was a problem, as indicated in Bank of Israel *Reports* which kept reiterating its dangers. Yet in spite of a continuous barrage of private and public warnings by professional economists, fiscal and monetary policy, sometimes singly and sometimes in tandem, continued to stoke inflation over the entire

1970–73 take-off interval.[6] Thus, when the Israeli economy had to absorb the major cost push of OPEC's first price hike, Israel was much more vulnerable than any other industrial country subjected to the same oil price shock. With inflation on the rise and already running at an annual rate three to four times the rate prevailing in those other countries, OPEC I pushed up Israeli inflation all at once into the 40–50 percent annual range.

The initial conditions underlying the point of departure to these post–OPEC I inflation rates were, of course, not reached by design. Runaway inflation was obviously the last thing a government in power would want at that particular (or any other) time. Although in the case of a small country the thrust of exogenous world market factors might be expected to have a major impact on the price level, experience suggests that this hardly ever happened in the twentieth century—the "century of inflation." In any case, this did not apply to the Israeli case. Although still above the low level of the early 1960s and high on the political agenda, inflation rates in 1970 in all industrial countries were moving down just as Israeli inflation was turning up; this holds for the entire take-off period (Table 19). We have seen that the Israeli inflation of 1970–73 had a clear domestic trademark. It was man-made, the result of the modus operandi of Israel's body politic, subject to the social constraints of the time along with the foreign and defense policy impositions. The politics of the matter were undoubtedly an inherent part of the economic policies adopted and implemented. We propose to focus on these in what follows.

While preelection posturing was clearly a factor in the refusal to adopt the necessary highly restrictive policies in the three prewar quarters of 1973, this does not apply either to the very first stage of the take-off (the revving-up phase) or to the following lull. The 1969 election campaign, in which the labor party was comfortably returned to power, was just out of the way. Electioneering was therefore not a pressing issue for the design and implementation of economic policy in 1970 and 1971, as inflation leaped from 2 to 10 percent and later moved to 13 percent. This is probably also true of the first half of 1972. This is supported by the fact that Golda Meir's government had the political courage in 1970/III to end the three-year National Unity Government experiment, allowing its other main faction, led by Menahem Begin, to move to the opposition benches on a highly delicate and politically divisive issue: the ceasefire terms with Egypt which ended the War of Attrition in August 1970 and suspended the confrontation along the Suez Canal for the next three years.

This is not to say that political considerations were irrelevant to economic policy making at the beginning of the take-off. Until August 1970, with the War of Attrition in full swing both along the Suez Canal and on the Jordan front and with almost daily notices of civilian and military casualties, morale was a highly sensitive issue. An economic boom was an obvious morale-boosting factor in these years of attrition (1968–70). Policies designed to call an even temporary halt to expansion might have been rejected out of hand in view of the high tensions that had to be endured as long as the border skirmishes were going on.

By September 1970, and once the shooting was over, the urgency of morale considerations abated significantly. Even the foreign policy-cum-defense stance at that time could have allowed the framing of a policy involving fiscal retrenchment and monetary constraint. Had there been any doubts on this score, the incoming data on losses of reserves and the rising price level made it quite clear that the need for action was acute.

The August 1970 measures, which involved a partial effective devaluation (see Chapter 3) and a rise in net fiscal absorption (hence also a reduction in the budget deficit—the only significant reduction in almost four years) were indeed an attempt to deal with the demands of the economy. The timing was, of course, not fortuitous. The government was using the political window of opportunity to pursue an unpopular policy. Yet, though perhaps not too late, it was too little to improve the current account of the balance of payments and, more so, as an attempt to nip the onslaught of inflation in the bud. The admission that the August 1970 measures were too weak to right the balance of payments came one year later (August 1971), when the government was forced to devalue again: this time a formal devaluation, across the board. Excluding verbal statements, mainly in Bank of Israel's publications, there was no operational admission that inflation needed shock treatment. The 20 percent devaluation in 1971 was not supported by a reduction in the budget deficit. The latter was allowed to rebound and expand substantially (Table 3). Furthermore, from the middle of 1970 on, monetary policy was highly expansionary (Table 16, and Chapter 3).

These expansionary policies were pursued, although the standard operating procedure for implementing a devaluation in a full employment environment requires a highly restrictive fiscal stance and clamping down on monetary aggregates, involving a substantial rise of short- and long-term interest rates. Since a substantial hike in the price of "essentials" was one of the instruments used in both devaluations, the reinforced cost-push effect of these devaluations required even more than the usual full compliance with such a procedure. Yet, although the upturn of inflation was well known by August 1970, and was a fait accompli a year later, as inflation crossed the single-digit threshold, these operational codes of behavior were flaunted. Monetary aggregates were allowed to expand at an unheard-of rate, real interest rates turned negative, real public sector demand was never reduced, and the budget deficit expanded massively from 1971 on. The ministries charged with economic policy were aware of what was happening and, at least until the end of 1972, would not have been constrained by pressing electoral considerations had they decided to implement unpopular measures. Yet they did not attempt to stem the tide. In fact, their policies worked in the opposite direction: they treated the mounting danger and challenge of inflation with what could, perhaps, best be described as "benign neglect."[7]

AN ECONOMIC RATIONALE AND A MISUNDERSTANDING

This attitude and behavior merits close examination. The conceptual background of the approach that regarded "some" inflation as part and parcel of full employment and rapid growth was the latent Phillips Curve notion. Although challenged by Friedman as early as 1968, this notion was still popular in mainstream macroeconomic thought. It was, of course, the conventional wisdom from the late 1950s to the early 1970s among a wide range of political groupings stretching from left of center to the center and even beyond. After World War II the social democratic parties and (somewhat more reluctantly) the parties of the center used the Phillips Curve notion as a rationalization for the price level implications of their expansionary policies. They admitted that these expansionary policies were endowing industrial economies with an inflationary slant, but maintained that the reward was an age of full employment, reduced social tensions, and the highest growth rates ever, in sharp contrast to the era of deflation and unemployment of the 1930s.

In retrospect, one might discern another conceptual train of thought that made "some" inflation admissible under the existing circumstances. The theoretical dimension of this issue shows up in an omission: the inflation models of this period hardly ever mention (in fact, often omit altogether) the relevance of inertial factors. These models implicitly assume that the rate of inflation can be contained by sheer volition on the part of the authorities.[8] The technical expression of this approach was the analysis of inflation by applying the "traditional" aggregate demand IS/LM general equilibrium setup. The focus on the price *level*, rather than on its *rate of change,* and the difficulties of handling cost-push effects emanating from labor markets or from deteriorating terms of trade and devaluations within an IS/LM framework led to the implicit suppression of the relevance of inertial factors. This suggested that an attempt to stop inflation could be relatively easy if handled by the judicious manipulation of conventional macroeconomic demand management.

This approach afforded the upper echelons of the civil service in the Israeli economic ministries an intellectually reasonable rationale for the continuation of highly expansionary economic policies, even though by 1970 the economy was already operating at its full employment ceiling and in defiance of evidence that inflation was on the move. The appeal of this undercurrent of thought in Israel was probably much more significant than elsewhere thanks to the ingrained belief in the power of government to shape and control the economic system. This belief could, indeed, call on the experience of two decades of government-controlled growth and structuring of the economy. It was personified by a powerful minister of finance, Pinhas Sapir, who by 1970 had already been at the helm for eight years and had a strong political standing in the governing party and in the country.[9]

It did not occur either to Sapir or to most others that the successful growth performance meant that by the early 1970s the Israeli economy had largely outgrown the option of shaping its structure and controlling its development by manipulating almost all the relevant levers from the treasury.[10] Furthermore, although they were aware of the comprehensive price linkage features in the economy, neither the minister nor many others in and out of government had an intuitive grasp of the momentum of the forces unleashed by the dynamics of the inflationary process due to such linkages. The major capital gains of businesses and households are an obvious case in point. The creation of greater uncertainty about the future was, of course, another imponderable, whose impact on real markets drew very little attention.[11]

ECONOMIC CONSTRAINTS: THE SOCIAL AND INSTITUTIONAL SETTING

Besides the intellectual setting which endowed the cavalier approach to the unfolding inflationary process with a veneer of academic respectability, there were, of course, pressing defense and political issues which required a proper economic response. Defense was undoubtedly of major economic significance in this context. One aspect of this issue was the rapidly rising oil revenues of the Persian Gulf states and of Libya, due to rapidly rising output, supplemented from 1970 onward by a significant rise in oil prices. These developments enabled Egypt, Jordan, and Syria to acquire modern weapons systems. Another issue was the decision made by the Soviet Union to finance and supervise the rearmament of Egypt and Syria—offering them state-of-the-art arms in almost unlimited quantity.

But it was not only the overall growth of defense costs that mattered. Israel fought and won the Six Day War with defense forces requiring about 7 percent of GNP *plus* (self-financed) defense imports of about 3 percent of GNP. It faced the Yom Kippur onslaught with a real domestic expenditure that in 1973/I–III was 11 percent of a GNP almost twice as great as in 1967, *plus* defense imports approaching 9 percent of GNP (not entirely self-financed). The difference in these figures indicates the tremendous increase in the burden imposed on the system and especially on government finances.[12] The effect of the timing of these defense requirements on the generation of aggregate demand pressures was no less relevant than their size. Just as the economy was nearing its capacity ceiling in late 1969 and early 1970, the War of Attrition was approaching its peak. Granting absolute priority to defense requirements—setting up fortifications along the Suez Canal and building defense works involving the erection of an electronically controlled fence along 100 miles of the Jordan—was inevitable at this particular juncture. The August ceasefire, initially set for six months, did not reduce these pressures. Rather, it increased the pressure on resources because of the agreed time limit. The decision to fortify the canal line led to a crash program to implement it before the end of the six-month deadline. The rise in domestic defense expenditures to an all-time high of 14 percent of GNP and more in 1970 and 1971 therefore coincided with the time when an attempt to control inflation was certainly due (in fact, overdue), requiring massive fiscal retrenchment.

Nor is this the whole defense story. The lessons of the French embargo, Britain's retreat from its commitment to sell Israel modern tanks, and the recurring difficulty in gaining access to first-line American weapons systems, even from the friendly Johnson and Nixon administrations, led to a strategic decision, made some time in 1968, to establish a state-of-the-art defense industry.

This all-out effort, not fully represented by defense budget estimates (Tables 3, 5, and 6), involved the rapid buildup of a sizable advanced, high-tech industrial sector. The 70 percent growth of the labor force in defense industries between 1968 and 1972 offers a clue to the magnitudes involved, although it underestimates the size of capital investment channeled into these endeavors.[13] The result of this effort was, among others, a state-of-the-art Israeli-designed and produced aircraft (the Kfir) which saw action in the Yom Kippur War. Yet the drain on resources which this policy imposed occurred at the very same time as the (over) full employment economy was running flat out.

The volume and timing of defense expenditures were not the only political constraint forcing the hand of the treasury. The second constraining factor was immigration. The surge in immigration, by a factor of two, to 40,000 immigrants annually, occurred at the very beginning of the take-off of inflation and continued through 1974. With immigrant absorption requiring a major public-sector-financed housing drive and the construction industry already strained by defense requirements and a private housing boom, a major increase in aggregate demand ensued. This occurred at the very time when restraint to fight inflation was the order of the day.

Civilian government demand was 9 percent of GNP and government investment rose in 1972 close to 7 percent, so that at least some of the defense and immigration related drain on resources could conceivably have been offset by reducing the civilian component of government demand for goods and services: a proper scale of priorities could, therefore, have allowed some retrenchment. But this meant reordering priorities by relegating welfare state features such as social services and income maintenance to the end of the line, a choice the government was very reluctant to make. On the contrary, claims that the economic benefits of the boom were not being evenly distributed put the welfare state proponents on strong ground. Whatever the facts of the pattern of distribution, what counted in political terms was the conviction of second-generation voters, the sons and daughters of immigrants from North Africa, born, or at least educated, in Israel, that inequality did exist. Their protest moved into the streets and its effect on the conscience of the community and in the political arena was both immediate and significant. Pushed by these events and the shifting demographic pattern of the electorate, the government embraced a far-reaching social policy in 1971. Its effects in terms of expenditure on income maintenance and public housing were already on the books in 1973. The collapse of net government absorption in 1972 and 1973, due to the rise of income maintenance payments (Table 3), indicates its very magnitude.

With full and overfull employment a fact of life, and a reduction of government expenditure on goods and services and/or lower transfers excluded, the textbook procedure called for another turn of the tax screw. But gross tax revenues were, since 1970, already above 41 percent of GNP (marginal tax rates were 60–70 percent for people in quite modest income brackets). Short-run macro considerations did justify higher tax rates, but such a move was clearly unwarranted from the point of view of long-run structural considerations, entrepreneurial incentives included. It goes without saying that the politics of a proposal to raise tax rates flashed a red signal.

With fiscal policy on an expansionary track, monetary policy should at least have attempted to hold the fort. As noted, however, monetary policy, too, had been highly expansionary since mid-1970. Although two consecutive governors (after a changing of the guard in November 1971) went on record with repeated warnings on the dangers of inflation, the central bank did not practice what it preached. We noted above (Chapter 4) that the constitutional framework of the Bank, as set out in the Bank of Israel Law of 1954, circumscribed its power vis-à-vis the political authority—the government, the treasury, and the Knesset. Its "independence" was therefore a far cry from the notion of power, responsibilities, and discretion traditionally associated with central banks in industrial countries. This was, of course, no accident. The perception in the 1950s of the role of government in economic management worldwide, and even more so in Israel, tilted the balance of the Bank of Israel Law in favor of the political element in the balance of power. The substantial fiscal deficits and the law, which forced the central bank to accommodate the treasury, reduced the freedom of the central bank and severely curtailed its discretion on the management of monetary policy.

Even with these constraints on its freedom of action, the Bank of Israel could have stepped a bit harder on the brakes. Of course, this would have taken its toll in terms of friction with the business sector and with a treasury run by a dominant personality. David Horowitz, the first and eminent governor of the Bank, was on his way out, and his willingness to join the fray in 1970–71, when a more assertive monetary policy might have been effective in reducing inflationary pressures, was presumably not strong enough to take on the government and the public at large. In 1972 the situation was already largely out of hand. In any case, the newly appointed governor, Moshe Sanbar, was in no position to confront the government's economic committee and the minister of finance (he did so two years later, in 1974, but this does not belong to our story). These two bodies, as noted, dragged their feet in the first place and never approved the governor's full set of quite modest proposals to hold back the monetary avalanche.

This left public opinion. A popular outburst against inflation could have had a political impact. Yet boom conditions supported by inflation-induced capital gains and rising real wages were not conducive to the appearance of a political group that would push for an effective and painful attempt to restrain inflation. With no pressure from public opinion (professional economists excluded), the government adopted a wait-and-see attitude.

The equanimity toward inflation was an expression of specific pressures whose emergence at crucial time intervals during the take-off period made fiscal retrenchment and a restrictive monetary policy difficult. It reveals the well-known reluctance of the political community to reordering priorities and making difficult political choices. A comparatively independent and determined monetary authority could have made a difference, but this was yet only a promise for the distant future—the legal requirement for greater independence was only very partially implemented 12 years or so later. The apparent theoretical support for (relative) indifference to inflation from the Phillips Curve notion, which implicitly excludes the relevance of inertial factors to inflationary dynamics, was of some relevance, too.

Naturally, the monetary and fiscal expansion of 1973 in face of a (surprising at that time) leap of inflation was affected by electoral considerations. But it also points to the fact that the two-year lull in 1971 and 1972 might have suggested to the authorities that the threat was not all that dangerous, and that after the elections the imp of inflation could be returned, with some effort, to its bottle. What they failed to take into account was the relevance of inertial factors which, in Israel's case, could gain momentum not only because of the inherent dynamics of an inflationary process, but also owing to the slippery sands of Middle Eastern politics.

WHAT MESSAGE FOR THE 1990s?

The most obvious lesson from the events of the take-off interval obviously refers to the rapid slide into inflation, due to the excessive fiscal expansion and monetary (over) accommodation of government deficits. Though history does not repeat itself—neither another OPEC nor a commodity price shock is in the offing in a world economy reeling from recession or anemic growth at best—the significance of even a 20 percent inflation, the rate reached at the very end of the take-off, is still very much in evidence. Israel's economy and political system, which in 1985 made a major and successful effort to pull back from the abyss of hyperinflation, has been struggling for seven years to pull that rate, at which it settled in 1986, further down to the lower single-digit rates of its main trading partners. This target, reflecting a sociopolitical consensus, was approached but not yet finally made only in 1992, as inflation dipped into the single-digit range. If anything had been learned from the traumatic experience of a generation of rampant inflation, it is presumably how easy it is to step onto the slippery slope of inflation and how costly and difficult—in terms of economic efficiency, equity, and sociopolitical turmoil—it is to regain the path to comparative price stability.

Although expansionary fiscal and monetary policies pushed the system into the rapid take-off, these do not necessarily always generate inflation. The three years' experience of 1966–69 is an obvious point case in point. Government domestic deficits of about 6, 9, and 7 percent of GDP in each of these years, supported by annual growth rates of monetary aggregates of about 20 percent, did not generate inflation at that time (Tables 3–15), although the economy was subjected to a significant cost shock from a substantial devaluation late in 1967. Only when the authorities failed to shift gears as the economy came within range of its capacity constraints in the early 1970s was the accumulating pressure inevitably released through the price outlet, by means of inflation.

The high rate of unemployment and the rising level of activity generating growth rates in the 6–7 percent range for three consecutive years, 1990–92, while price inflation had been declining, appears to be quite similar to the 1967–69 situation. The analogy seems even stronger in view of the machinery which has been pulling the economy from its torpor. As in 1967, when the immediate requirements of the defense buildup and of the absorption of the first wave of (significant) immigration from Russia and Eastern Europe were met by an expansion of public sector expenditure, the requirements of the second wave of mass immigration were met in the same way. The *domestic* sector deficit swung from 1 percent of GDP, to which it had been reduced in the wake of the 1985 stabilization policy, to over 6 percent for 1990–92. It financed the expansion of health and education services and, by means of the monthly absorption grants to new immigrants, contributed to the leap of household consumption expenditures. Finally, as in 1967, the construction industry, responding to the pull of an all-out effort to provide (government subsidized) housing to immigrants, has been leading the upturn of economic activity.

In view of the (1992) almost 11 percent unemployment rate, pressures to increase government expenditures, even though this would swell the current budget deficit, were mounting. This unemployment rate, implicitly identified as a measure of (excess) capacity, might suggest that these claims, made by many members of the political community, do not increase the danger of stopping in its track and even reversing the recent downward pattern of inflation. Accordingly, a further pull on aggregate demand by opening the expenditures tap even further, to boost employment and social services, would increase output rather than inflation. Such a line of reasoning could be supported by reference to the option to increase the import surplus financed by foreign (U.S.-guaranteed) credits. A rising import surplus, putting more resources at the disposal of the economy, would accordingly push the relevance of the capacity constraint, and the danger of a renewal of inflationary pressures, further down the road.

But this analogy with the late 1960s, often made in political circles, is overdrawn. Consider, first, the unemployment rate. Its use as an exclusive capacity indicator is fraught with danger, even in economies with a comparatively stable labor force, industrial structure, and composition of demand. This is so because labor is not the only factor of production, and furthermore, the labor force is quite heterogeneous. Thus, a change in the composition of demand, and/or in the technology applied in production, could generate substantial unemployment in spite of growing output and productivity, as labor with skills not adapted to the structure of demand would have to retrain or upgrade skills to be reemployed in another niche of the system.[14]

This feature, the skill and know-how composition of Israel's labor force, is undoubtedly at the root of present unemployment levels. These reflect first and foremost the quest for employment by new immigrants. Indeed, the unemployment profile of veterans, showing up in almost unheard-of unemployment rates of 9 percent as recently as 1989, had certainly improved in the wake of and due to the mass immigration, as in the 1950s. Their skills, know-how, and labor market linkages offered them, rather than the immigrants, the openings which made for an increase of more than 10 percent in employment through 1992. This, of course, means that a substantial fraction of unemployment, perhaps almost all of it, is clearly structural. The skill composition, know-how, and standard of training of the new (mass immigration) immigrants is quite different from that reflecting the demand structure of Israel—a comparatively advanced industrial economy. This, however, means that present unemployment data are a much less reliable proxy for capacity than the same data in 1967–69.

Another feature which makes unemployment data much less representative of excess capacity, and underlines its structural features, are the dire straits of the defense industry. This component of Israel's manufacturing sector was, in 1967–69, in the vanguard of rapid expansion and growth. Yet the significant lower demand for armaments and defense-related products at home and abroad has forced this group of firms to reduce output and the size of its work force, which in 1985 had been close to 20 percent of total employment in manufacturing. The important feature in our context is the fact that a significant fraction of its capital equipment is highly specific to the high-tech production processes of state-of-the-art armaments. This means that a significant fraction of this equipment cannot be used or easily be converted to civilian production. The strain which recently came into the open due to the shedding of labor of the flagships of the defense industry suggest a simultaneous increase in the rate of obsolescence of their capital equipment. Since the share of defense industries in the capital equipment of Israel's manufacturers is greater than their share in employment, this suggests a significant effect on the capacity of Israel's manufacturing industry.

Though highly relevant, the issue is not just merely the identification of the most relevant capacity indicator as a guide to policy. The proper calibration of the size and duration of an expansionist policy in the 1990s has to take into consideration an underlying feature woven into the fabric of the system by the traumatic experience of the "great inflation." The fiscal and monetary expansion of the late 1960s was implemented in a non-inflationary environment. Indeed, Israel's 2–3 percent inflation rates at that time were lower than those of the industrial countries. Even the single-digit (9.6 percent CPI) rate of inflation of

1992 is twice the current rate of its main trading partners. Furthermore, with much lower government credibility (the inevitable result of a generation of inflation) the management of an expansionary policy is quite another story than that of 1967–69. It has to perform a highly delicate feat—to maintain annual growth rates of, say, 5–6 percent while pulling down inflation several percentage points to the 2–4 percent range of its trading partners. This is clearly a difficult maneuver under any circumstances; and it is made still more difficult owing to the inertial factors which, though of lesser momentum, are as relevant now (perhaps more so) as they were in 1966–69. An adverse change in expectations might shift the demand for money *relatively* downward (this demand does seem to be increasing at a much lower pace than it did hitherto). This alone might have an immediate effect on domestic prices, and at least arrest the winding down of inflation and generate currency speculation. The present, much greater freedom of short-term capital mobility could thus easily put the authorities into a corner. It might force them into a significant devaluation to defend international reserves. The ensuing cost-shock effect could easily reverse the downward trend of the rate of change of prices and rekindle inflation.[15]

The fiscal expansion through 1992, involving a domestic deficit of almost 6 percent of GDP, proved a risk worth taking. Yet a further increase of that dose, both in size and duration, is a much riskier undertaking. A significant fraction of the inflationary potential of the expansionary fiscal dosage was neutralized by a (30 percent) leap in imports, and the corresponding import surplus. Unilateral transfer data and budget figures indicate that this increase in the net inflow of resources—about 3 percent of GDP—was mostly financed by public sector funding from UJA contributions and U.S. aid.[16] These two sources of unilateral transfers were, however, exceptionally high and are probably not sustainable at these levels. It was availability of these funds which reduced the overall deficit of the public sector to about 3 percent of GDP (*Report 1991,* table V-1, p. 156), a level which probably would not reignite inflation as long as an (increased) import surplus of about 7–8 billion dollars could be maintained. An import surplus of this size, higher by 3–4 percent of GDP than that of the late 1980s, could probably be financed in the foreseeable future even if, as expected, U.S. aid and UJA funds are lower than they were in 1991 and 1992. This, however, assumes greater reliance on foreign credits supported by U.S. guarantees.

This scenario involves greater risk. In the first place, it encourages an increase in foreign debt, which together with its domestic counterpart is now at a level of approximately 100 percent of GDP (*Report 1991,* table V-1, p. 156). The 6 percent of GDP budget deficit might also require excessive funding by the creation of base money, which, in turn, would force monetary authorities to reduce the size of the money multiplier in an attempt to prevent excessive money growth. But that would induce a higher interest-rate structure than the one which could be maintained with a lower rate of base money creation.[17] The only short-run alternative to base money creation imposed by high domestic deficits is increased sales of government debt, pushing up long-run interest rates and signifying a reversal of the highly warranted policy, implemented in the wake of the 1985 economic stabilization policy, of lowering government involvement in the capital market.

Perhaps the most important lesson from the expansionary policy of the take-off period is the risk of missing the boat. The authorities were probably late to identify the surfacing of the capacity constraint, nor did they fully comprehend its significance. And in any case, the very large size of the government deficit meant that a significant reduction in expenditures had to overcome strong political resistance. An attempt at reversal was also hamstrung by the major new departure in social policy put in place at that time, which involved a leap in entitlements. The attempt to reduce the clout of the fiscal expansion, when finally made in 1970, was therefore confined to a significant rise in (gross) taxation. The prevailing very high tax rates meant that, by excluding expenditure reduction from the menu, the fiscal retrenchment, even during the short interval in which it was made, was insufficient. It was, of course, also quite late, and was soon (within one year) abandoned (Table 3).

The message of all this is first and foremost to avoid having to start from a high benchmark. This suggests that it is imperative to immediately contain the budget deficit—even the 6.2 percent domestic deficit run up in 1992 might be excessive. It also suggests that a further increase in entitlements should be avoided at all costs. This component of government expenditure is politically almost impossible to cut, even if there is a reasonable case for it, in terms of equity (the social security issue in the United States is an outstanding case in point).[18] Finally, the maintenance of standards of services in education, health, and in particular, retraining and skill upgrading of the immigrants in the wake of the record wave of mass immigration, undoubtedly requires an increase in government expenditure. With further defense expenditure reductions very unlikely, after a 30 percent cut in terms of GDP since 1985, and the urgent need for more expenditure on infrastructure, tightening of eligibility standards and prevention of any widening of the scope of transfer payments is imperative.

The increase in government consumption expenditures does not necessarily imply a corresponding growth in public sector employment. This, as past experience has shown, reduces the scope of action whenever temporary retrenchment is the order of the day. Options for greater flexibility in budget commitments, thus more rapid response as indicators of strain surface, are available. One technique is farming out to business sector entities some in-house public sector activities, a move which would increase efficiency. Investment in infrastructure is the most obvious case in point, but not the only one. The retraining and skill-upgrading operations, which in the coming decade will be a major component of Israel's education system, are another obvious example of operations, which, although requiring public expenditure, could be farmed out to the private sector.

The greater flexibility, efficiency, and options for controlling fiscal policy promised by allowing business sector entities to provide a greater fraction of goods is not the only technique allowing more flexible and rapidly responsive macroeconomic management and control. The main avenue for this purpose is the change of balance between monetary and fiscal policies: this would involve the reduction of the clout of fiscal policy by means of a lower budget deficit in particular, and allow the capital market and monetary policy more leeway to promote growth and a high level of activity.

Indeed, the rebound of the fiscal deficit since 1989, in the inherent context of low government credibility, led to the maintenance of an overrestrictive monetary policy. Short-term and particularly long-term real interest rates had been maintained at levels which closed many investment opportunities. A lower budget deficit would immediately reduce government demand for funds in capital markets, making more resources available to the business sector. The relatively high household and business saving rates would be quite helpful on this score. Indeed, a major institutional change can be quite handy for that purpose: a reduction of the quota of non-traded, long-term government bonds placed directly with pension funds and insurance companies at real interest rates significantly above the market rate would push more funds into the capital market. Correspondingly, it would, of course, reduce the cost of the new issues of the national debt.

The same line of reasoning applies to monetary policy, whose impact on activity is much more rapid. Lower budget deficits would require less base money creation, thus making bank credit a greater component of (the increase in) the supply of money. In other words, a more restrictive fiscal policy, reducing domestic deficit to, say, 2–3 percent of GDP, which could be fully funded by unilateral receipts and some foreign credit, would allow a more expansionary monetary policy. The resulting lower short-term interest rates would offer additional degrees of freedom to the business sector. What might be more significant in the short run is the greater ease with which this instrument of macroeconomic policy could be used to control aggregate demand and the developments in the market. Its much shorter reaction interval could nip in the bud an expansion which might endanger monetary stability.

Errors in macroeconomic management are obviously unavoidable. In a world of uncertainty, an error on the side of restrictions—especially fiscal restrictions—is obviously preferable to errors which allow overexpansion. For better or for worse, this is the main lesson of the take-off for economic management in the 1990s as the rapid absorption of mass immigration rises to the top of the agenda, as it was in the 1950s.

NOTES

1. See Tables 1 and 2, and Figure 3.

2. The reference to housing stock follows *Report 1973*, table V, p. 149.

3. Neither the public nor the economic leadership cared for the mirror image of these capital gains—the *capital loss* of the government sector. The strain that the rapid erosion

of its claims against the business and household sectors would impose in the future, at the redemption dates of the linked government debt, was considered very remote in terms of the political timetable.

4. A far-reaching social policy, especially regarding income maintenance devices—children's allowances, and old-age pensions—was put in place and/or raised substantially between 1970 and 1973. Every indicator suggests that the lower income brackets bene-fited, too, in *absolute* terms at least, from that economic expansion (see Kop, 1989, tables 1 and 4, pp. 48–53). In relative terms, though, some groups might have been sliding down the ladder. Reliable data on this subject are unavailable.

5. A major component of this wave of immigration, from 1969 onward, were persons from the Soviet Union. The Six Day War generated a resurgence of Jewish identity among Soviet Jews and the spirit of detente between the blocs, which induced the Brezh-nev regime to a partial opening of the gates, combined to allow this unexpected process which for 50 years was considered an unrealizable dream.

6. A weekly column appearing on Fridays in *Ma'ariv* (at that time the newspaper with the highest circulation in the country), was the instrument used by five members of the Hebrew University economics department to describe the dangers of inflation at such rates and criticize government and Bank of Israel policies. From the very first columns in the autumn of 1971, contributors to the panel repeatedly focused on inflation and the slippery path along which the economy had been moving, once it moved toward (and past) the single-digit threshold. See Barkai et al. (1975) and especially the following contributions: Patinkin (October 3, 1971, March 31, 1972; April 24, 1972, June 23, 1972, July 18, 1972); Barkai (November 5, 1971, February 2, 1972, March 24, 1972); Michaely (October 10, 1971, April 4, 1972).

7. The expression is attributed to Senator Moynihan of New York and refers to the highly charged and pressing race problem in the United States, seemingly unresponsive to policy measures.

8. In the late 1970s and the 1980s the monetarist counterrevolution was in full swing and the rational-expectations approach was gathering momentum, whereupon these fac-tors were put at the focus of macroeconomic modeling.

9. His famous "little notebook," in which he entered data and information acquired in the field—meeting workers, entrepreneurs, industrialists, bankers, and the man in the street—was a symbol of government involvement and control.

10. GDP in 1970 was 2.3 times larger than in 1960 and in the six-year interval be-tween the two wars just about doubled (Metzer, 1983, table A-1, p. 67). The sheer change in size and, perhaps more importantly, in variety and sophistication, inevitably reduced the relative power of government to control the system.

11. Although the *Economic Panel* (see Barkai et al., 1975) columns on inflation, published between the fall of 1971 and the summer of 1973, correctly predicted the future pattern of inflation, referred to the danger of its acceleration, underlined its real costs, and suggested (in 1971) an immediate about-turn of macroeconomic policy, a retrospective rereading of these articles suggests that the inertial features of the process should have been addressed much more emphatically. Greater emphasis on the effect of inflation on uncertainty and on decision making would have also been in place. It goes without saying that these retrospective comments reflect more recent developments in macroeconomic theory and in the theory of inflation.

12. Loans from the U.S. government financed about 40 percent of defense imports in

1970–72 (*Report 1973*, tables III-2 and IV-23, pp. 44 and 85, respectively). Most of these loans were to purchase grain and animal feed from U.S. agricultural surpluses.

13. The almost five-fold increase in defense exports between 1966 and 1970 and by another 70 percent or so between 1970 and 1971 offers another indicator of the rapid buildup of the defense industries. The data are from Barkai (1987), tables 1 and 2.

14. The events of the lackluster upswing of the U.S. economy in 1992 are an obvious case in point.

15. This kind of scenario is not just a matter of speculation—it reflects the developments in exchange markets in 1988, the resultant significant devaluation, and the corresponding reversal of the trend of inflation: consumer and "domestic uses" price inflation rose from 16 and 18 percent respectively in 1988, to 21 and 20 percent in 1989, though the level of activity in the latter year was stagnant, involving an all-time high unemployment rate since 1966 (8.9 percent).

16. *Report 1991,* table V-1, p. 156; table VI-1, p. 187; table VI-11, p. 200.

17. The average annual rates of increase at M_1 and M_2 in the first three quarters of 1992, 34 and 23 percent, appear excessive for the maintenance of a lower than single-digit rate of inflation in 1993.

18. An expansion of social policies should be halted during the first years of the absorption of the new immigration inflow. The demographic structure of this new wave of mass immigration is imposing a heavy burden on the social security and other components of the social policy basket. In any case, an economy with a per capita income of approximately $10,000, between 45–65 percent of that of the major industrial countries, can hardly afford to maintain a flow of income-maintenance transfers of 14 percent of GDP—the level reached in 1992.

Figures and Tables (Part I)

Figure 1
Price Trends, 1965–89 (Index: 1969 = 100)

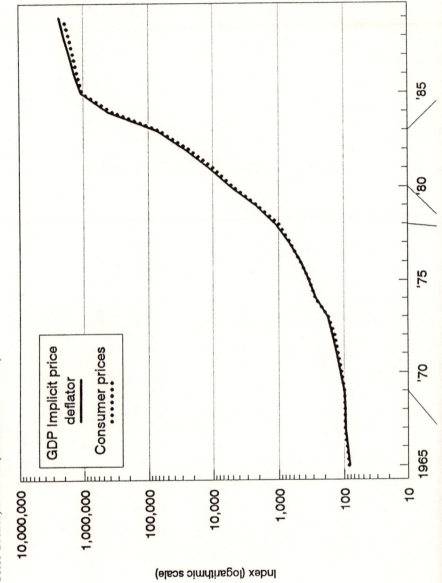

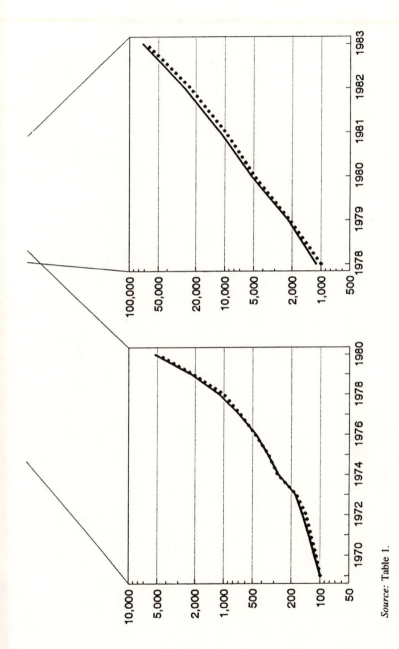

Source: Table 1.

Figure 2
Price Trends, 1969–89 (annual rate of change, percent)

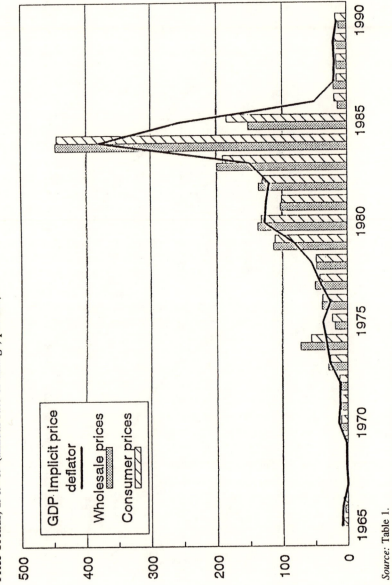

Source: Table 1.

Figure 3
Quarterly Price Indicators (quarterly rate of change, percent)

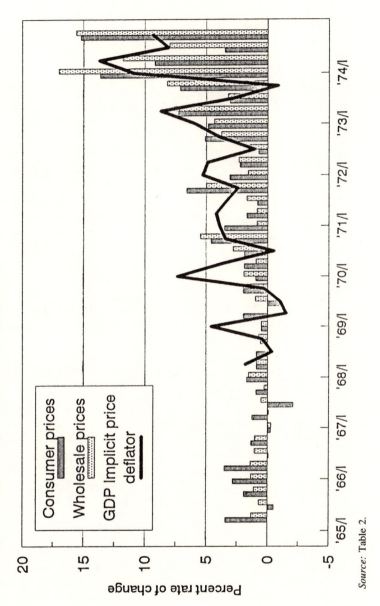

Source: Table 2.

Table 1
Price Trends, 1969–92[a]

(Percentage rate of change; calendar years)

| | U.S.$ | | Shekels[b] | | GDP[c] implicit price deflator (5) | Whole-sale prices (6) | Consumer prices (7) | Formal exchange rate (Sh/$) (8) | Effective exchange rate ($) | |
	Export (1)	Import (2)	Export (3)	Import (4)					Imports (9)	Exports (10)
1965	..	..	..	..	9.6	4.7	7.1	0.0		0.3
1966	-2.0	1.9	..	..	8.0	-0.1	7.8	0.0	1.5	1.6
1967	6.5	0.0	5.7	1.7	0.7	3.0	0.2	7.6	-0.5	4.5
1968	-1.0	-3.0	14.0	12.9	2.2	3.2	1.9	8.3	0.5	13.8
1969	5.0	5.0	4.5	5.5	2.3	11.3	3.9	0.0	14.2	0.0
1970	-1.0	1.0	3.0	4.5	14.3	10.3	10.1	0.0	2.7	2.4
1971	3.9	3.4	15.4	16.2	12.6	9.6	13.4	20.0	0.7	10.0
1972	7.2	6.0	15.5	20.2	12.2	21.8	12.4	0.0	10.0	0.0
1973[d] (9)	37.3	47.1	..	..	30.9	29.5	21.9	0.0	-3.6	9.8
1974	22.9	27.9	18.4	20.4	27.3	72.8	26.4	24.2	14.2	9.1
1975	18.4	37.0	37.8	42.7	32.3	19.0	56.2	34.9	7.4	41.6
1976	4.7	4.5	39.1	42.8	37.9	39.2	23.5	21.6	34.6	26.2
1977	1.8	-2.4	28.6	32.0	26.8	50.0	38.0	59.7	30.4	34.4
1978	16.0	8.8	41.7	41.1	42.6	47.0	42.5	36.2	29.9	49.6
1979	27.2	17.3	75.1	74.8	55.7	113.9	48.1	71.3	56.9	49.9
1980	13.3	21.4	73.1	70.8	83.0	138.1	111.4	111.1	48.5	79.6
1981	11.7	30.4	128.4	134.3	127.7	103.5	132.9	115.1	92.4	124.0
1982	-3.7	-3.0	118.4	115.8	126.0	136.9	101.5	115.5	124.2	113.9
1983	-5.7	-8.5	107.8	107.1	121.3	199.7	131.5	185.2	122.3	134.2
1984	-3.2	-4.6	134.6	125.1	151.0	446.9	190.7	554.0	134.4	424.5
1985	-2.3	-0.4	395.5	403.3	379.7	152.8	444.9	176.0	412.1	287.0
1986	-1.0	-2.3	275.3	301.7	257.2	15.1	185.2	10.4	303.4	25.0
1987	2.8	2.1	31.1	26.2	24.4	20.9	19.6	5.6	29.8	7.2
1988	8.5	10.4	17.4	19.3	18.4	15.8	16.1	2.1	7.4	0.3
1989	10.3	5.8	11.7	7.3	22.7	19.5	16.4	20.2	0.6	19.4
1990	1.2	5.6	10.5	16.4	17.7	12.6	20.7	5.2	13.7	
1991	5.2	8.9	9.3	11.8	14.9	14.6	17.6	12.8		
1992	-1.5	-2.3	15.4	10.1	21.8		18.0			
							9.6			

[a] The series in columns (1)–(4) present annual average price data, while the series in columns (5)–(7) reflect end-of-year (December) prices. The former series accordingly "lead" the latter series by an approximate interval of six months. The series in columns (8)–(10) represent annual average exchange rates.

[b] Sheqel import and export prices are from data in chapters on prices in Bank of Israel, *Annual Reports* for the 1967–77 interval, and from the chapters on Resources and Uses for 1965/6 and 1978/9. The series for both types of tables are derived from the social accounting data and reflect the social accounting database which was revised backward from time to time.

[c] Entries represent annual average, and not calendar (December) prices. Data for 1965–68 refer to GNP prices.

[d] Refers to the first three quarters of 1973 (1973/I–III).

Sources:

Columns (1), (2)—CBS, *Monthly Bulletin of Statistics.* For 1986–1991 *Reports 1988–1991*, table 6-3.

Columns (3), (4)—*Report 1971*, table III-15; *1974*, table IX-1; *1977*, table X-3, tables II-1, and III-2 in subsequent *Reports*, through 1991.

Column (5)—*Report, 1966, 1969, 1980*, table I-1; and *Report 1985*, and *1989*, table B-1. Entries for the years 1969–1974 were derived from GDP in current and constant prices series in CBS, *Monthly Bulletin of Statistics*, Supplement: May 1971, table 13 for 1969–70; December 1973, table F-1 for 1971–72; and December 1975, table F/1 for 1973–74.

Columns (6)–(7)—CBS, *Abstract 1989*, tables 10-1 and 10-9; and *Report 1969* and *1970*, table VI-2; *1972*, table VI-2; *1974*, table IX-3, and similar tables in the "Prices" chapters of subsequent *Reports.*

Column (8)—Bank of Israel, *Foreign Currency Exchange Rates, 1948–85*, Jerusalem, 1986, and *Reports* (various years).

Columns (9), (10)—Bank of Israel database, April 1, 1990.

Table 2
Quarterly Price Indicators

(Quarterly percentage rate of change)

	Consumer prices	Whole-sale prices	GDP implicit price deflator	Shekel prices[a]		Dollar prices		Formal exchange rate
				Exports	Imports	Exports	Imports	
	(1)	(2)	(3)	(4)	(5)	(6)	(7)	(8)
'65:I						−3.7	1.0	0.0
	3.43	1.32				5.7	0.0	0.0
	−0.52	0.70				−4.5	−1.0	0.0
	1.92	1.11				2.8	−1.0	0.0
'66:I	2.82	1.35				1.8	3.0	0.0
	3.51	1.39				0.9	0.0	0.0
	−0.09	1.07				3.6	1.0	0.0
	1.34	1.03				0.9	1.0	0.0
'67:I	−0.25	−0.27				−3.4	0.0	0.0
	1.27	−0.09				−0.9	−0.9	0.0
	−2.09	0.54				0.9	0.0	0.0
	0.94	0.27				−0.9	−1.0	16.7
'68:I	1.69	1.53				−2.7	−1.0	0.0
	0.92	0.88	0.5			0.9	0.0	0.0
	0.91	0.01	1.8			0.9	0.0	0.0
	0.58	0.70	1.8			1.8	0.0	0.0
'69:I	0.50	0.50	4.6	1.9	2.6	2.7	1.0	0.0
	1.98	0.00	−1.5	−1.2	1.6	−4.3	2.9	0.0
	−0.97	0.99	−1.0	3.8	1.9	4.5	0.9	0.0
	1.96	1.96	0.3	−0.3	1.9	1.7	0.9	0.0
'70:I	0.96	1.92	4.9	3.4	−0.2	−4.2	1.8	0.0
	1.90	0.94	4.1	0.0	−1.3	0.0	−1.9	0.0
	1.87	2.80	0.1	0.8	3.7	1.0	−0.9	0.0
	4.59	5.45	4.6	0.7	2.6	1.0	0.0	0.0
'71:I	3.51	0.86	6.5	2.3	0.8	1.9	1.0	0.0
	1.69	0.85	2.7	0.0	1.5	0.0	1.9	0.0
	0.83	1.69	−0.9	11.3	13.7	−0.9	0.9	20.0
	6.61	5.00	3.9	10.8	7.4	3.8	0.9	0.0
'72:I	3.10	1.59	6.9	1.8	2.5	1.8	1.8	0.0
	2.26	2.34	3.0	3.0	3.1	3.6	3.6	0.0
	0.74	1.53	1.1	1.2	−0.6	0.9	−0.9	0.0
	5.11	3.76	3.0	6.3	3.6	8.6	3.5	0.0
'73:I	4.86	4.35	9.9	5.4	4.6	3.2	5.0	0.0
	7.28	7.64	9.1	11.3	12.1	10.2	11.2	0.0
	3.09	3.23	2.1	4.9	8.7	6.7	15.1	0.0
	7.13	8.20	4.0	3.5	−14.4	1.6	10.2	0.0
'74:I	13.65	17.0	8.7	35.2	6.5	4.7	13.9	0.0
	9.19	11.8	12.2	−6.7	13.2	9.6	3.5	0.0
	3.49	8.0	7.2	−11.7	−1.6	8.1	3.9	0.0
	15.21	15.6	11.3			1.9	1.1	42.9

Table 2 (Continued)

ᵃThe quarterly rates of change of sheqel import and export prices were derived by multiplying an index of import and export dollar prices by corresponding entries of an index of effective exchange rates of import and export. The latter quarterly index was approximated by calculating ratios of quarterly sheqel values of imports (including duties, etc.) and the corresponding dollar values of imports. Similarly, the current sheqel value of exports (including export subsidies) was divided by the corresponding dollar value of these exports.

Sources:

Columns (1), (2)—CBS, *Monthly Bulletin of Statistics*, Supplement, various years.

Column (3)—Derived from GDP current and constant price series in CBS, *Monthly Bulletin of Statistics*. See full references in sources to table 1, column (5).

Columns (4)–(7)—Calculated on the basis of the value of trade data in various issues of CBS, *Foreign Trade Statistics* and *Monthly Bulletin* (Supplement), March 1970–78.

Column (8)—CBS, *Abstract 1984*.

Table 3
Public Sector Measures: Demand, Absorption, and Deficit, 1966–74 (percent of GNP)

| | Government domestic consumption | | | Gov't invest-ment | Total domestic government demand (3)+(4) =(5) | Gross taxation[a] | Subsidies, transfers, domestic interest payments[b] | Net domestic absorp-tion (6)-(7) =(8) | Domestic excess demand (5)-(8) =(9) | Defense imports | Total govern-ment demand (5)+(10) =(11) | Budget deficit[c] (11)-(8) =(12) |
| | Civilian | Defense | Total | | | | | | | | | |
	(1)	(2)	(3)	(4)		(6)	(7)			(10)		
1966	11.8	6.9	18.7	5.1	23.9	33.4	13.0	20.4	3.5	3.4	27.4	7.0
1967	11.4	10.3	21.7	4.7	26.5	31.9	11.7	20.2	6.3	4.4	30.9	10.7
1968	10.4	11.9	22.3	5.3	27.6	32.1	13.3	18.8	8.8	6.3	33.9	15.1
1969	9.2	12.6	21.8	5.8	27.6	34.2	13.2	21.0	6.6	7.6	35.2	14.2
1970	9.6	13.9	23.5	4.8	28.4	40.8	16.3	24.5	3.9	11.8	40.2	15.7
1971	9.7	14.5	24.3	4.8	29.0	44.7	22.3	22.4	6.6	9.1	38.1	15.4
1972	9.5	12.3	21.8	6.9	28.7	42.4	24.3	18.1	10.6	8.6	37.3	19.2
1973(9)	10.0	10.9	22.0	(6.9)	(28.9)	35.8						
1973	10.0	15.1	25.1	5.4	30.5	42.2	31.4	10.8	19.7	17.4	47.9	37.1
1974	9.9	17.9	27.8	5.7	33.5	45.8	39.6	6.2	27.2	12.9	46.4	40.2

[a]Includes income from government property, which in only two out of these years was somewhat above 1 percent of GNP.

[b]This column also includes an imputation for the implicit credit subsidies to the private sector—to households and firms. These are dependent on the (ex post) rate of inflation and did not appear as a current charge on government in public sector accounting. If these private, wealth-increasing imputations are excluded, entries in column (7) [and correspondingly columns (8) and (9)] are lower. These are shown in Table 4.

[c]This series exaggerates the total public sector deficit, since it excludes donations from UJA and similar organizations in other countries and the grant component of foreign aid.

Sources:

Bank of Israel data bank, July 11, 1990. These estimates follow the "old" classification of government activities. A similar series, based on a "new" classification, goes back to 1980 only. Data for the latter classification appear in *Report 1985* and onward, tables V-1 and V-11. Entries for 1973(9), which refer to the pre–Yom Kippur War interval, were derived from *Report 1974*, tables II-1 and III-10.

Table 4
Public Sector Subsidies, Absorption, and Excess Demand, Alternative Estimate[a]
(percent of GNP)

	Subsidies, transfers, domestic interest		Net domestic absorption		Domestic excess demand[b]	
	(7)	(7')	(8)	(8')	(9)	(9')
1966	13.0	11.7	20.4	21.7	3.5	2.2
1967	11.7	13.7	20.2	18.2	6.3	8.3
1968	13.3	14.5	18.8	17.6	8.8	10.0
1969	13.2	14.0	21.0	20.2	6.6	7.4
1970	16.3	15.3	24.5	25.5	3.9	2.9
1971	22.3	17.9	22.4	26.8	6.6	2.2
1972	24.3	18.0	18.1	24.4	10.6	1.6
1973	31.4	22.0	10.8	20.7	19.7	9.8
1974	39.6	24.1	6.2	21.7	27.2	11.8

[a]Column (7) includes and column (7') excludes the cost of implicit interest rate subsidies to households and firms. See note *b* to Table 3.

[b]The figures in column (9'), which correspond to entries in column (7') rather than to those in column (9), were the data which figured in the budget records and thus served as signals and guidelines for policy making.

Table 5
Public Sector Real Demand and Absorption Measures, 1967–74
(average annual percentage change)

	Government domestic consumption	Domestic defense expenditure	Total domestic direct government demand	Total government demand	Gross taxation	Subsidies, transfers, domestic interest payments[a]	Subsidies and transfers
	(1)	(2)	(3)	(4)	(5)	(6)	(7)
1967	18.5	51.3	13.1	15.0	−2.3	−7.8	21.3
1968	17.4	30.2	17.9	24.3	15.1	28.3	21.3
1969	9.6	17.7	11.8	15.6	18.3	11.0	10.6
1970	15.7	18.3	10.9	22.2	27.2	31.5	16.1
1971	13.5	14.4	12.2	14.8	19.7	46.9	24.2
1972	1.7	−3.1	10.9	9.9	6.8	21.0	10.0
1973(9)	6.9			8.6	1.7		
1973	21.1	29.2	11.5	33.6	4.7	34.4	26.5
1974	30.1	22.8	14.5	1.6	13.2	30.8	16.8

[a]Includes implicit credit subsidies to the private sector; see note *b* to Table 3.

Sources: Table 3 and GNP data from *Report 1970* and *1974*, table II-1.

Table 6
Public Sector Demand and Absorption Measures (Index: 1966 = 100)

	Government domestic consumption	Domestic defense expenditure	Total domestic direct government demand	Total government demand	Gross taxation	Subsidies, transfers, domestic interest payments[a]	Subsidies and transfers
	(1)	(2)	(3)	(4)	(5)	(6)	(7)
1966	100	100	100	100	100	100	100
1967	118	151	113	115	98	92	121
1968	139	197	133	143	113	118	147
1969	152	232	149	165	133	131	163
1970	176	273	165	201	169	173	189
1971	199	313	186	212	203	254	235
1972	204	324	206	233	216	307	258
1973	246	415	229	311	227	413	327
1973(9)	219				220		
1974	286	511	263	316	256	540	381

Source: Table 5.

Table 7
Selected Demand Indices (1966 = 100)

| | Total domestic government demand | Private consumption expenditure | Gross domestic investment | Non-defense imports | New housing starts | | Apartment prices | Ratio of non-tradable to tradable prices | Real wages[a] | Employment | Unemployment rate |
| | | | | | Public | Private | | | | | |
	(1)	(2)	(3)	(4)	(5)	(6)	(7)	(8)	(9)	(10)	(11)
1965		92	121		221	136	102	97	93	101	3.6
1966	100	100	100	100	100	100	100	100	100	100	7.4
1967	113	102	78	98	106	70	99	100	106	95	10.2
1968	133	113	116	131	98	113	105	100	101	105	6.1
1969	149	125	146	150	157	169	120	102	100	109	4.5
1970	165	129	165	160	249	181	143	104	110	110	3.8
1971	186	135	201	190	206	243	175	103	113	114	3.5
1972	206	148	227	198	353	257	235	105	116	122	2.7
1973(9)	---	168	271	252							
1973	229	162	248	237	302	213	303	108	127	125	2.6
1974	263	173	240	250	350	174	447	108	121	125	3.0

[a]Derived from hourly wage series (for Israeli and registered workers from the territories) deflated by the CPI.

Sources:

Column (1)—Table 6.

Columns (2), (3)—*Report 1974*, table II-1, and corresponding tables in previous issues.

Columns (5), (6)—CBS, *Monthly Bulletin*, July 1975, p. 84, and corresponding tables for previous years.

Column (7)—Index of Apartment Prices in *Report 1972*, table XI-6; *1974*, table IX-6; *1970*, table IV-8; *1967*, table VI-12.

Column (8)—Halevi (1983), derived from Cukierman and Razin Series of "Tradables and Nontradables" in CPI, in Halevi and Kop (1976).

Column (9)—*Report 1972*, table IX-1, and *Report 1974*, table XII-1.

Column (10)—CBS, *Monthly Bulletin*, July 1975, pp. 47–55, and corresponding tables in previous issues.

Column (11)—CBS, *Abstract 1989*, table XII-1, p. 325.

Table 8
Selected Quarterly Demand Indicators

			Index: 1967 = 100				Quarterly rates of change (percent)	
		Gov't domestic consumption expenditures	Private consumption	Gross domestic investment	New housing starts		Non-tradable prices	Employment
					Public	Private		
		(1)	(2)	(3)	(4)	(5)	(6)	(7)
1966							8.7	
1967	I	100	100	100	100	100		-4.1
	II	145	103	66	94	71		0.2
	III	113	116	102	149	84		1.7
	IV	101	113	102	101	114		1.1
1968	I	112	173	134	47	123		3.3
	II	135	174	109	73	151		2.5
	III	122	191	153	146	168		1.2
	IV	130	176	155	139	154		1.9
1969	I	126	127	137	147	179	3.7	0.9
	II	171	132	203	174	206	2.7	1.7
	III	142	140	214	182	232	3.4	0.7
	IV	143	140	165	147	232	4.7	-0.3
1970	I	162	137	217	207	224	5.6	-0.2
	II	162	137	213	262	217	3.5	1.4
	III	215	145	169	277	226	3.2	0.7
	IV	211	138	201	257	208	4.8	0.5
1971	I	203	137	270	187	250	7.3	0.7
	II	193	139	225	221	322	6.8	0.3
	III	181	147	264	225	350	10.8	3.0
	IV	183	145	256	227	325	8.7	-0.4
1972	I	181	146	259	257	232	6.4	2.4
	II	179	152	261	255	249	5.2	0.8
	III	182	160	279	250	258	7.6	1.4
	IV	185	160	284	206	288	6.0	-0.1
1973	I	177	166	308	252	280	6.1	1.5
	II	180	171	354	266	322	6.0	1.3
	III	188	181	361	266	336	5.0	1.0
	IV	530	154	255	163	245		0.2
1974	I	289	173	243	214	227		-1.7
	II	275	185	391	291	260		1.6
	III	270	187	340	368	260		-1.7
	IV	270	177	346	276	258		-1.7

Sources:
Columns (1)–(5)—CBS, *Monthly Bulletin* (May Supplement), various years.
Column (6)—See sources to Table 7, column (8).
Column (7)—CBS, *Monthly Bulletin*, various years.

Table 9
Selected Measures of the Real Economy (annual percentage rate of change)

| | GDP | | GDP (private sector)[a] | | National income[b] | Private disposable income[c] | Non-defense imports[d] | Import surplus[e] | | International reserves | | Population |
| | | Per capita | Total | Per employed person | | | | | Non-defense | Total | Ratio[f] | |
	(1)	(1')	(2)	(3)	(4)	(5)	(6)	(7)	(7')	(8)	(8')	(9)
1966	1.4	-1.2	-0.6	0.7	0.6	-0.7	2	-14	-20	-3.5	5.6	2.6
1967	2.5	-0.7	0.4	6.7	2.6	6.0	-2	18	-26	13.7	5.8	3.3
1968	14.7	10.9	19.1	7.5	15.4	16.7	34	29	77	-7.2	4.3	3.4
1969	12.8	9.9	15.0	10.2	13.2	12.3	14	36	37	-46.0	2.5	2.6
1970	8.9	5.9	9.7	8.1	7.7	-5.4	7	40	13	6.6	1.8	2.8
1971	10.1	7.5	11.6	6.8	10.2	10.7	19	-1.4	7	59.2	2.1	3.0
1972	12.0	8.4	14.0	6.3	12.6	18.9	4	-11	-10	86.0	3.9	3.3
1973(9)	6.9	3.5	6.6	1.7	(6.7)	7.5	27	61	(110)	56.0	3.8	3.3
1973	6.5	3.1	3.9	3.0	6.7	6.8	20	136	121	58.7		3.3
1974	4.3	1.2	3.7	3.4	2.3	-3.8	5	128	59	-36.9	1.9	3.0

[a]Excluding housing.
[b]Nominal income deflated by implicit GDP price index.
[c]Private disposable income from domestic resources net of "compulsory loan" payments. Nominal income deflated by COL price index.
[d]Non-defense imports at constant dollar values.
[e]Current dollar values of import surplus.
[f]Ratio of end-of-year reserves to total imports in terms of "import months."

Sources:

Columns (1)–(4), (8) and (9)—*Report 1974*, table I-1.

Column—*Report 1974*, table II-12; *1972*, table II-10; *1969*, table II-7.

Columns (6)–(7) and (8)—Imports: *Report 1970*, table II-1, and *Report 1974*, table IV-1; Reserves: tables XIX-2, XX-2 and similar tables in *Report 1966, 1967, 1968, 1969*, and *1971, 1972, 1973*.

Table 10
Selected Balance of Payments Indicators ($ millions)

	Import surplus (1)	Unilateral transfers (2)	Current account (1)−(2) (3)	Long-term capital (4)	Short-term capital (5)[a]	PATACH deposits (6)	Interbank credit (7)	Change in reserves[b] (8)
1965	−520	327	−193	230	66	17	−10	−106
1966	445	292	153	184	−8	10	−3	19
1967	−532	521	−11	303	−51	5	−8	−212
1968	−648	435	−213	164	−10	35	6	−42
1969	−869	459	−410	168	−55	115	2	187
1970	−1,234	649	−585	559	−36	121	65	−120
1971	−1,227	765	−462	642	−54	326	−35	−593
1972	−1,081	1,052	−29	580	−75	323	−24	−975
1973(9)	−1,288	777	−511	417	28	419	−362	−678
1973	−2,560	2,190	−370	812	43	346	−288	−885

[a]Non-financial sector.
[b]Increase in reserves indicated by minus sign.

Sources:
Columns (1)–(5)—*Report 1973*, table III-1; *Report 1970*, table III-22.
Columns (6)–(7)—*Report 1973*, table III-24, *Report 1970*, table IV-22.

Table 11
Selected Cost Indicators

	Exchange rates			Wage per employee post[b]		Labor cost per employee		Labor produc- tivity[c]	Labor cost per unit of product[d]	Total Factor produc- tivity[e]
	Formal[a]	Effective		Nomi- nal	Real	Nomi- nal	Real			
		Imports	Exports							
	(1)	(2)	(3)	(4)	(4')	(5)	(5')	(6)	(7)	(8)
Annual percentage rate of change										
1965	0	1.5	0.3	17.5	-	18.5	14.0	7.4	10.3	5.5
1966	0	−0.5	1.6	18.9	10.9	15.8	10.5	0.7	15.0	-2.3
1967	16.6	0.5	4.5	0.3	-0.5	4.6	3.4	6.7	−2.0	5.1
1968	0	14.2	13.8	3.6	0.2	1.3	−0.9	7.5	−5.8	6.9
1969	0	2.7	0.0	5.1	3.8	3.3	1.1	9.1	−5.2	7.9
1970	0	0.7	2.4	8.6	2.5	15.1	7.5	8.1	6.5	5.6
1971	20.0	10.1	10.0	15.2	4.4	15.8	5.4	6.8	8.4	6.0
1972	0	14.0	9.8	13.7	2.4	19.2	1.5	6.3	−5.0	4.9
1973(9)				..	..	..	..	3.3		3.2
1973	0	−3.6	0.0	27.4	7.7	30.2	9.3	3.0	4.2	3.4
1974	42.8	7.4	9.1	36.3	-	36.1	−10.1	3.4	0.0	0.5
Index: 1966 = 100										
1965	100.0	99.5	98.4	84.1	84.0	86.4	90.4	99.3	86.9	102.3
1966	100.0	100.0	100.0	100.0	100.0	100.0	100.0	100.0	100.0	100.0
1967	116.6	100.5	106.2	100.3	99.5	104.6	103.4	106.7	98.0	105.1
1968	116.6	114.8	120.8	103.6	99.7	106.0	102.4	114.7	92.6	112.4
1969	116.6	117.9	120.8	108.9	103.4	109.6	103.5	125.1	88.1	121.2
1970	116.6	118.6	123.7	118.3	106.1	126.1	111.2	135.2	93.7	128.0
1971	139.2	130.7	136.1	136.3	110.7	146.0	117.3	144.5	101.6	135.7
1972	139.2	150.0	149.4	155.0	113.4	174.0	119.1	153.5	98.3	142.3
1973(9)					..			163.6		146.8
1973	139.2	144.3	149.4	197.4	122.1	226.5	130.1	158.3	102.4	147.2
1974	199.8	155.0	163.0	269.1	..	308.3	118.2	163.7	188.6	147.9

[a]Rate of change of formal rate imputed to the year in which it occurred.
[b]Wage and labor cost per employee post according to National Insurance Institute data. Real wage and real labor cost entries in columns (4') and (5') are corresponding nominal entries deflated by wholesale price index. Deflators are annual averages and not calendar year averages.
[c]Gaathon series of labor productivity per employed in the business sector only.
[d]Labor costs refer to the economy as a whole, and productivity series reflect performance of the business sector only. The series is accordingly a rough approximation only for unit labor cost in the business sector. Note also that the entries for 1965–71 are derived from the entries of columns (5) and (6); the entries for 1972–74 are according to Bank of Israel estimate (*Report 1989*, Diagram IV-1, p. 130).
[e]Gaathon definition: "man-hours," and 0.66 weight for labor in input basket.

Sources:
Column (1)—*Abstract 1989*, table IX-12; Columns (2), (3)—Bank of Israel data bank, April 1, 1990; Columns (4)–(5)—Silberman series (May 11, 1987). Column (4) derived from National Insurance Institute data; Column (5) derived from Social Accounting data; Columns (6) and (8)—Gaathon series, in Bank of Israel, *Report 1972*, table II-8 for 1965–69, and *1974*, table II-9, for 1970–74. Column (7)—for 1965–1971, derived from the entries in Columns (5) and (6); for 1972–74, *Report 1989*, Diagram IV-1, p. 130.

Table 12
Selected Quarterly Cost Indicators

		Import prices[a]	Exchange rate		Average monthly wage per worker	Wages per unit of product[c]	Product per workhour (annual % change)
			Formal	Effective[b] (imports)			
		(Quarterly	percentage	change)			
		(1)	(2)	(3)	(4)	(5)	(6)
1967	I	2.9	0.0		-0.1	2.9	
	II	-1.0	0.0		-2.3	8.2	11.3
	III	0.0	0.0		4.6	-18.3	
	IV	-0.9	16.66		0.5	-6.5	
1968	I	-0.9	8.36		-1.1	-5.2	
	II	1.0	0.0		1.4	-5.0	3.7
	III	-0.9	0.0		2.2	-4.1	
	IV	0.0	0.0		0.0	-1.1	
1969	I	1.0	0.0	-6.0	1.1	-5.5	
	II	2.9	0.0	18.1	0.0	3.1	8.8
	III	0.9	0.0	-2.8	2.2	-2.2	
	IV	0.9	0.0	-10.2	-0.8	-2.8	
1970	I	1.8	0.0	2.1	3.1	2.2	
	II	-1.8	0.0	2.3	3.7	2.0	7.9
	III	-0.9	0.0	33.7	2.9	0.8	
	IV	0.0	0.0	-7.4	1.3	0.3	
1971	I	1.0	0.0	-8.0	8.5	-3.5	
	II	1.9	0.0	-0.3	0.5	3.4	7.2
	III	0.9	13.0	10.6	5.1	-2.9	
	IV	0.9	6.2	13.5	1.0	-0.1	
1972	I	0.9	0.0	1.6	6.2	5.5	
	II	3.6	0.0	-2.0	2.2	-0.7	5.3
	III	-0.9	0.0	-0.4	3.9	-0.7	
	IV	3.5	0.0	2.2	1.4	1.2	
1973	I	5.0	0.0	-0.5	11.1	5.5	
	II	12.0	0.0	-2.1	8.3	0.7	7.3
	III	13.6	0.0	-1.4	8.0	6.9	(3–4.6)[d]
	IV	5.5			0.1	–	
1974	I	12.0	0.0		13.2	-6.2	
	II	3.6	0.0		5.3	3.6	3.2
	III	3.5	0.0		15.1	–	
	IV	0.6	42.86		3.9	–	

Table 12 (Continued)

[a]Current dollar prices.

[b]The derivation of the quarterly exchange rate series is described in Table 2, note a. The significant variance in the series is due to the changing composition of imports over the quarters. Imports were subject to widely different duties and impositions.

[c]Wage per unit of product, calculated from index of ratio of workers' nominal daily wages and product per man-day in manufacturing (seasonally adjusted).

[d]Private sector only. The range refers to the first three quarters of 1973.

Sources:

Column (1)—CBS, *Monthly Bulletin of Statistics*, various issues, table H-2.

Column (2)—CBS, *Abstract 1989*.

Column (3)—Calculated from value of imports series in CBS, *Foreign Trade Statistics*, and *Monthly Bulletin* (Supplement), May 1978.

Columns (4), (5)—CBS, *Monthly Bulletin*, various issues, tables M-1, K-3.

Column (6)—*Report 1974*, table II-2, p. 30, and *Report 1972*, table II-8, p. 24.

Table 13
Monetary Indicators: Velocity of Circulation and Interest Rates

| | Velocity of circulation[a] | | | Nominal interest rate (short-term bank credit[b]) | Real interest rate[c] (%) | Real interest rate on "development" credit (%) | Real rate of return on government bonds (%) | Nominal rate return on treasury bills[d] (%) |
| | M_1 | M_2 | Bank deposits | | | | | |
	(1)	(2)	(3)	(4)	(5)	(6)	(7)	(8)
1964	5.91	..	19.2	16.0	11.5		4.6	..
1965	5.98	..	21.2	16.2	8.5	0.87	4.1	..
1966	5.01	..	21.9	17.9	9.4	0.18	4.4	7.7
1967	4.97	..	18.5	16.5	16.3	7.8	5.1	6.3
1968	5.35	..	17.8	14.3	12.1	6.0	6.2	5.8
1969	5.99	3.35	19.9	15.3	11.0	4.9	5.1	6.3
1970	6.01	3.29	21.5	17.8	7.0	-1.0	6.2	7.75
1971	5.91	3.21	23.0	18.6	4.6	-3.9	4.9	8.5
1972	6.09	3.52	24.5	19.0	5.9	-3.0	5.3	8.5
1973(9)			26.1	..	..	-13.8	5.6	8.5
1973	5.99	3.52	24.2	20.5	-4.7	..	..	8.5
1974	6.96	4.71	28.7	24.6	-20.2	-30.2	2.8	9.25

[a]Velocity of circulation of M_1 and M_2 with respect to GNP; M_2 defined as M_1 *plus* non-linked bank deposits and short-term treasury bills.

[b]The series represents average effective interest rates on "brokered bills" through 1969; from 1970 it represents the interest rate on a major fraction of short-term, "non-directed" bank credit—the substitute for the former type of bank credit after the abolition of the legal ceiling on interest rates in March 1970.

[c]Real rate: nominal (marginal) rate (column 4) deflated by the CPI.

[d]Rates (rounded) on 3-month bills. The entries represent annual averages if and when the (predetermined) set supply prices of these bills (sold at a set discount) were changed within a given year. This occurred three times in 1966, four times in 1967—within which the 7.5 percent (discount) rate set at the end of 1966 was reduced to its all-time low of 5.75 percent; and finally three times in 1969 in which the rate was raised to 7.75 percent in November. The 8.5 percent rate was maintained from August 1971 through October 1974.

Sources:

Columns (1)–(3)—*Report 1974*, table XVII-2; *1973*, table XIII-2; *Report 1969*, table XIV-3, and *1967*, table XV-6.

Columns (4)–(7)—Bank of Israel data bank, July 6, 1990.

Column (8)—Sanbar and Bronfeld (1973), table 10, p. 227, and *Report 1974*, p. 482.

Table 14
Nominal and Real Interest Rates on "Non-Directed" (Free) Bank Credit

(Percent)

		Nominal rate of interest[a]	Real rate of interest		Real rate of interest	
		(1)	Quarterly[b] (2)	Annual[c] (2')	Quarterly[e] (3)	Annual[c] (3')
1967	I	4.20	..		4.33	17.53
	II	4.00	..		4.14	
	III	3.80	..		4.82	
	IV	3.55	..		3.20	
1968	I	3.51		13.2	1.91	10.55
	II	3.43	2.90		2.58	
	III	3.26	5.10		3.07	
	IV	3.35	1.50		2.69	
1969	I	3.34	−1.20	12.6	3.38	12.03
	II	3.55	5.10		2.90	
	III	3.70	4.70		2.69	
	IV	3.91	3.60		2.55	
1970	I	4.22	−0.60	3.47	2.35	5.97
	II	4.15	0.40		3.18	
	III	4.16	4.10		1.38	
	IV	4.20	−0.40		−1.02	
1971	I	4.20	−2.10	5.26	3.07	8.71
	II	4.37	1.60		3.71	
	III	4.40	5.30		2.47	
	IV	4.42	0.50		−0.75	
1972	I	4.44	−2.30	3.84	2.58	8.80
	II	4.41	1.40		2.69	
	III	4.41	3.30		2.31	
	IV	4.49	1.40		0.96	
1973	I	4.61	−4.80	−5.95[d]	0.28	−0.08[d]
	II	4.66	−4.10		−2.10	
	III	4.78	2.60		1.26	
	IV	5.05	1.00		−2.61	
1974	I	5.07	−2.80	−14.49	−8.70	−19.7
	II	5.35	−5.90		−5.20	
	III	6.03	−1.10		−1.60	
	IV	6.19	−4.60		−7.30	

[a]See note *b* to table 13.
[b]Quarterly nominal rate deflated by GDP implicit price index.
[c]Derived from the quarterly averages.
[d]Refers to the first three quarters of the year only.
[e]Quarterly nominal rate deflated by wholesale price index.

Source:
Ben-Zion et al. (1986), table 8, p. 120.

Table 15
Monetary Indicators: Monetary Aggregates, Bank Reserves, and Cash Ratios[a]

	Monetary base H	Money M₁	Money M₂[b]	Money M₃[c]	Out-standing bank credit	Outstanding Treasury Bills[d] 1966 = 100	Effective reserve ratio[e]	Currency/deposit ratio	Money multiplier M₁
	(1)	(2)	(3)	(4)	(5)	(6)	(7)	(8)	(9)
	(Percent annual rate of change)						(P e r c e n t)		
1964	6.2	6.1	7.3	15.3	23.4	..	45	53	1.56
1965	11.8	11.2	5.2	13.0	17.7	..	47	55	1.52
1966	4.3	5.7	14.4	18.2	27.4	100.0	45	57	1.54
1967	28.7	26.4	39.9	25.4	9.4	140.0	45	64	1.50
1968	16.4	14.2	24.0	19.1	17.8	183.0	43	60	1.55
1969	-1.8	2.5	1.9	10.9	20.3	173.0	39	62	1.60
1970	19.8	13.4	39.6	19.5	20.7	207.0	38	63	1.61
1971	47.6	29.2	29.8	34.7	22.2	265.0	48	60	1.48
1972	41.4	28.7	27.6	17.6	18.9	277.0	58	57	1.37
1973(9)	21.3	26.4	..	..	31.0		52	57	(1.44)
1973	25.9	32.3	14.2	24.7	34.0	139.0	52	58	1.43
1974	9.2	18.0	7.7	28.7	70.7	60.0	50	57	1.47

128

[a]Entries for monetary aggregates refer to end-of-year balances. Reserve and cash ratios are averages for the year.

[b]M_2 is M_1 *plus* Israeli currency denominated time deposits *plus* treasury bills (non-linked monetary assets) held by households and firms.

[c]M_3 is M_2 *plus* foreign-currency-linked deposits (PAZAK, TAMAM and others).

[d]From 1966 onward, treasury bills served as a monetary instrument handled by the Bank of Israel.

[e]End-of-year ratios.

Sources:

All entries are ultimately based on Bank of Israel published and (frequently) revised data.

Column (1)—1964–1971: Sanbar and Bronfeld (1973), table 3, p. 225, and *Report 1974*, table XVII-4.

Column (2)—1964–1971: Sanbar and Bronfeld (1973), table 4, and *Report 1974*, table XVII-1.

Columns (3), (4)—Derived from data in Sanbar and Bronfeld (1973), table 4, and *Report 1974*, table XVII-7.

Columns (5), (6)—Sanbar and Bronfeld (1973), tables 4 and 6, and *Report 1974*, tables XVII-10 and XVII-4.

Column (7)—1964–1971: Sanbar and Bronfeld (1973), table 5, and *Report 1974*, table XVII-5.

Column (8)—*Report 1974*, table XVII-6, and corresponding tables in previous *Reports*.

Column (9)—Derived from columns (7) and (8) by application of the formula which involves the currency deposit ratio and the effective reserve ratio.

Table 16
Semiannual Monetary Indicators: Monetary Aggregates and Reserve Ratios[a]

		Monetary base H	Money		Out-standing bank credit[b]	Treasury bills (Index: 1966=100)	Effective reserve ratios
			M_1	M_2			
		(1)	(2)	(3)	(4)	(5)	(6)
		(Semiannual rates of change -- percent)					(Percent)
1966		..	..	..	..	100	43.9
1967[c]	I	..	21.0	27.9	4.9	..	48.2
	II	..	4.5	10.9	4.3	140	48.2
1968[c]	I	4.0	12.1	16.0	7.0	..	47.7
	II	14.9	1.8	6.2	10.1	183	43.2
1969	I	2.7	5.6	4.5	12.2	178	40.3
	II	-3.8	-2.9	-2.4	8.1	173	38.8
1970	I	9.9	5.1	19.4	7.1	204	42.7
	II	8.5	8.5	16.9	12.7	207	38.2
1971	I	31.2	14.9	17.1	8.2	230	50.1
	II	12.4	11.7	11.5	12.4	265	48.2
1972	I	29.2	16.9	14.9	5.5	293	59.7
	II	9.5	10.1	10.5	12.9	277	57.4
1973	I	6.8	10.9	5.0	13.8	254	53.2
	II	17.9	19.3	8.5	17.7	139	52.5
	(9)	9.1	19.3	10.0	23.2		52.1
1974	I	-18.8	-2.5	-6.6	26.6	43	32.9
	II	34.6	21.1	15.4	34.8	60	50.0

Table 16 (Continued)

aRates of change reflect end-of-June and end-of-December balances. The third entry (9) for 1973 reflects end-of-September balance. Entries for treasury bills and reserve ratios refer to end-of-period balances.

bThe credit series definitions, thus end-of-year balances, were changed twice—in 1970 and 1972. The rates of change were accordingly calculated from the monthly series represented for each year in the corresponding *Annual Report*.

cEntries for 1967 and 1968 exclude treasury bills from the definition of M_2. These are included in the subsequent entries.

Sources:

Column (1)—*Report 1974*, table XVII-4; *1973*, table XIII-5, and similar tables in *Report 1969* through *1972*. Data for 1967–71 derived by a summation of outstanding currency and banking system liquid assets in *Report 1971*, tables XIV-5 and XIV-6, and similar tables in previous *Reports*.

Column (2)—*Report 1974*, table XVII-6 and similar tables (Means of Payment) in *Report 1967* through *1972*.

Columns (3), (5)—*Report 1974*, tables XVII-6 and XVII-7, and similar tables (Other Parameters, Assets, and Means of Payment) in *Report 1967* through *1973*.

Column (4)—*Report 1968*, table XIV-10; *Report 1969* to *1971*, table XIV-10; *1972*, table XIII-14; *1973*, table XIII-11; *1974*, table XVII-10.

Column (6)—*Report 1974*, table XVII-5, and similar tables (Bank Liquidity Indicators) in *Report 1969* through *1973*.

Table 17
Main Items of Bank of Israel Balance Sheet, Outstanding Treasury Bills, and Monetary Base (IL mill.)

	Net foreign reserves	Government net debt[a]	Credit to public and banking system	Banking system foreign currency deposits	Outstanding treasury bills	Total $(1)+(2)+(3)-(4)-(5)=$	Monetary base	Residual[b] $(7)-(6)$
	(1)	(2)	(3)	(4)	(5)	(6)	(7)	(8)
1966	1,849	344	249	1,047	270	1,125	1,353	228
1967	2,445	530	399	1,470	379	1,525	1,734	209
1968	2,280	1,464	408	1,803	495	1,854	2,017	163
1969	1,197	2,717	694	2,345	467	1,796	1,981	185
1970	1,226	3,818	738	2,790	560	2,432	2,382	50
1971	2,299	5,238	880	4,169	714	3,534	3,540	6
1972	4,689	4,980	859	4,755	745	5,028	5,004	-24
1973(9)	6,542	5,064	1,312	6,355	823	5,740	5,717	-23
1973	7,398	4,179	1,383	6,092	433	6,435	6,303	-132

[a]Total government and Jewish Agency net credit balances with the Bank of Israel.

[b]The summation of columns (1)–(5), with the two last columns as negative values should, by definition, sum to the corresponding entries for the monetary base—column (7). Since some minor Bank of Israel balance sheet items are not available, and monetary base figures were published from 1972 onward (going back to 1970) the quality of the monetary base data for 1966–69 in particular is somewhat questionable. Hence the relatively large residuals for those years. These would have been smaller if entries in a column of Sanbar and Bronfeld (1973), described as "other factors," had been used in the compilation of Table 17. Note that the residuals for 1970–73 are of an order of 0.5–2 percent only—thus negligible.

Sources:

Columns (1)–(8)—*Reports 1973* and *1972*, tables XIII-3 and XIII-4, respectively, for 1970–73; Sanbar and Bronfeld (1973), table 3, for 1966–69.

Column (4)—*Reports 1973* and *1972*, table XIII-3; *Report 1968*, table XV-4.

Column (5)—*Reports 1973* and *1972*, tables XIII-3 and XIII-4, respectively; *Report 1970*, table XIV-6; and Sanbar and Bronfeld (1973), table 4.

Column (7)—*Reports 1973* and *1972*, table XIII-5; and Sanbar and Bronfeld (1973), table 3.

Table 18

Annual Inflows (+) and Outflows (−) of Bank of Israel Assets and Liabilities, and Changes in Outstanding Treasury Bills and in Monetary Base, 1967–73 (IL mill.)

	Net foreign assets	Government net debt	Credit to the banking system and public[a]	Commercial bank foreign currency[b] balances	Outstanding treasury bills	Total[c] (1)+(2)+(3) −(4)−(5)C	Monetary base	Residual (6)−(7)
	(1)	(2)	(3)	(4)	(5)	(6)	(7)	(8)
1967	596	186	150	423	109	400	381	19
1968	−165	934	9	339	116	329	283	46
1969	−1,083	1,253	286	542	−28	−58	−36	−22
1970	29	1,101	44	445	93	636	401	235
1971	1,073	1,420	142	1,379	154	1,102	1,158	−56
1972	2,390	−258	−21	586	31	1,494	1,464	30
1973(9)	1,853	84	453	1,600	78	712	713	−1
1973	2,709	−801	524	1,337	−312	1,407	1,299	108

[a]Entries in this column reflect mainly the change in the nominal volume of bills, arising from the "directed" credit component of total bank credit. The purpose of these operations was to finance privileged sectors (e.g., agriculture and manufacturing) and activities (reports) at interest rates lower than the going market rate.

[b]These balances held at the Bank of Israel were actually foreign-currency-denominated reserves which commercial banks had to maintain as backing for non-resident PATACH deposits and long-term resident deposits arising from German reparations and pension payments.

[c]See Table 17, footnote b. Note that if the data from the Sanbar and Bronfeld column "other factors" were included, the "residual" for 1970 would be 149 only, and the residual for 1971 almost nil.

Sources: Derived from Table 17. An entry for year *t* is the difference between corresponding entries for years (*t*) and (*t* − 1) in Table 17.

Table 19
World Price Indicators

	GDP deflators (annual percentage rate of change)				Consumer prices		Index: 1975 = 100					Industrial countries export prices (annual rate of change[a])	Industrial countries import prices (annual rate of change[a])
	Indus-trialized countries	U.S.	Germany	U.K.	Europe	U.S.	Total	Food	Metals	Petro-leum fuel		
											Commodity prices		
	(1)	(2)	(3)	(4)	(5)	(6)	(7)	(8)	(9)	(10)	(11)	(12)
1965	3.0	2.2	3.5	5.0	33	59	43	39	71	12	2.0	1.0
1966	3.6	3.2	3.6	4.5	39	60	56	39	77	12	1.9	1.0
1967	3.2	3.0	1.4	2.9	41	62	52	40	66	12	0.0	0.0
1968	4.0	4.4	1.8	4.2	43	65	52	39	67	12	-0.9	-1.0
1969	5.0	5.1	4.2	5.5	46	68	56	42	74	12	3.8	3.3
1970	6.0	5.4	9.2	7.3	49	72	58	44	78	12	6.4	5.3
1971	5.9	5.0	7.6	9.4	54	75	55	45	68	15	4.3	5.0
1972	5.3	4.1	7.8	8.3	60	78	63	51	68	18	8.6	5.0
1973	7.5	5.7	5.4	7.1	70	83	96	79	99	25	19.3	8.6
1974	11.8	8.8	6.5	14.8	85	92	122	127	124	91	25.0	22.8
1975	11.3	9.9	6.0	27.3	100	100	100	100	100	100	11.1	42.1
1976	8.4	6.3	3.7	14.6	115	106	113	82	106	107	1.0	8.7
1977	7.8	6.7	3.7	14.0	138	113	137	79	114	116	7.9	1.0
1978	7.7	7.4	4.2	11.1	172	121	130	90	120	119	11.9	9.9
1979	8.3	8.8	4.1	14.6	230	135	152	102	156	158	16.4	9.9
1980	10.4	9.1	4.5	19.7	345	153	166	137	173	267	12.7	18.9

[a]For quarterly breakdown, 1969/IV to 1974/IV, see Table 20.

Sources:
Columns (1)–(4)—IMF, IFS, Yearbook 1984, p. 125.
Columns (5)–(6)—Economic Report of the President, 1986, p. 376.
Columns (7)–(10)—IMF, IFS, Yearbook 1984, p. 133.
Columns (11)–(12)—IMF, IFS, Yearbook 1984.

Table 20
Import and Export Prices, Industrial Countries

(Quarterly rates of change, percent)

		Export prices	Import prices
1969	IV	2.8	2.8
1970	I	1.8	2.8
	II	1.8	0.0
	III	0.9	0.0
	IV	0.9	0.9
1971	I	1.7	1.8
	II	0.8	1.7
	III	1.7	1.7
	IV	3.3	1.7
1972	I	4.0	4.1
	II	0.8	0.8
	III	0.0	0.8
	IV	1.5	0.8
1973	I	7.0	7.0
	II	8.2	10.1
	III	8.3	8.8
	IV	2.1	4.0
1974	I	4.1	13.6
	II	11.1	14.3
	III	3.5	4.0
	IV	4.0	2.4

Source: IMF, *IFS, Monthly Financial Statistics.*

—— PART II ——

The Role of Monetary Policy in Israel's 1985 Stabilization Effort

Introduction

Argentina's Austral, Brazil's Cruzado, and Israel's Sheqel plans, all launched
in 1985/86, involved a combination of devaluation, exchange-rate pegging, and
price-wage freezes, supported by price controls and tighter fiscal and monetary
discipline.

While the Cruzado and Austral plans failed, the Sheqel plan achieved the goal
of reducing inflation to an annual rate of 15–20 percent (somewhat later than
expected); inflation stayed within that range for six years before dipping further
to 9–10 percent. This study shows that the failure of the two South American
plans and the success of the Sheqel plan can be attributed to the absence (or at
best, weak application) of traditional aggregate demand control instruments, both
fiscal and monetary, in the first two cases, and their strict and persevering application in the Israeli case. A necessary condition for such success was an all-
out effort to tighten the fiscal screws so as to eliminate the bulging public sector
deficit.

Israel's monetary policy was restrictive from the very beginning, as evidenced
by very high real interest rates; its role was crucial because of the enormous
liquidity overhang and the very openness of the economy. Monetary policy was
used to lure highly liquid economic agents away from real assets into financial
instruments, while increasing the cost of maintaining inventories, thus pushing
goods into the markets. The rapid decline in the sizable government deficit
allowed the Bank of Israel to keep money scarce. This was the only way to
maintain the dollar peg in the short run without resorting to foreign currency
allocation, and to sustain the peg in the longer run as the influx of funds improved the foreign reserve position.

Scarce money inevitably meant a prolonged spell of high real interest rates,
which raises the question of "overshooting": could the same purpose have been

served with less onerous real rates? In retrospect, there clearly was some over-shooting, as revealed by real marginal lending rates in the upper two-digit range for almost a whole year. Assigning the highest priority to the credibility and success of the program, the Israeli monetary authorities, unlike their counterparts in Argentina and Brazil, preferred to err on the side of caution, that is, the side of high real interest rates.

These three programs, launched almost simultaneously, were described in the financial and economic literature as "heterodox" stabilization programs. To most people, especially those in political circles, the hallmark of heterodoxy is a wage-price freeze, enforced by controls and supported by pegging a key variable, for example, the nominal exchange rate. Using the exchange rate as a nominal anchor is obviously not specific to heterodox cures of inflation; it was the condition sine qua non of "orthodox" stabilization schemes in the 1920s and post–World War II stabilization programs based on the Bretton Woods rules. The true distinguishing feature of heterodoxy is its income policy component, with universal price controls as the linchpin. Together with the pegged exchange rate these two instruments were assigned the main role in taming and ultimately subduing the inertial forces that many adherents of the heterodox view identify as predominant in generating runaway inflation.

In the two Latin American programs wage and price controls were to bear the main burden of pulling the sting out of inflation. Israel's program also had an incomes policy component, but unlike the Latin American program, it had a specific content: one of its instruments was an immediate (though not longer-run), substantial, across-the-board cut in real wages. Social psychology and political considerations, as represented by claims made by the labor unions (the Histadrut), therefore required the imposition of a universal price freeze supported by controls as quid pro quo.

Although similar in appearance, the programs were really quite different. While some professionals and the political community in Argentina and Brazil believed—or at least behaved as if they believed—that price controls and pegging the exchange rate, with minor (if any) support from demand management, could reduce inflation painlessly (i.e., without eroding real wages and entailing significant fiscal and monetary restraints), the Israeli program was run along altogether different lines: what counted was the *signal* that controls were at work, rather than their actual use. True, price freezes were formally imposed, but in practice market forces, generated and supported by traditional fiscal and monetary policy instruments, were what maintained price discipline. These highly restrictive policies bore the brunt of enforcement and led to the winding down of inflation from an annual rate of 400–500 percent to the first target—annual rates of 15–20 percent—within six months. It was adherence to a strictly restrictive stance, especially in the monetary arena, that helped keep inflation within this two-digit range through 1991, at which time it was finally pulled down one step further, to around 10 percent.

The move toward (upper) single-digit inflation did not occur before a significant improvement was made in one of the fundamentals. The wage–productivity ratio finally fell into place in the wake of the major 1988–89 recession, when unemployment rose to 10 percent, with a significant erosion of real wages. A rise in unemployment (and a corresponding loss of foregone output) could not be avoided altogether at the time the 1985–86 stabilization program was implemented, but it was relatively small at first, gaining force only in 1988–89, due to the pervasive and drawn-out restrictive monetary policy. This policy had to be maintained for so long, in order to keep inflation in check until the institutional resistance to an improvement in the fundamentals of the labor market—a proper meshing of wage and productivity—was overcome.

A comparison of the performances of the Austral, Cruzado, and Sheqel programs, with special reference to the role of monetary policy, shows that the notion that a heterodox stabilization program can be implemented without tight fiscal discipline to support a highly restrictive monetary policy, though welcome in the political arena, is unwarranted. Freezes, pegs, and controls are bound to lead to dismal failure. On the other hand, a highly restrictive monetary policy, sustained by a tight fiscal stance for a lengthy interval (in terms of the political horizon), supported by a stable exchange rate as a highly visible nominal anchor and a significant (temporary) erosion of real wages, combined to successfully contain Israel's runaway inflation.

6

A Comparative Review of the Austral, Cruzado, and Sheqel Plans

In a 1988 Economic Focus article, "Hype on Inflation," *The Economist* described the Israeli stabilization effort as follows:

Israel's stabilization plan was launched in July 1985, a month after Argentina's. It contained roughly the same ingredients. The budget deficit was to be cut, while prices, wages, and the exchange rate were frozen. (July 16, 1988, p. 59)

In the same article, which also refers to the Cruzado Plan, the three stabilization programs of Argentina, Brazil, and Israel are classified as "heterodox" inflation cures, designed to overcome inertial inflation at minimal cost in terms of output and employment. None of the three paragraphs outlining the design and implementation of the Israeli program and its comparative success in reducing inflationary momentum mentions monetary policy. Similarly, in an article dated March 14, 1987 (p. 69), *The Economist* describes the demise of the Cruzado Plan, and squarely attributes the Israeli success to "wage and price controls . . . and big cuts in the budget deficit."

This image of Israel's stabilization policy is widespread even among economists. Thus, the preface of a volume of proceedings of the recent Toledo Conference on Inflation Stabilization states that "there are strong similarities among the programs in different countries—for example, Argentina, Israel, and Brazil—but evidently major differences in the outcomes" (Bruno et al., 1988, p. vii).[1]

The imposition of price and wage controls, the pegging of the exchange rate, and the planned substantial reduction of the budget deficit—all part and parcel of the three programs—do indeed create an appearance of similarity. The fixing of the exchange rate was, however, a sine qua non of orthodox stabilizations, involving a return to the gold standard implemented in the 1920s, and of several of the post–World War II stabilizations carried out on the basis of the Bretton Woods rules. The same applies to the reduction of the budget deficit, the distinguishing feature that warrants the heterodox label for these three plans is thus the universal price controls that were to break, or at least weaken, inflationary inertia. It was hoped that these controls would allow the economy to move quickly and without substantial cost in foregone output to a (comparatively) stable price environment.

EXCHANGE RATES AND PRICE PATTERNS

Table 21 and Figure 4 show price and quantity data for two pre-stabilization quarters and eight post-stabilization quarters for the three countries.[2] They reveal both the similarities and some of the crucial differences between these attempts at stabilization. Table 21 and Figure 5 show that the official exchange rate—a major policy instrument—was virtually stopped in its tracks at the beginning of the program in all three countries. This was also true for the parallel exchange market in Argentina, but not in Brazil. In the latter, only the rate of change of the "official" exchange rate dropped from a monthly rate of 11.4 percent in the last pre-stabilization quarter to 1.5 percent in the first, and to zero in the second post-stabilization quarter. A reduction of the premium on the exchange traded in the comparatively free parallel market occurred in Argentina but not in Brazil, where this premium initially stayed at 40 percent (see Table 21 and Figure 6), suggesting that in Argentina the credibility of the policy at the beginning of the process might have been higher.

In Israel, the substantial 30 percent devaluation supported by the highly publicized first tranche of special U.S. aid of $750 million was most effective in calming expectations in the Israeli exchange market. In the first quarter after stabilization, depreciation of the domestic currency in the official (and dominant) exchange market slowed down immediately, from monthly rates of 10 percent or more to a virtual crawl. Even more significant as an indicator of expectations was the substantial reduction in changes in the black-market rate, from monthly rates of 15 percent and 12 percent in the two pre-stabilization quarters to 2 and zero percent, respectively, in the two post-stabilization quarters. This is underlined by the immediate reduction of the black-market premium from 26 to 8 percent (Table 21), a further reduction to 7 percent in the second post-stabilization quarter (after which it remained stable through the next three quarters), and finally, its virtual disappearance during the fifth to eighth quarters. This pattern suggests a gain in the credibility of the program over time. At these premiums the price of black-market foreign exchange was substantially lower than the price of the "passenger"[3] dollar in the official exchange market.

Since official exchange rates were to serve as instruments, the slowdown of devaluation to a virtual standstill in the first quarter or two after the launching of the programs is obviously not even an approximate test of the policy. The

target was prices: the trend of their rate of change could provide an early indication of which way the wind was blowing and could ultimately serve as an
indicator of success.

However, with controls in place, price data are not the only relevant indicator
of the market process. Under these circumstances only relevant quantity indicators could offer the required supplementary information. The appearance and
persistence of shortages would suggest suppressed inflationary pressures not captured by the price data. This happened in Brazil in the first stage of implementation, where, between March and June 1986 (the first quarter of the Cruzado
Plan), shortages of milk and meat, and waiting lists for automobiles became
widespread (Modiano, 1988; Simonsen, 1988).

A comparison of the first post-stabilization quarter in the three countries suggests that Brazil, with a rate of price increase of less than 1 percent, came in
first in terms of the prime target of the exercise.[4] These official price index
figures led Brazil's finance minister to describe Brazil as "a country with Swiss
inflation and twice the Japanese growth rate." The appearance of shortages,
however, was hardly consistent with such a reading of these signals. An inspection of the decomposed wholesale price index should have suggested, by
June 1986 at the latest, that the prices of some components of the wholesale
price index basket were far from settling down at the predicted low-inflation
pattern. By June, the price series for agricultural products was already rising for
the second consecutive month (0.7 percent), while the other major component
of this index—industrial products, a much more stringently controlled sector—
which had declined in May, rose in June by 0.3 percent. By August and September, with agricultural prices rising at a monthly rate of about 2.5 percent,
the game was already lost, though the consumer price index, rising at only 1.5
percent in the second post-stabilization quarter (Table 21), was still "reasonable" in terms of the plan's price targets.[5] With inflation as measured by the
consumer price index again rising and at monthly average rates of 4.1 percent
in the third post-stabilization quarter (7.3 percent in December), the last quarter
of 1986, it was evident that the Cruzado Plan was a flop.

Argentina's inflation at the time of stabilization was significantly higher than
that of Brazil and also higher than the 14 percent monthly inflation rate of Israel.
Though the Argentine inflation rate dropped to about 2.5 percent in the first two
quarters after stabilization—higher than the initial Brazilian rates—the process
of disinflation was steeper than that of Brazil (Figure 4). The 2.5 percent inflation of the first post-stabilization quarter—down from the very high rate of 25
percent in the preceding quarter—could therefore rightly be rated satisfactory.
The absence of shortages also support this reading.

The signals from the comparatively "free" parallel exchange market were
also reassuring. For the first three post-stabilization quarters, this rate, which did
not serve as an instrument, as did its official counterpart, was declining at
monthly average rates of 0.6 percent (Table 21). Furthermore, the premium on
the official rate went down from 23 percent to 7 percent in the second and third

post-stabilization quarters. Similarly, the black-market rate declined toward the official market rate and hardly moved during the three first quarters after the launching of the program.[6]

Figures 4 and 5, which describe the rates of change of prices and exchange rates, respectively, show that the Austral Plan survived somewhat longer than the Cruzado Plan. The price entry for the third post-stabilization quarter in Argentina, 3.1 percent average monthly inflation (Table 21), overstates the timing of reversal, since it mainly reflects the high figure for the rate of price change at the end of the quarter (March 1986). Yet an average monthly inflation rate of 4.4 percent for the fourth post-inflation quarter meant, in effect, that within less than a year the Austral Plan, which was initially promising, was a disaster.

This occurred while Argentina's exchange rate instrument—the pegging of the official rate—was kept in place throughout the third quarter. Since the parallel market rate did not stray out of line even through the fourth post-stabilization quarter (when inflation was rising by leaps and bounds to an annual rate of more than 65 percent), the official rate during these two quarters is fairly representative of the cost of foreign exchange. The reasons for this substantial lag of the exchange rate after prices are undoubtedly of some interest for the study of the dynamics of the process in the Argentine environment. But what is relevant in this context is the lag in the adjustment of the parallel exchange rate to prices.[7] This indicates that the reacceleration of inflation can hardly be ascribed to balance-of-payments factors.

Compared with the price series for the other two countries, the Israeli series does not decrease as steeply (Figure 4). Though the unofficial target was to bring inflation down to 1–2 percent a month in the second month of implementation, price resistance shows up clearly in the 3.5 percent monthly average for the last two months of the first post-stabilization quarter. Only in the third quarter did price inflation dip to a quarterly average of less than 1 percent a month, the target that Brazil apparently succeeded in reaching in the first quarter. In the fifth quarter after stabilization the rate declined again, to the 1–2 percent a month target, and stayed within this range through the succeeding four quarters and ever since.

Thus, though somewhat slower in reaching the low inflation target, Israel succeeded where the other two failed—to stay within the stabilization program's prescribed price range as price controls were relaxed in successive stages. This process, which involved the exclusion of groups of commodities and services from the controlled list, began in January 1986, that is, the beginning of the third post-stabilization quarter. An inspection of the price series in Table 21 and Figure 4 indicates that inflation in this quarter did not surge upward. On the contrary, it declined to its trough in terms of rates of change.

The next and major stage in the relaxation of controls came in April-June 1986, that is, during the fourth post-stabilization quarter. This is reflected in the rise of the quarterly mean of the monthly inflation rate, which moved upward somewhat beyond the upper limit of the 1–2 percent target range. With inflation at 1 percent through the fifth quarter it was obvious that the economy did not succumb to a new bout of high inflation, though a further relaxation of controls was implemented during this quarter. This stage, like the earlier stages of the dismantling of controls, inevitably involved some upward adjustment of prices frozen by fiat and of prices of public utilities and essentials directly determined by the government. The Israeli price curve in Figure 4 and the series in Table 21 indicate that by the beginning of the fifth post-stabilization quarter the system was well within the Sheqel Plan's inflation target.

A comparison of the Argentine and Brazilian price data for the third and fourth post-stabilization quarters suggests that it was some time during this interval that these stabilization programs began to break down. The viability of the programs was subjected at this time to a crucial test—the attempt to allow for a realignment of relative prices by relaxing price controls. Relative prices were, of course, not necessarily at their longer-term equilibrium values when the price freeze was imposed, which created pressures expressed in terms of shortages (mainly in Brazil), and in a loss of profitability in the industrial sector in particular. It was this attempt to adopt more flexible price controls, at which prices reflect costs more closely, that caused the seams of the straitjacket imposed by fiat on the price system in these two economies to burst wide open (Machinea and Fanelli, 1988, pp. 141–42; Canavese and Di Tella, 1988, pp. 159–61; Modiano, 1988, pp. 233–39; Simonsen, 1988, pp. 281–84).

But this did not occur in Israel, where, at the same stage (the third post-stabilization quarter) and in quite rapid stages, price controls were abolished, which suggests that the failure of the Austral and Cruzado Plans was not necessarily the result of tampering with controls. These controls were, in any case, designed as a temporary, mainly demonstrative device in the case of Israel, and should have been conceived as such in the two Latin American countries.

THE MACROECONOMIC ENVIRONMENT

A review of the macroeconomic environment and the policies pursued by the three countries during the early stages of the stabilization attempts offers some insight into the reasons for the success of one and for the failure of the other two programs.

Economic Activity and Employment Levels

The differences in the long-term pattern of prices inevitably reflect differences in macroeconomic developments. Without comparative quarterly GNP series, unemployment rates are the most relevant indicator of the level of activity. This socially sensitive indicator could also shed some light on the political strains and stresses of implementing such a program.

Figure 7 and the corresponding series in Table 21 underline the contrast in the macroeconomic situation between the two South American economies and

Israel. The Argentine unemployment figures (their technical deficiencies notwithstanding) do not show a lower level of activity through the crucial first quarters of the Austral Plan. For the first two quarters they even suggest a slight improvement in the labor market. GDP figures indicate a small slowdown in the third quarter of 1985—the first post-stabilization quarter—but this disappeared in the next quarter.[8]

The case of Brazil, with better coverage of unemployment data, is even more outstanding. The unemployment figures for the three first quarters after the launching of the Cruzado Plan reveal a clear trend of falling unemployment. Moreover, industrial production series showing annual growth rates of more than 12 percent during each month of the first three post-stabilization quarters, and the 8.2 percent growth rate of GDP in 1986 (also in 1985) suggests a booming economy.[9]

The situation was different in Israel. The 6.3 percent average unemployment rate in the two pre-stabilization quarters was exceptionally high by Israeli standards. Declining employment in manufacturing, while the real capital stock of the industry was still growing (at an annual rate of about 5 percent), indicates excess capacity in this sector. Data for the whole business sector suggest that this was true everywhere during these two quarters.[10] Thus, in stark contrast with the situation in Argentina and Brazil, the macroeconomic setting in Israel at the launching of the stabilization program was hardly one of full employment.

An inspection of the unemployment record in the immediate aftermath of stabilization through the succeeding five quarters underlines a crucial feature of Israel's stabilization policy on the macroeconomic plane: it was carried out from a base of relatively high unemployment and within an environment of declining activity.[11] The immediate rise in the unemployment rate to an even higher level of more than 7 percent for the next four quarters was therefore meaningful. Yet the perception of declining activity and employment through the first two or three crucial quarters was worse than the reality. The corresponding increase in uncertainty about employment and income as inflation was rapidly declining helped rather than hampered in pushing the economy toward the stabilization targets. The tightening of markets for goods and services reduced the temptation to mark up prices and weakened resistance to the substantial (temporary) cuts in real wages that, following an agreement with the unions, were an integral element of the program.

An objective measure of the immediate stabilization costs in terms of output and employment would not be as high as the impression that they made at that time on economic agents—households and businesses—and on the political community. Yet it was this contrast between the initially low and subsequently declining pattern of activity in Israel and the boom conditions in Argentina and Brazil that created an altogether different environment for the attempt to reach lower inflation.

The Fiscal Dimension

The figures in Table 21 for government deficit and real interest rates offer a first approximation of an explanation of the contrast between the macroeconomic environments within which the Sheqel Plan on the one hand and the Austral and Cruzado Plans on the other were implemented.

Consider first the government deficit—whose reduction had been an integral element of all the so-called heterodox stabilization plans. Quarterly series of a real measure of government deficit for Brazil are unavailable. Annual series of the public sector borrowing requirement (PSBR) suggest a slight improvement (from 4.3 percent of GDP in 1985 to 3.7 percent in 1986) in the "operational" deficit, defined to exclude the monetary correction element of the interest cost of the public debt. The planning team of the Cruzado program had assumed that a December 1985 fiscal package would reduce the operational fiscal deficit to almost zero as the plan progressed. However, this did not happen in 1986, as the public sector neither reduced expenditures nor kept the operational deficit below the 1985 level.[12]

In contrast, Argentina's public sector deficit curve (Figure 8) shows that price controls were supported by the second element of the Austral program—a reduction in the government deficit. During the first post-stabilization quarter, the government deficit on a cash basis declined from 7 percent and more to only 1.8 percent of GDP. With deficits that in only one of the first five post-stabilization quarters slightly exceeded 2 percent of GDP, the non-financial public sector undoubtedly exerted a restraining influence on aggregate demand during this period. A deficit series that includes the central bank's operations (interest payments on the national debt) shows correspondingly higher deficit ratios. Yet the pattern of the total is similar to that of the deficit of the non-financial sector. And even those ratios, except for one quarter, are well within the 2–3 percent of GDP range, suggesting that during the first five quarters the fiscal policy stance was on the whole restrictive. This policy was, however, implemented indirectly; government expenditures on goods and services were only slightly reduced, if at all. The significant scaling down of the deficit was achieved by measures designed to increase the revenues of the government and public enterprises: a substantial cut in the subsidies to public utilities supplemented by a rise in foreign trade and income taxes and by the fiscal benefit of the (reverse) Tanzi effect that comes into effect as inflation rates decline (Machinea and Fanelli, 1988, pp. 127, 134; Canavese and Di Tella, 1988, p. 160; de Pablo, 1988, table 1, p. 196).

The restrictive impact of rising government revenues affects aggregate demand indirectly: it reduces disposable income and thus might affect expectations by creating, or increasing, uncertainty about the disposable income pattern in the near future. Both lower income and higher uncertainty are expected to instantaneously reduce consumption expenditures. An even more important immediate effect of a lower government deficit is monetary: lower deficit means lower borrowing requirements by the public sector, which allows for the scaling down of central bank accommodation, thus reducing base money creation. Lower borrowing requirements may also reduce the issuing of more (indexed) highly liquid government debt. The significant reduction of the Argentine government's deficit, maintained through the first five post-stabilization quarters, undoubtedly supported attempts at monetary restraint designed to reduce aggregate demand pressures.

In Israel, fiscal policy was also assigned the same role, first and foremost to support restrictive monetary policy. Figure 8 shows the drastic reduction of the government deficit, which was even larger than the significant effort by Argentina. The deficit moved from over 9 percent of GDP in the first pre-stabilization quarter to 0.5 percent immediately after stabilization, and even became a small surplus in the second post-stabilization quarter. Yet, in contrast with Argentina (which abandoned its attempt at fiscal discipline in the sixth post-stabilization quarter) and Brazil (which barely attempted it) the Israeli government stuck to its guns. Strict fiscal discipline was maintained, as the series indicates, through the second year of stabilization when the public sector was again in surplus.

Israel's deficit reduction also involved only a small cut in expenditures. Real government demand for goods and services, including labor services, was hardly cut. Most of the cut in expenditures reflected the significantly lower public sector wage cost made possible by an agreement with public sector employees to allow a substantial, though temporary, cut in their real salaries. At the trough, in the second quarter after stabilization, wages and salaries of public sector employees were about 20 percent lower in real terms.[13] A substantial increase in net tax absorption, involving the escalation of gross tax revenue to 50 percent of GNP, served as the main instrument of imposing fiscal constraint.

Thus, in Israel too, the impact of fiscal policy on aggregate demand was on the whole indirect, implemented mainly by means of temporary reductions in disposable income, and by what amounts to a strong demonstration effect. The major cut in food subsidies (the obverse of the initial price shock) and the substantial temporary cut in real wages and salaries sent a highly visible message to economic agents that restraint was to be the order of the day. This increased the credibility of both government finances and the stabilization policy.

The monetary impact of this drastic change of absorption, from high negative values to (low) positive ones, was far-reaching. The central bank could almost stop accommodating the treasury, thereby reducing a major source of base money creation. It also initially reduced (and later stopped altogether) government net absorption of funds from the capital market, affording significantly greater access to business which hitherto had been crowded out. Finally, the corresponding stabilization of the real level of the domestic national debt offered far greater leeway for the pursuit of a restrictive monetary policy.

The Monetary Dimension

The above discussion of the fiscal stance underlines the major difference between Brazil's fiscal policy—which did not offer any support to the stabilization effort—and that of the other two countries. It also points to the differences in terms of persistence and duration between the Israeli and Argentinian attempts at fiscal restraint: the Brazilian boom and Argentina's high level of economic activity, compared with that of Israel during the first stage of implementing the respective programs, might also reflect differences in the monetary stance; if so, it should have found expression in terms of the monetary dimension of each economic system.

Insight into the comparative developments in the money and capital markets in the three countries is offered by the real interest-rate series in Table 21 and Figure 9.[14] Such a series suffers from several familiar technical deficiencies. The use of an ex post deflator, reflecting ex post real interest rates, means that the deflator is at best only a proxy. The choice of a proper deflator is another matter. Substantial variance of the inflation rate, typical of periods in which stabilizations are attempted, casts the significance of quarterly averages in doubt. Finally, the availability of information on interest rates in credit markets that are highly segmented by government fiat imposes an obvious constraint on international comparative analyses. In spite of all their shortcomings, these series offer substantial insight into the reasons for the far-reaching differences in the macroeconomic environments within which the three programs were tested.

Brazil has the poorest data coverage on nominal interest rates. This made it necessary to use a very short-term rate—the interest rate for overnight money—to gauge the cost of credit. Though the absolute level of real rates is also significant for a cross-country analysis of the functioning of money markets, the time trend of this price measure is a more meaningful indicator of developments in financial and in real markets.

In retrospect, knowing that the Cruzado Plan failed, an inspection of the pattern of the Brazilian overnight rate should not come as a surprise. Even though the 5 percent average annual real interest rate, maintained through the first post-stabilization quarter, represents the floor of the Brazilian interest-rate structure, it still seems very low. The cost of short-run bank credit was higher, but even if real rates on longer-term bank credits were twice or even three times as high, so that the cost of short-term bank credit was 10–15 percent in real terms, such interest rates would seem low at a point when an attempt to reduce inflation from annual rates of 300 percent to low single-digit rates is being made. Figure 9, displaying the levels and patterns of real interest rates in the three countries at the same stage of implementing their specific programs, shows dramatic differences. The Argentine rates, and even more so the Israeli ones, were several times higher than even a 10–15 percent real rate.

The most important insight offered by the Brazilian interest-rate series is its pattern: it rose from a rather low negative level of 11 percent (the quarterly average two quarters before stabilization) to 2 percent in the quarter before stabilization. It then rose to 5 percent when the stabilization price shock was implemented and to 12 percent in the second post-stabilization quarter, and subsequently turned negative. Another available series—interest rates on certificates of deposit (CDs)—shows similar features: extremely low absolute rates following a similar declining pattern (Modiano, 1988, p. 253, table 5A.9).

These data suggest that whether by design or by not attempting to prevent accommodation, the monetary stance adopted by the Brazilian authorities was at best neutral, and later on, in the third post-stabilization quarter, even expansionary. There can thus be little doubt that the Cruzado Plan was launched and implemented without any (effective) attempt at monetary restraint. A supporting restrictive monetary policy was apparently considered unnecessary by those in charge of designing and implementing the program.[15] Rising demand pressures that exploded in the third post-stabilization quarter, and the failure of what three months before was considered the Brazilian "miracle" by some people, should have surprised no one in view of the pent-up demand pressures that monetary and commodity market monitors were clearly showing.

An inspection of the continuous Argentinean and Israeli monetary indicators emphasizes this reading of the Brazilian series.[16] The accelerating price inflation in Argentina preceding stabilization involved highly negative interest rates in the regulated (effectively, though perhaps not formally), subsidized segment of the credit market. This did not apply, however, to the non-regulated market, where a real annual interest rate of 38 percent in the last pre-stabilization quarter was extremely high by Brazilian standards. What is even more significant is the very steep jump of this rate to 15 percent and 53 percent in the regulated and non-regulated markets, respectively, coinciding with the launching of the program, which suggests that a restrictive monetary stance was initially adopted by the authorities. Note in particular the move to the 15 percent real interest rate on "regulated credit," the largest component of the Argentine credit market, in the immediate aftermath of stabilization.[17]

These figures suggest that the monetary screw was initially tightened to support the Argentine stabilization effort, though the segmentation of the credit market meant that these high rates did not apply across the board. This squeeze was undoubtedly quite persuasive, and inevitably resented by industry and particularly by trade because of the unusual hike in the cost of carrying stocks. The latter were quite high in terms of the annual flow of production and sales— a typical feature warranted in economies with rampant inflation. Real rates of interest of such magnitudes also have long-run effects: they reduce investment levels and thus impede or prevent growth, and, of course, also mean a high cost of servicing internal debt.

Long-run considerations on the level of real investment, the budgetary costs of debt service with high interest rates, the imposition on business as a result of the economic cost of carrying inventories, and presumably, also the political clamor building up on the fear of recession, combined to request some relief from the monetary squeeze. Though the authorities did not take active steps along this route, as clearly indicated by a quantity measure—the rate of growth of the nominal money supply which did not accelerate—they did not lean against the wind: the surfacing trend of lower nominal lending rates. (This might have reflected lower demand for domestic credit owing to an increased inflow of foreign funds.) Though following a downward trend, real interest rates in the third post-stabilization quarter were still formidable—18 percent and 27 percent in the regulated and non-regulated money markets, respectively (Table 21). Partial relaxation of price controls pushed inflation rates upward to a 3.1 percent monthly average for the quarter, and thus reduced ex post (and, more significantly), expected real interest rates.

At this stage, when further relaxation of the price freeze was inevitable, the major consideration should have been the short-run requirements of stabilization. Yet the warning signals from the commodity markets, in which prices were again rising at monthly averages of 3 percent and more, were ignored. Monetary expansion was hardly slowed down to bring it more in line with demand for money during the third and fourth post-stabilization quarters. Nominal interest rates in both markets thus did not rise, so that the somewhat more rapid price increases, which undoubtedly reawakened only partially dormant inflationary expectations, pushed real interest rates rapidly downward toward zero in both the regulated and the unregulated markets during the fourth post-stabilization quarter.

Stable nominal interest rates while prices were rising more rapidly than before should have served as a warning.[18] But monetary expansion continued at the same rate as previously through the fifth post-stabilization quarter, in which rising inflation rates pushed real interest rates into negative figures. An inspection of Figure 9 shows a strong reversal of the trend of falling rates in the sixth post-stabilization quarter (toward the end of 1986), but this so-called monetary crunch, which was to save the day and pull inflation down again, came too late. With inflation at a monthly rate of 4.4 percent in the fourth quarter and 7.6 percent in the fifth, the Austral Plan was dead.[19]

The timing of monetary relaxation just when the price freeze was being relaxed could not have been worse. But the error was not due to an actively expansionary policy pursued by the authorities. This is suggested by the fiscal stance: the fiscal deficit reached its trough in the fourth and fifth quarters after stabilization (Figure 8) when real interest rates turned negative and inflation accelerated, suggesting that it was not fiscal laxity, leading to an expansion of the monetary base, that turned the inflation tide at this crucial juncture.

This fact is supported by the data on the (nominal) monetary aggregates. The rate of growth of M1 and M2 did not increase at all during the fourth and fifth post-stabilization quarters. Yet, though not an error of commission, monetary relaxation was undoubtedly one of omission. Ignoring the nominal interest-rate signals, which implied lower real rates, the authorities presumably did not consider that the natural initial leap in demand for money in the immediate aftermath of a currency reform should settle down to a slower rate of increase. With growth of money supply maintained at the same rate in these crucial post-stabilization quarters, and the rate of growth of demand falling, nominal interest rates were held at a level that entailed a downward drift of real rates. At the beginning of the fourth post-stabilization quarter, deposit rates turned negative. By the beginning of the succeeding quarter, debit rates were also negative, which, of course, suggests that in this situation the monetary authorities should have tightened their grip on the market and reduced the rate of expansion of monetary aggregates.[20]

A stronger case in support of the interpretation that it might have been an error in monetary policy at a crucial juncture that led to the demise of the Austral Plan is, of course, the Israeli example.[21] The interest-rate series in Table 21 and Figure 9 underlines the two most important features of the monetary policy pursued in Israel during the crucial period at which stabilization policies were initiated. First, in terms of interest-rate measures, Israel's monetary policy was much more restrictive than Argentina's. Israeli marginal interest rates were also much higher before and in the early stages of the program.[22]

What may be even more significant is the persistence of the highly restrictive monetary policy. During the eight quarters for which data are presented in Table 21 (and in effect through 1988) as indicated in the series presented in Tables 26–27 (and Figures 10–11) the cost of money was kept very high. This restrictive monetary stance is also reflected in the average interest rates on total bank credit. The average rate rose through the third post-stabilization quarter, even though marginal interest rates were already allowed to decline to an average annual rate of 66 percent, so that in spite of this decline, rising interest rates for 90 percent of outstanding bank credit were maintained through this quarter too.[23] In any case, the average interest-rate series indicates that, through the eight post-stabilization quarters, even the most favored bank customers had to pay a real interest rate of, say, 10 percent, while most credit accommodations involved an interest cost of at least 14 percent in real terms. Similarly, marginal rates on deposits (CD rates) were maintained through the first three post-stabilization quarters within a range of annual real rates of 10–40 percent.[24]

The above comparative review clearly indicates that price and exchange-rate freezes are not enough to carry a stabilization policy through. It does suggest that monetary policy made feasible by fiscal discipline, in the Israeli case, saved the day. This policy stance maintained the lower rate of price increase as controls were gradually relaxed from the third post-stabilization quarter onward. Whether the Israeli stabilization effort, which involved an incomes policy too, should be classified heterodox is, of course, a matter of semantics. A more detailed study of the design and implementation of the Israeli program and of the economic and institutional environment in which it was carried into effect appears in the following chapters.

NOTES

1. References to the three programs of Argentina, Brazil, and Israel as "heterodox" in the papers and comments in this book are numerous. See, for instance, p. 102.

2. The Argentine and Israeli programs were launched at approximately the same time—June 14 and July 1, 1985, respectively. The Brazilian plan was launched later—in February 1986. The quarterly data presented in Table 21 are therefore effectively identical in terms of calendar time for Argentina and Israel; their first post-stabilization quarter is accordingly the third quarter of 1985, whereas the first post-stabilization quarter for Brazil was defined to cover the four months March through June 1986. The data for Brazil refer to five post-stabilization quarters only.

3. A surcharge of 15 percent was imposed on exchange for foreign travel. Designed as an equivalent to a value-added tax, it was to serve as a source of fiscal revenue and a measure of equity, while simultaneously raising the relative cost of foreign travel.

4. The entries for the first post-stabilization quarter are a mean of price changes for two months out of three for Argentina and Israel, and for three months out of four for Brazil. The price change during the first month after the launching of the programs has been excluded. The rate of change in prices and exchange rates in the first month of implementation is entered in the "shock" column of Table 21.

5. The wholesale price series is derived from Fundaçao Getulio Vargas data.

6. On the black-market rate, see Canavese and Di Tella (1988), p. 159.

7. The so-called parallel markets for foreign exchange in Argentina and Brazil transact a comparatively substantial volume and are not just a fringe of the official market. Though quantitative data on volume are hard to come by, the rates established in these markets are, by common consent, a meaningful signal on the flows of exchange and on economic trends.

8. See GDP series in Canavese and Di Tella (1988), p. 179.

9. Industrial production and GDP figures are presented in Modiano (1988), table 5A.1, p. 245, and table 5A.4, p. 248.

10. Relevant production and employment data for the business sector and the manufacturing industry is presented in Bank of Israel, *Annual Report 1985*. Detailed employment and unemployment data from 1983 through 1986 are presented in Bank of Israel, *Recent Economic Developments*, 39 (April 1986), and in succeeding issues.

11. GDP declined in the first two post-stabilization quarters by 6.2 percent, after rising in the first two quarters of 1985, the two pre-stabilization quarters, by 4.5 percent. At a rate of 2.2 percent for the whole of 1986, not much more than the population growth, the economy was hardly booming. For GDP and other production data, see Bank of Israel, *Annual Report 1986*.

12. The operational deficit excludes the "monetary correction," that element of the interest cost of the domestic national debt that the government pays to adjust the value of outstanding debt for inflation. Only a fraction of the latter are current payments that, together with the operational deficit, are financed by printing money and/or by new borrowing.

The planning team's operational assumption on the size of the deficit is stated by Modiano (1988), p. 232. Simonsen (1988), pp. 282, 284, refers to a 4.7 percent fiscal deficit and refers to "loose fiscal policies." The comments of Eliana A. Cardozo, the highly critical comments of Roberto Macedo, and the comment by Miguel Urrutia (ibid., pp. 288, 295–96, and 302), support this reading of the actual fiscal stance.

13. Beginning in the third post-stabilization quarter, this cut was gradually restored, but it was only after eight quarters that wages returned to the April–June 1985 level. The temporary reductions in wage rates were implemented according to the contract signed with the unions upon the launching of the plan. This contract also applied to the business sector, though the size of the cut, about 12 percent at its trough in the second post-stabilization quarter, was lower, and its duration shorter. The real wage data are treasury estimates (treasury memoranda dated September 16, 1987, and August 7, 1988).

14. Nominal quantity data—the quantity of money according to various definitions, or the quantity of bank credit—are unsatisfactory indicators of transactions in money markets when stabilization policies are implemented. The cost of money—relevant interest rates—is an alternative gauge of the state of these markets, the mood and expectations of the financial community, of business, and of households. Data on the net inflow of foreign short-term funds, and particularly the direction and volume of the flow of funds of the banking system, if available, would also be helpful for this purpose.

15. See Modiano (1988), p. 232. In his postmortem of the program, Simonsen (1988), p. 285, refers to the belief that "Brazilian inflation of January and February [1986, H.B.] was purely 'inertial,' and not due to 'loose monetary and fiscal policies.' " A similar remark on the identification of the nature of inflation by "policy makers" is made in Cardozo (1988), p. 227.

16. The Argentine and Israeli data are effectively coterminous, not only in terms of stabilization stages but also in calendar time. Not so the Brazilian series, with an eight-month difference in the launching date of the Cruzado program.

17. The non-regulated market accounted for about 45 percent of total credit; see Machinea and Fanelli (1988), p. 149, note 13.

18. The rate of growth of M1 and M2, which came down from monthly rates of over 20 percent before stabilization to 5–6 percent in the second post-stabilization quarter, did not change at all through the seventh quarter, but shot up in the eighth quarter to 9.4 percent. These data alone are not a reliable indicator of the state of the money market in these specific circumstances (see also note 14 and especially Chapter 8). The M1 and M2 series are from Canavese and Di Tella (1988), table 4A.2, p. 174. Nominal interest rates are from their table 4A.10, pp. 186–87. See also Machinea and Fanelli (1988), table 3.9, p. 135.

19. On the government (monetary) stabilization dilemma, see Canavese and Di Tella (1988), pp. 160–61, especially their suggestion, based on information from opinion polls, that after the launching of the program ex ante real interest rates were lower than ex post rates, which means that the credibility of the will of government to see the policy through was rather low.

20. See interest-rate data in Machinea and Fanelli (1988), p. 135.

21. The lack of political stamina of the Argentine government might have also contributed to the relaxation, by omission rather than by commission, of a highly unpopular policy.

22. Line E.3i in Table 21 and the corresponding curve in Figure 9 offer a close approximation to the marginal interest rate, in the free credit market. The actual marginal rate was somewhat higher.

23. The volume of the free sheqel credit lines, which carried (almost) the marginal

interest cost at that time, was only about 10 percent of total outstanding bank credit. An outline of the structure of the Israeli credit market is presented in Chapter 7 and in Table 23.

24. Real rates on CDs are presented in Table 27.

7

The Factual and Conceptual
Background of the Sheqel Plan

THE INFLATIONARY SETTING

The stabilization plan of July 1985 was launched after a 15-year spell of inflation, which took off in 1970 from an annual rate of 2 to 3 percent in 1969. By the end of the decade inflation was running at 130 percent; the three-digit threshold was crossed in 1980 and, with inflation accelerating to an annual rate of almost 400 percent in the last quarter before stabilization, the cumulative five-year rise in prices reached a factor of about 335.

The duration, the high rates, and the force of the price thrust as inflation accelerated toward hyperinflation rates meant that by 1985 the economy had long since adopted and adapted a full complement of defense mechanisms. Though surfacing piecemeal, these "technical arrangements," initially designed to immunize specific activities or groups from the direct impact of inflation, evolved into an elaborate web of formal and implicit contracts aimed at preventing a mismatching of relative price signals facing economic agents in the private and public sectors. A complementing feature of these arrangements was the appearance of a host of linkages for a continuously growing number of financial assets, finally covering almost the whole spectrum of the capital and money markets, including money. The actual expression of these structural features was the almost universal price and exchange-rate linkages of flows and of stocks. Linkages of wages, and cost-of-living allowances, prices, and exchange rates were the most significant ones relating to the flow of production, employment, and foreign transactions in goods and services.

A related technique to overcome the inflationary erosion of incomes and revenues appeared in the early 1980s: reducing the time reference for nominal contracts. Thus, from January 1983 on, cost-of-living allowances were paid every month. Banks began debiting the accounts of credit card holders every two weeks. Finally, to reduce the impact of the Tanzi effect on government revenues, the lag of business sector tax transfers to the treasury on account of sales and income taxes was reduced to one month only; arrears were indexed and subject to high interest rates. The implementation of these rules from 1983 onward signified the transition to universal price or exchange-rate linkages.[1]

After an unwarranted delay, in view of the upper-bracket two-digit inflation, median- and long-term government credits for housing and business investment were finally fully indexed in 1981. Similarly, nominal interest rates for short-term bank credits were gradually adjusted to price changes. From the first quarter of 1984, interest rates on overdraft facilities, the marginal rate on bank credit, moved within nominal brackets that implied positive (low) real rates. The indexation of all types of long-term government credit and the continuous adjustment of nominal interest rates to prices completed the process.[2] Stock variables such as the whole spectrum of financial assets thus finally joined indexed flow prices.

The obverse of this process of universal price linkage was a continuous erosion in the volume of domestic money—the non-linked money balances which come under the M2 heading. This shows up in the time series of the ratio of "money" to "domestic uses" and is also reflected in the "foreign currency assets" ratios presented in Table 22.[3] Note in particular the almost complete demise of the M1 ratio, which reached its trough by the middle of 1985, and the corresponding decline of M2, which is composed of non-linked sheqel assets. M3, which is the sum of M2 and foreign-currency-linked deposits (PATAM), was in effect the relevant "money" variable in the early 1980s. Note that the M3 ratio in 1984 and 1985 is quite similar to, indeed somewhat lower than, the M2 ratio in 1970—this supports the suggestion that M3 had taken over most of the M2 functions.[4]

The foreign currency component of M3 was only about 13 percent of total monetary assets in 1970. At its all-time peak, just before stabilization in 1985, it was between two-thirds and three-fourths of the total. In contrast with 1970, one of its components was a highly liquid current account denominated in terms of foreign exchange.[5] The time pattern of the foreign currency/financial asset ratio (Table 22, column 5) shows similar features. By June 1985, 37 percent of long- and short-term financial assets were directly linked to the exchange rate. A large part of these assets, such as saving accounts, were not as liquid as the PATAM accounts, but even these less liquid accounts were more than an expression of the financial environment within which a policy of stabilization had to be implemented and had a potentially direct monetary implication owing to the immediate and proportional wealth effect of a devaluation, a standard component of a stabilization program. PATAM accounts also had a potential immediate liquidity effect, if and when a devaluation was put into effect.

The impact of such an effect can be inferred from Table 22. With foreign-currency-linked assets about 14 percent of net domestic uses in June 1985, a 10 percent devaluation would directly, through its effect on "base money," increase M3 by 1.4 percent of domestic uses; the full monetary potential, due to the workings of the monetary multiplier, is obviously higher. An estimate of the wealth effect also requires information on the net financial asset GDP ratio. Since the net financial asset portfolio was about the same as GDP in 1985, and the foreign-currency-linked assets/financial asset ratio was 40 percent, the expected direct increase in wealth of a 10 percent devaluation would be about 4 percent of GDP.[6] The wealth effect on demand in real markets is obviously the product of this magnitude and the wealth elasticities of demand.

An induced immediate and substantial liquidity effect, topped by a corresponding wealth effect caused by devaluation, endowed the system with significant inertial monetary potential, which would, of course, be activated only if the stabilization program involved a devaluation. This was, however, a foregone conclusion. In Israel, as elsewhere, a stabilization program was put in place only when the political community was forced by the sheer dynamics of inflation to attempt to contain it. As in other countries, it was launched in Israel when its driving force had created an unbridgeable gap in the current account and accompanying capital flight. Correspondingly, and in a sense its obverse image by that time (the first half of 1985), inflation had also played havoc with government finances, generating an unmanageable fiscal deficit. The long haul along a high inflation track was by that time reflected in a structural setup involving economic contracts pegged to myriad price linkages. The usual acceleration of price inflation induced by discussion of a stabilization program strengthened the inflationary expectations of economic agents that generate strong inertial forces.

The Sheqel Program of June 1985 was an attempt to cope simultaneously with both the fundamentals and the inertial forces of the system: (a) a balance-of-payments crisis, a large fiscal deficit, price inertia induced by expectations and by the wage contracts pegged to previous rates of inflation; and (b) the accommodation of the price thrust provided by induced monetary expansion due to the price-linked setup of the financial and monetary sectors.

THE PROGRAM AND ITS MONETARY FACET

The main elements of the stabilization program designed to deal with the various dimensions of the crisis were spelled out in a document, "A Comprehensive Economic Stabilization Program," submitted to the government in the last week of June 1985. These elements included a large devaluation of the sheqel to take care of the balance-of-payments problem and a substantial cut in the budget deficit. The latter, which was to induce a reduction in aggregate demand and thus support the attempt to correct the balance of payments, would be implemented mainly by an increase in government absorption.[7] At the same time, reduction in the size of the deficit would help to reduce the liquidity of the system by lowering its requirements for central bank accommodation (creation of base money), and its borrowing requirements from the capital market.

These two steps were to generate a major price shock at the very launching of the program on account of a devaluation-induced rise of import prices and the inevitable significant price boosts required to reduce the level of the fiscal subsidy to "essential" goods and services.[8] This opening move was thus the very opposite of the declared target of the exercise—to reduce the momentum of inflation. In any case, this was the image generated by its immediate effect on prices. Bitter experience suggested this kind of public reaction in view of several previous attempts to reduce inflation that had involved price shocks, yet had pushed inflation rates even higher.

In this case the image was warranted by the absence of a monetary anchor. With M2 balances at their lowest—4.6 percent of "domestic uses"—the demise of non-linked money balances had by then almost reached the hyperinflation threshold. The deflationary real balance effect of a rise in the price level—the "classical" factor helping to contain inflation in non-linked monetary systems—would have been negligible.[9]

A *universal price freeze,* supported by legally enforceable controls, was therefore an indispensible plank in this program. Economically, this freeze was to rely, on the one hand, on pegging the nominal post-devaluation dollar exchange rate, which was to serve as a highly visible signal of "stability," and was simultaneously to prevent cost-push effects caused by further rises in import prices. On the other hand, it was to be supported by a substantial (temporary) cut in real wages, implemented by means of (two) adjustments of nominal wages at a rate lower than the initial price shock, to be followed by a three-month freeze at the newly set nominal level. The wage arrangements and particularly the wage freeze were formalized for the private sector through union contracts, and for public sector employees through a legal device. The price freeze was to be legislated, but no physical control system to police the freeze was instituted. It was assumed, at least tacitly, that except for some flagrant abuses that would be prosecuted, the price freeze would be implemented by market forces, marginally supported by legal enforcement.

Though the relevant passage in the program's section on the "main elements of the program" states that the government will " . . . act to impose a freeze on wages, prices, the exchange rate and credit . . . ," the price-wage freeze and the exchange-rate peg were deliberately put in the limelight. They were to serve as the major instruments for containing inertial forces by reducing inflationary expectations. The stable dollar exchange rate, a highly visible, continuously available price of great significance in Israel's highly open economy, was to serve as a major instrument underlining the new, stable price environment.[10] Since the exchange rate was tightly controlled, its stability would serve as an indicator of government perseverance in maintaining the policy.

Monetary policy was assigned an instrumental role in the implementation of the program.[11] The relevant passage in the "main elements" section states that "the Bank of Israel will initiate a policy to restrain the nominal amount of Bank credit." This facet of the program, which required quantitative specification, was formulated in the last days before implementation, in consultation with the central bank, which was brought into the deliberations at that time. Its targeted ceiling was specified simultaneously with the rate of devaluation, set at close to 20 percent (about 25 percent if the depreciation of the sheqel in the last days of June is included), and the size of the cut in subsidies. The decision on the size of the latter was, in effect, a decision on the magnitude of the price boost of "essentials."

The proposed magnitude of the devaluation and the overall cut in subsidies were spelled out in the "main elements" section of the program, while the designed credit restrictions were outlined in the following section, "details of the program." Total bank credit was specified as an interim operational target: during the first month of implementation the nominal volume of bank credit was to grow at a rate lower by 10 percent than the price rise during that month. The volume of bank credit on August 1 (the beginning of the second month of implementation) would serve as the credit ceiling for the next three months. Thus, bank credit was designed to serve as an additional nominal anchor—the nominal (temporarily pegged) dollar rate and nominally frozen wages were the other two—which, by "roping in" the system, were to lead to a deceleration of inflation.

The setting of the monetary target in terms of bank credit meant that the other component of the money supply (M2 or M3)—base money—was left on its own. This did not apply to short-term Bank of Israel credit to the government, hitherto a regular source of additions to base money, which had previously served as a regular source of government financing, restricted only by the size of the government budget. To prevent the treasury from operating the printing presses directly, the clause in the Bank of Israel Law of 1954, allowing direct access to the Bank, was repealed.[12] Though it appeared under the heading of fiscal policy, this part of the stabilization program had mainly monetary implications. It did not prevent the creation of base money on the basis of other "sources"—changes in foreign currency reserves, open-market operations, or business sector accommodation by discounting commercial paper.

The program included another element with direct monetary implications: it revoked the eligibility of residents to open new current account PATAM deposits or to increase the sums invested in existing deposits. Owners of such accounts were not forced to close them, but existing current PATAM accounts were to carry no interest. Residents could still open and maintain interest-bearing PATAM deposits invested for a year or more. The move to encourage delinkage was fully in line with the major, longer-term target of the program—lower price inflation. Delinkage of PATAM accounts (or for any other financial contracts) was never compulsory, being left to the volition of individuals. By maintaining the option of long-term linkage and avoiding any change in the linkage of existing financial assets—a highly sensitive nerve and a major variable of Israel's economic body—the public's confidence in the security of its financial assets was to be upheld. This meant, however, that monetary policy had to cope with a potential onslaught of massive movements from linked to non-linked accounts and their immediate expansionary monetary implications.[13]

INSTITUTIONAL AND STRUCTURAL CONSTRAINTS

The Bank of Israel and the Treasury

The executive power of the government in the realm of macroeconomics is exercised in Israel, as in most European countries, by the treasury. But, owing to the responsibilities of the central bank, which is charged with operating the exchange market and controlling the supply of money, day-to-day practice requires coordination between the finance minister and the governor of the central bank. In Israel, this is formally implemented by the (non-voting) membership of the governor in the Cabinet Committee on Economic Affairs, chaired by the minister of finance.

The influence of the central bank also depends on the governor's stance in public opinion, which happened to be low in 1984/85, mainly because of the so-called "bank shares crisis" of late 1983, which shattered the image of the country's financial leadership. That crisis was the subject of a public investigation by a special committee of enquiry appointed by the president of the High Court of Justice and chaired by a member of the court.[14] The governor's delicate personal situation on the one hand, and the personal involvement of the new prime minister in the preparations for the program on the other, virtually excluded the Bank throughout most of the final days of the program's preparation. The program was shaped by a team of officials from the treasury and the prime minister's office, reinforced by outside advisors chosen by the prime minister. When the Bank of Israel was officially advised about the program, its basic contours, including its monetary dimension (particularly the inclusion of an intermediate nominal credit target) were already in place. In response to a suggestion by the Bank's monetary department, the Bank was allowed some flexibility in handling the volume of credit by adding a nominal interest-rate provision. The Bank was instructed to stick to the highly restrictive intermediate bank credit target, but was allowed to "intervene ... from the second month (after implementation) onward, if nominal interest rates rise above 25 percent per month."[15]

The mission of the Bank was thus spelled out in terms of two operational variables: maintaining the exchange rate evenly against the dollar (after a devaluation of about 25 percent), and supporting it, and the price target of the program, with highly restrictive monetary control managed through a credit instrument. Though the Bank was not involved in the planning, the separation of powers and Israeli coalition politics endowed it with substantial freedom to wield the monetary weapons at its disposal as long as it maintained the exchange rate at its preordained peg. The latter, specified as the cardinal instrument of stabilization, was undoubtedly the key figure closely watched by the prime minister, the minister of finance, and the planning team.[16]

Structural Features

Monetary policy is obviously circumscribed by the environment in which it operates, both on a regular basis and even more so in a crisis situation, such as an attempt to cope with runaway inflation. In Israel, the most relevant factors to be considered were the comparative size of foreign trade, the flow of funds, the domestic public debt, the significant segmentation of the credit market, and the oligopolistic features of the banking system.

The Foreign Sector. The openness of the Israeli economy imposes constraints on monetary policy, as it does in small open economies everywhere. This is especially true in crisis situations, when steps affecting the official exchange rate are expected. Some insight into the potential monetary effects of this factor is gained by reference to the comparative size of the foreign trade sector. With civilian imports and exports of goods and services at about 58 percent of GDP, the size of a one-month lead and a one-month lag in the purchase and transfer of foreign exchange by importers and exporters, respectively, before and after a devaluation would mean a reflow of close to 5 percent of GDP across the exchanges. Thus, even if the central bank did not partly sterilize the outflow before a devaluation, the reflow would involve not only a return to the previous level of monetary assets, but also an increase in their volume proportional to the rate of devaluation. With a 25 percent devaluation implemented on July 1, the one-month lead and lag assumed above would involve an increase in the (base) money supply of about 1.5 percent of GDP within one month after devaluation. Even a low money multiplier (say, 1.3) would mean that the reflow would raise the money supply by close to 2 percent of GDP over and above its immediate pre-devaluation level.[17] As the M3 ratio for the middle of 1985 was 23 percent, the size of the reflow effect on the supply of money came close to 10 percent of the relevant money supply within one month after the launching of the program.

This rough, though quite indicative estimate of the monetary implications of a devaluation ignores the possible effects of lags caused by pre-devaluation delays in private transfers and donations and to the quite feasible lags in medium- and long-term capital inflows. It also assumes that the outflow of funds before devaluation was not even partly sterilized by the central bank to prevent a domestic credit crunch and corresponding effects on short-run interest rates. If the bank had partly sterilized the impact of the outflow, the corresponding effect of the reflow on the monetary base and the supply of money would have been even greater.

This rough estimate of the size of feasible leads and lags is supported by the fact that a net inflow of $1 billion was recorded within five weeks of the launching of the plan. This amounts to a lead and lag on the civilian goods and services account (net of capital services) of about three weeks,[18] suggesting that monetary policy had to plan to cope with an inflow to the foreign account, that is, an increase in foreign reserves in an amount that could easily have increased the liquidity of the system by more than 10 percent (in terms of M3) within the first month after the launching of the program. The expected inflow could have been even more substantial if long-established controls on capital flows had not been in place.

The Domestic Public Debt. The expected increase in foreign reserves, an immediate policy target, was not the only liquidity overhang that monetary policy was expected to cope with in the immediate aftermath of the plan's launching. Deposits directly linked to foreign exchange were an immediate source of inflating liquidity, standing at about 16 percent of GDP in June 1985 (equivalent to 13.9 percent of domestic uses (Table 22). The 25 percent devaluation involved an immediate increase of 4 percent of GDP in M3 money. Conversion of part or all of that increase into non-linked deposits would involve an even higher expansion of M2 and, correspondingly, of M3 owing to the lower reserve ratios for non-linked sheqel deposits. In any case, if the move into non-linked deposits were delayed, a devaluation would immediately boost M3 money supply by 17–18 percent.

The nominal value of price-linked assets would also be boosted. The immediate monetary impact would be limited to issues with close redemption dates, but in an economy with a domestic public debt to GDP ratio of over 100 percent, the flow of redemptions would in any case be significant.[19] Both the devaluation and the corresponding price shock, the first steps in the program, generated increases in financial wealth. Though not immediately translated into rising consumption expenditure and effective demand, the flow of redemptions that provided immediate liquidity virtually eliminated the cashing-in costs of financial assets in order to finance purchases in real markets. To prevent an onslaught on real markets and to induce owners of redeemed assets to reinvest in financial assets, monetary policy had to offer attractive financial alternatives.

Monetary policy was therefore expected to counteract the momentum of the automatic monetary accommodation, a feature built into the system for more than a decade in the form of an ever-increasing ratio of national debt to relevant aggregates. In view of the rate of devaluation and the steep increase in the price of "essentials," the monetary blow, when the plan was first implemented, should have been extremely strong, reinforcing the innate inertial factors (price expectations) that had been driving the system. The strength of the countervailing force had to be adapted to the momentum unleashed by the policy. But monetary policy, which had to face this expansionary impact, was impeded by two features: segmentation of the credit market and the monopolistic features of banking.

Credit Market Segmentation. The segmentation of the credit market, created by government fiat in the early 1950s, was designed to offer privileged access to bank credit to specific groups of customers. The quantitative significance of this feature, typical of economies subject to lengthy and substantial inflation, is presented in Table 23, which shows total bank credit by major categories. "Free" credit was granted at the banks' discretion in terms of choice of customer, volume, and specific charges and rates. "Directed" credit involved credit lines over which banks had no control either in terms of volume or of price; credit volume was determined by the export performance of firms, and interest rates were set by interdepartmental government committees in "consultation" with the central bank. For example, the value of fuel imports proscribed the size of the credit lines to the three fuel corporations operating in the country, and the interest rate on these credits was set by the government. Until the middle of 1985 these arrangements involved implicit interest-rate subsidies, whose level depended on the category to which a customer belonged.

The quantitative constraint imposed by such segmentation on monetary policy as the stabilization program progressed is demonstrated by the data for 1984, when directed credit made up 55 percent of total bank credit. The situation was undoubtedly much the same on July 1, 1985. Thus, and though the stabilization program prescribed the use of total bank credit as an operating instrument and specified a highly restrictive target in terms of that total (see also Chapter 8), the directed credit component was explicitly excluded from any quantitative restrictions. This, of course, implied that the monetary target was to be achieved by operating on the 45 percent "free" component of total outstanding credit. Hence, the squeeze on the free segment of the market was about twice as strong as the one designed for total credit. Since the free segment also included a linked component—commercial credits for one year or more were usually linked to prices or to the exchange rate—the brunt of the policy was borne by the even smaller (non-linked) segment that accounted for about 19 percent of the credit market.

The Oligopolistic Structure of Banking. With close to 90 percent of Israel's banking business handled by three major banking groups, the oligopolistic structure of Israel's banking industry has obvious effects on efficiency and on income distribution.[20] The monetary significance of this feature is demonstrated by a rough estimate of the financial margins—the difference between lending and deposit rates—presented in Table 24. Nominal financial margins of 6.7 percent, as in the second quarter of 1985, are high by any standard and underline the non-competitive feature of the industry, especially on the credit side. Competition is significantly stronger for deposits, which have to be pulled in from a great number of depositors.

The extra burden that this structure imposed on monetary policy was due to the fact that monetary management at this juncture was expected to restrain business activity, especially investment in inventories and fixed capital equipment. At the same time, it sought to restrain households from using their highly liquid positions to plunge into real markets when only lower demand could prevent another spurt in the price spiral. This was to be accomplished in the wake of a major price shock, which could only strengthen inflationary expectations. To do this, households had to be persuaded to stick at least to the financial assets at their disposal. Similarly, business real investment was to be discouraged—firms were to be induced to reduce the level of inventories.

The only way to succeed in this task, in view of several past stabilization policy failures, was to boost the rate of return on financial assets to households and other holders of liquid funds, implying even higher lending rates. Thus, the requirement of significantly higher interest rates than previously (particularly high creditory rates) inevitably meant much higher lending rates, owing to the wide spread between the rates imposed by the oligopolistic structure of banking. If the level of lending rates were to call the tune, this would have implied significantly lower deposit rates, and corresponding effects on households' choice between real goods and financial assets.

NOTES

1. The availability of continuous exchange-rate information for every business day turned the latter into a coefficient for adjusting sheqel prices on a daily basis. More and more transactions, many of them with little direct foreign exchange component, moved into this dollar-related pricing orbit.

2. Long-term government debt has been price- or foreign-exchange-linked since the mid-1950s.

3. The various money ratios are the reciprocals of corresponding income velocities. This does not apply, of course, to the entries in columns (4) and (5) of Table 22. In view of the substantial import surplus (about 15 percent of GDP) "domestic uses"—the sum of GDP and the import surplus—are a better "income" measure of what monetary theory identifies as the income-determined component of demand for money.

4. The lower M3 in the 1980s could reflect the beginning of widespread use of credit cards, which, of course, reduce the demand for "conventional" money. This is a structural change, which has only a slight link, if any, with inflation. A supplementary argument to explain the falling and later rising pattern of the M3 ratio through 1984 could refer to the time required for the process of adjustment—substituting one kind of money (foreign-currency-linked) for another.

5. Initially, effective until 1977, foreign currency accounts were a privilege accorded to Israelis receiving restitution payments from Germany. These accounts were not fully subject to foreign currency controls. They could be used to purchase foreign currency for foreign travel and were thus, in effect, long-term accounts, similar in nature to foreign-currency-denominated bonds but less liquid. The so-called 1977 economic turnabout, which liberalized exchange control regulations, allowed residents to open foreign-currency-linked current and long-term accounts. (Initially, these could be transferred, in terms of foreign currency, to other Israeli residents.) The high inflation brought about by the energy crisis and the almost complete liquidity of these accounts made them a popular liquid, relatively inflation-proof asset. The advent of three-digit inflation in 1980 turned them into the dominant component of total monetary assets.

6. The net financial asset-to-GDP ratio was derived from data for the 1986 values of these two variables. The ratio of assets to GDP for this year is about 1.17 percent. The asset data are from Bank of Israel, *Annual Report 1988*, table H-17, p. 287; the

current prices GDP data are from *Annual Report 1986,* table B-1, p. 12. An estimate of the 1985 asset portfolio is unavailable.

Note that this estimate of the wealth effect of a devaluation does not refer to the indirect, price-induced wealth effect. The impact of price rises works through the price-linked component of the financial assets portfolio. M2 figures for June 1985 in Table 21, which imply that the M2 ratio to GNP was close to 10 percent, and the corresponding entry for the asset ratio in column (5), suggest that price-linked financial assets were more than 50 percent of total net financial assets. The indirect wealth effect thus depends on the size of the induced price effect.

7. The reduction of the deficit was to be implemented mainly through raising net taxes—by reducing subsidies to goods and services including public mass transit. Gross taxes were also raised, though the major "source" of this increase in absorption was a hefty cut in subsidies to "essentials," which early in 1985 reached an all-time high of 5 percent of GDP. These were to be cut by more than 50 percent, to close to 2 percent of GDP (Bank of Israel, *Annual Report 1985,* p. 125).

8. The expected price shock of the planned halving of subsidies can be visualized from the support levels of specific commodities: the subsidy for some dairy items was 125 percent of the price to the consumer in January 1985. Public bus transportation was subsidized by 250 percent (Bank of Israel, *Annual Report 1985,* p. 125).

9. The obverse of this is the high ratio of foreign-exchange-linked money (M3-M2), and the price-linked, longer-term financial instruments which, in this financial and monetary setup, provide automatic monetary accommodation.

10. The foreign exchange rate has far greater substantive significance in Israel than in Argentina and Brazil. It reflects the fact that with an import bill of more than 40 percent of GDP and export revenues close to 30 percent of GDP, Israel's economy depends much more on foreign trade than do the two South American economies. This applies in particular to the dollar exchange rate, to which most of the foreign-exchange-linked financial assets are pegged.

11. This feature is discussed in Liviatan (1984): "The freeze period would allow for transition to monetary restraint. . . ." In a diagram summarizing the essentials of the stabilization policy, used in the presentation of the program to the cabinet meeting, monetary policy specified in terms of "credit restriction" is accorded equal footing with the wage freeze and the pegging of the exchange rate as determinants of "stabilization of the price level." The diagram is presented in Bruno (1985), p. 213 (see also p. 212 and note 6 of Bruno).

12. According to this clause, repealed several weeks before implementation of the plan, the government was permitted to borrow up to 10 percent of its total expenditure on goods and services from the Bank. At the end of each fiscal year this short-term "debt" to the central bank was "repaid" by means of a book entry—the short-term debt was converted to long-term outstanding debt. This clause effectively endowed the government with money-printing rights. The central bank could attempt to sterilize such money printing by, say, open-market sales of government securities. This never happened and could hardly be implemented in the Israeli capital market, owing to the small quantity of negotiable government bonds in the portfolio of the central bank.

13. In contrast to Brazil and Argentina, the Israeli program did not attempt to prescribe rules for the de-indexing of contracts between private parties. But eliminating the right to open new PATAM current accounts was a move that pushed the system into a pattern of de-indexation, as, and if, credibility of the policy was sustained.

14. This committee published its report in April 1986. One of its main recommendations called for the resignation of the governor of the Bank of Israel and the chairmen of the boards of directors of the three major commercial banks. Public uproar forced the implementation of this recommendation in the summer of 1986.

15. See "A Comprehensive Economic Stabilization Program," Section 3-f. This "flexibility" provision qualified the credit target spelled out earlier.

16. The outsider status of the central bank in the planning stage of the program was public knowledge. The economic adviser to the prime minister in 1985, himself a member of the planning and implementation team, confirmed this fact in a newspaper interview two years later (Plozker, 1987).

17. The money multiplier here is the coefficient of Friedman's model of money supply: $M_i = m(\ )H$, the supply of money is the product of base money (H) which represents liabilities of the central bank, and the money multiplier, m. The latter is an increasing function of interest rates, of (uncertain) expectations about the future trend of interest rates and prices, and of variables under the direct control of the central bank—liquidity ratios and its own discount rate. In what follows, the argument will sometimes be pegged to the alternative formulation according to which the supply of money is the sum of base money (H) and outstanding (commercial) bank credit.

18. This figure was reported in a privately circulated memo. Expectation-induced outflows and inflows of funds of a similar size were again recently recorded. In anticipation of a devaluation, Israel's reserves registered a loss of about $2 billion in the last two months of 1988. In response to a devaluation of about 14 percent in the last week of the year, these funds were regained within about two months (Bank of Israel, *Recent Economic Developments,* No. 46, table A, p. 10).

19. The ratio of domestic public debt to GDP averaged about 120 percent of GDP in the 1980s (Bank of Israel, *Annual Report 1988,* table 5-1, p. 110, English version).

20. This is the share of these three banking groups in terms of balance sheet totals (Bank of Israel, Supervisor of Banking, *Annual Report 1985,* table A-1, p. 2, and table A-3, p. 18). Their share in terms of credit balances and deposits might be somewhat lower.

___ 8 ___

The Monetary Dimension

TARGET AND INSTRUMENTS

The intermediate monetary target set in the outline of the Sheqel Plan was spelled out in terms of the level of nominal bank credit. Since it was quantitatively specified in terms of the expected rate of inflation during the first month of implementation, it put monetary management in a quandary. The inflationary environment and the expected added momentum to prices as a result of the price shock to be administered at implementation meant a leap in the inflation rate. However, during the first two weeks of July 1985, before the publication of the June price index, officials were in no position to "guesstimate" the expected value of the very variable that was to determine the credit target.[1]

Information on the rate of net inflow of foreign funds and the flow of conversions from PATAM (foreign-exchange-linked) deposits into sheqel deposits provides (almost) real time data on the potency of the flow that directly affected the liquidity of the system, and especially the second component of money—the monetary base. The expected substantial reflow of foreign funds was obviously a major potential source of expansion for the monetary base.[2] At the same time, the countervailing planned improvement in the cash flow of the treasury could not yet have surfaced. The expansionary influence of these three factors is underlined by the extraordinary growth of the monetary base in July: 163 percent (Table 25).

The Bank of Israel prepared for this expected avalanche by applying two classical central bank instruments. Preferring not to put a ceiling on domestic credit by fiat, it attempted to reduce the "effectivity" of bank reserves as a source of money, and at the same time restrict their expansion.[3] The attempt to reduce "reserve effectivity" was implemented by raising required liquidity ratios three times in July, as indicated in Table 26. A final upward adjustment was made on August 1 and maintained through March 1986. The third rise, on July 25, was undoubtedly affected by the data then available to the authorities about the June price jump, which suggested an even higher leap for July. The rapid expansion of the monetary base, which toward the end of the month was almost a fait accompli, inspired both the third and the fourth increases, raising these ratios fourfold for CDs (to 43%), and almost fivefold for time deposits (to 50%) within one month.[4]

At the same time, the Bank attempted to restrain the rate of increase of bank reserves by raising the interest rate on the ''monetary loan'' to what was (then) an all-time high nominal rate of over 19 percent. This was a small rise from the June level of 18 percent; it was probably more an expression of the prevalent expectations on the July price index than of the natural reluctance of the monetary authorities to rock the boat.

The interest rate on the monetary loan—the source for supplementing reserve shortages—is the Israeli equivalent of the discount rate in major money centers. The discount rate can push the structure of rates upward only if the banking system, short of reserves, is forced to use the central bank's credit window. Open-market sales are thus indispensible for making discount rates effective. In a small, open economy with a stable exchange-rate regime, pushing domestic rates upward is quite unfeasible. The relevance of the domestic equivalent of the discount rate, given a free flow of short-term foreign funds, is of minor significance. Any attempt to push interest rates above world market rates (*plus* some premium for exchange rate risk) would be thwarted by an immediate inflow of funds. Israel's good credit standing, which improved in the immediate aftermath of the program's implementation, allowed Israeli banks to borrow abroad in order to supplement their reserves.

Thus, although a rapid reversal of the falling trend of international reserves was undoubtedly one of the immediate targets of the program, monetary considerations required tightening existing controls on short-term capital flows. Among other devices, this was put into effect by a 15 percent reduction of the ceiling imposed by central bank fiat on the volume of ''free'' foreign-currency-linked commercial bank credit. Customers who had hitherto enjoyed this kind of credit were pushed into the sheqel credit market, generating an increase in the demand for bank reserves. The substantial rise to 45–50 percent in reserve requirements and the relevant LIBOR dollar rates (at that time about 10 percent for dollar credits) raised the cost of using foreign funds to supplement bank reserves, although it was still lower than the cost of borrowed sheqel reserves, at the extraordinary rates of the first restabilization quarter (Table 26 and Figure 10). Supported by some controls on the flow of the short-term funds, the Bank of Israel could nonetheless make use of the interest-rate instrument.

The reflow of funds and induced conversions of dollar-linked deposits into sheqel deposits made the banks highly liquid.[5] Thus, in the first week of July, the banking system did not need any accommodation from the Bank of Israel.

But as liquidity ratios were rapidly tightened and open-market sales of treasury bills by the Bank were substantially expanded by offering higher real rates of return (Table 27, column 5), the Bank managed, toward the end of July, to tighten its grip on the market. The July 27.5 percent price shock, which induced a corresponding jump in the demand for nominal credit, and the dwindling effect of PATAM conversions supported by expanded open-market sales, forced the banking system to rely increasingly on accommodation through the central bank.[6] This accommodation, both in absolute and in relative terms (as a ratio of the resources of the banking system) grew substantially toward the end of the third quarter of 1986.[7] The size of the monetary loan and the rate of interest charged on it thus became a major instrument of monetary control during the crucial first three to four quarters of the stabilization effort.[8]

Such a situation is prima facie inconsistent with the realities of the marketplace, if the market is to clear. The Bank could either set a quantity—the size of the loan—and sell it at the highest price consistent with that quantity, or set a price and supply the quantity of required "borrowed reserves" at that price. It could not set both and expect the market to clear unless the dual criteria were superfluous. However, simultaneously setting both quantity and price could be possible if the supply of funds were controlled through several "credit windows," representing a step function, infinitely elastic at each step. At each of these preset quantities, accommodation will be offered at this step's specific interest rate. The highest step would not be constrained, however, in terms of quantity; the quantity borrowed at this rate would be determined by the demand of the banking system. Therefore, only the interest rate at the highest step on this supply curve of reserves would set the marginal cost to banks of central bank accommodation. Also, by varying the quantities offered at the cheaper credit windows, to which banks would first turn, the Bank of Israel could directly affect the total quantity of borrowed reserves, their marginal, and their average cost.[9]

The rationale of this technique is to keep tight control over the quantity of reserves, and thus over the volume of nominal bank credit. Also, it gave the central bank some direct influence on the size of financial margins.[10] Although this had income distribution implications too, the major purpose of this backdoor control was monetary. In view of the monopolistic structure of Israeli banking, the central bank used this control technique to ensure that changes in interest rates would affect business and households—debtors and creditors—as similarly and simultaneously as much as feasible under the circumstances.

Data on expected prices were thus used in setting the marginal (and other) rates on the weekly "sales" of the "monetary loan," while end-of-week data on the actual reserve position of the banks was used to set the corresponding quantities on the step function. The intention was to force the banks to borrow a substantial fraction of their required reserves at the marginal interest rate. This set of instruments—liquidity ratios, open-market sales, setting the marginal rate on the "monetary loan" supported by capital account controls—was used to try to reach the prescribed monetary target.

An evaluation of the performance at the outset of implementation of the sheqel program seems to offer confused readings. Interest-rate data for July 1985 hardly suggest monetary tightening; the relevant real interest rates in July show highly negative rates (Table 27). This, and particularly the Bank's use of its monetary loan instrument, is highlighted by a comparison of the CPI and the marginal monetary loan rate in Figure 10. The former, representing a 27.5 percent price rise in July, towers above the corresponding marginal loan rate curve that peaks at about 19 percent.

At the same time, however, the Bank performed much better than expected in terms of the credit target. With a 27.5 percent monthly rate of inflation—not yet known to the authorities in July—the "90 percent of the price rise" rule as the nominal credit target meant that a rise of about 25 percent in nominal outstanding credit balances would be in line with the defined nominal target. The actual increase in total credit for July 1985 (17.5 percent; Table 27) indicates better performance than prescribed by the monetary rule set out in the program, and even more so with respect to "free" credit (FC), which is a closer approximation to the "actual" credit target used by the Bank of Israel.[11] The July figures for the money aggregates, particularly the 163 percent increase in the monetary base, however, cast doubt on the usefulness of rating performance solely in terms of the volume of credit.

These apparently confusing signals suggest that an analysis of the financial and monetary sectors in the unsettled economic environment of an attempted stabilization and the evaluation of the policies pursued requires a more detailed discussion of the expected and actual pattern of prices and their impact on the corresponding ex post (proxying for the ex ante) real rates of interest.

REAL INTEREST RATES AND PRICE PATTERNS

Real Interest Rates and Price Forecasting Errors

The impression of a rather loose monetary policy suggested by the July base money and interest-rate data disappears once the relevant measures are considered in the context of a longer time period. Note, in particular, that the overshooting of the price index (CPI) curve in July (Figure 10) is followed by a continuous decline in which the monetary loan rate curve follows the downward direction of the rapidly declining price curve, although with a substantial lag. Similarly, the estimated series of monetary aggregates in real terms in Table 28 shows a substantial decline in M3 and the corresponding credit series in the third quarter of 1985.

Finally, the real interest-rate figures for August and September (Table 27 and Figure 11) offer an altogether different perspective on the nature of monetary policy in the immediate aftermath of the plan's launching. An average monthly (ex post) real interest rate of 11.7 percent during these two months for "effective" overdraft facilities suggests a highly restrictive monetary policy through this quarter. It required about one month to take effect, though. Moreover, real annualized interest rates of about 277 percent for the "effective" overdraft facility, and even the 13 percent figure for the average rate on total credit—not to mention the annualized 41 percent rate on CDs and a 70 percent real rate of return on treasury bills—underscore the highly restrictive features of monetary policy.

Figure 11 shows the cyclical pattern of the CPI both when it was high before stabilization and when it was low afterward, which is the major factor generating the frequent and substantial fluctuations in ex post real interest rates (Figure 11). This erratic behavior of prices, in terms of momentum rather than in terms of direction, offers some insight into one of the major uncertainties facing those charged with monetary policy in a highly inflationary environment. These uncertainties are probably highest in the early stages of an attempt to reduce inflation. The unpredictability of the price momentum over the short term goes a long way toward explaining the apparent "looseness" of monetary policy in the first month of the plan's implementation.

The July feature of negative real interest rates across the board probably reflects a forecasting error (Table 27, part A). Note that the monetary loan rate curve peaked at a nominal rate of 19.3 percent (Figure 10), a value similar to that of April 1985, the previous all-time high inflation rate. Thus, with the May inflation rate at 6.8 percent, far less than the April rate of 19.4 percent, the hiking up of the rate on the monetary loan from a nominal rate of 18 percent in May to over 19 percent was presumably expected to at least prevent a negative real cost of funds to the banking system, which suggests that the monetary authorities had been expecting the planned price shock of July to push prices upward at a rate of, say, 20 percent at most.

Figure 12, which shows the most important lending rates, supports this interpretation of a price forecasting error. During the first half of 1985, banks had maintained lending rates above the rate of change of prices, except for April, when the unusually high (local) peak of the price curve intersected the rate for that month. The effective overdraft rate had been adjusted upward from that of March, but still yielded a negative real rate of 1 percent (Table 27, part A, column 1). This took place even though, since late 1983 and throughout 1984, banks had maintained nominal rates on overdraft facilities that yielded (ex post) high real rates of interest.[12] By raising their nominal rate for July to an all-time high of 21 percent, the banks were probably assuming that real interest rates would at least not turn negative.[13]

This was, however, not the only price forecasting error. An inspection of Table 25 and Figure 10 shows that as forecast by the planning team, the rate of change of prices fell abruptly. It did not reach the 1–2 percent target before November 1985, however, and it took four months to bring the monthly rate down toward the hoped-for 2 percent. Moreover, a low inflation pattern finally emerged only about six months after the launching of the policy when the low November CPI figure was published on December 15, followed a month later by another low inflation reading.

Price Resistance

This "price resistance" in the system, reflected in the time elapsed before the price pattern adjusted downward to the predicted range, indicates that the disinflationary process in Israel was put into effect mainly by market forces. A price freeze was imposed at the outset of the program but, except for attempts to involve "public opinion," no enforcement mechanism was put in place.[14] Shortages—the inevitable counterpart of controlled prices when the latter are widely off the mark—did not surface. Goods and services were available at the prices set during the second half of 1985, before the repeal process was set in motion.[15]

Consider now the modus operandi of the system that relied essentially on market forces to bring down the rate of inflation. During the first month or two after implementation, the forces unleashed by expectations and the price shock induced a deceleration of the rising price pattern. "Essentials"—which were about 20 percent of the CPI basket—were freely available at much higher but stable prices. Supplies of other goods, including inputs (raw materials), reacted much more strongly to the whims of the marketplace and thus, in the short run, to the size of relevant business inventories and the pricing policies adopted for business purposes. Given the pre- and post-stabilization availability of foreign exchange—as in Israel—it was the momentum of the inflationary process itself that provided for ample inventories on the one hand and, on the other, created a cushion of wide price margins. This same process, which generated the high inventory ratios and assured ample price margins to start with, created a lull in demand immediately after the launching of the program.

Consider first the practice, acquired over time, by businesses (and later by households) of maintaining high inventory/sales and inventory/consumption ratios in a system subject to high and continuous inflation. Anticipation of a stabilization attempt—which is known to involve an upward adjustment of prices and of the exchange rate—induces economic agents to raise their inventory ratios over and above the high ratios typical for systems subject to long spells of inflation. The immediate expression of such behavior is the well-known run on stores.

This wave of anticipatory purchases had been a well-known occurrence in Israel. The run on stores in May and June was, as usual, highly publicized in the media. The obvious response of business to brisk demand and to the expected unveiling of a stabilization program is twofold: to increase orders, particularly for goods with a high import content, and to raise prices more rapidly. This not only increases current profits, but also raises the base at which prices are to be "frozen" if the program is launched.

This inventory policy has a macroeconomic expression in terms of anticipatory purchases of foreign exchange, implemented by a movement from foreign-currency linked bank and trade credits to domestic currency credit accommodation.[16] In view of the expected "new economic policy," usually involving a price freeze, substantial anticipatory price increases that, when implemented, involve some "overshooting" are obviously rational business behavior. The timing of such a move in advance of the policy change, with brisk demand and "soft" price resistance by consumers, is also optimal. The 15 percent price hike of June 1985—one of the highest monthly price leaps in Israel during 15 years of high inflation—thus involved an anticipatory component. Part of this price hike must have spilled over into the administered price shock of July, formally "warranted" in terms of the price control rules, though not necessarily justified economically by the rise in the cost of both foreign and domestic inputs.

The momentum of these price adjustments decelerated, of course, after July. But the natural lag involved in finding an "appropriate" price in the new situation, compounded by administrative delays in approving cost-warranted price adjustments, led to a spillover into August and September.[17] The non-controlled sector (mainly fresh farm produce), which could adjust its prices to market circumstances, worked in the same way. Although the rates of price change of 3.9 percent, 3.0 percent, and 4.7 percent for August, September, and October 1985 were higher than the sheqel program's targeted price pattern, since they reflected the realities in markets not subject to shortages, they were quite reasonable. Nonetheless, although beyond the desired range, they were a breakthrough on the inflation front and offered the breathing space required to increase the credibility of the program.

As long as post-stabilization prices are not simply decreed, that is, as long as these are prices at which merchandise is sold, all that price deceleration from high two-digit monthly rates requires is time. Though it is impossible to set a rule on the length of time necessary, the four months required for Israeli inflation to decelerate from two-digit monthly rates to a 1–2 percent range, with no shortages, seems quite reasonable. However, the public's awareness that the target had been reached inevitably lagged by two more months. The behavioral and political implications of a six-month interval before the policy could finally be considered a success are obvious, with implications for the management of monetary policy during these crucial six months.

MONETARY POLICY

The Objective

Though not spelled out, the objective of monetary policy during the first and crucial stage of the stabilization effort was to support the attempt to lower price inflation and to improve the balance of payments. In the next stage, beginning with the repeal of controls, it was to maintain a restrictive stance of aggregate demand to prevent a reacceleration of inflation in the wake of the inevitable adjustment of some relative prices to market realities. The onset of the second stage obviously depended on success in the first—the timing could not be predicted. The differences in monetary policy during these two stages (the transition between them is not clear-cut) are a matter of quantity rather than of quality, but both require a restrictive stance. The real issues are, therefore, the tightness of this stance and the choice of quantitative proxies to evaluate the impact of the policy.

Indicators and Measures

As already noted, and in line with the "nominal anchor" strategy of the stabilization program, the intermediate target of monetary policy was specified in terms of a quantity: the level of nominal commercial bank credit. In the final version of the plan, however, this aim was subjected to a price constraint—the credit target was to be adhered to as long as a leading nominal lending rate did not exceed a certain level.

The planned 10 percent cut in the volume of real bank credit, which was to be maintained for three months (four, according to an alternative interpretation of the relevant text), was never implemented, as shown by both real credit series in Table 28. This point can also be made in terms of the nominal credit series of Table 25. The July figures were indeed on target, but reflected the high liquidity created by the tremendous reflow of funds from abroad, financing a corresponding increase in the monetary base. However, by the end of September, credit balances had already overshot the target by a wide margin. Furthermore, the evolution of M1 and M2—with monthly growth rates of about 17 and 26 percent, respectively, through the first post-stabilization quarter—suggests that an expansionary rather than a restrictive policy was in place. Neither of these quantity indicators really signifies a non-restrictive policy stance. Rather, the real interest-rate figures for both the credit and the debit side of the market underline the highly restrictive monetary policy operated by the Bank of Israel during the first two post-stabilization quarters (Table 27). The interest-rate data show that this stance was, on the whole, maintained through the next two quarters, though at a significantly reduced strength.

The failure of the nominal quantity measures to properly gauge the monetary situation, and the main thrust of the policy, in this specific environment is no coincidence. It resulted from an assumption implicit in the use of quantity targets and measures that does not hold good in an economic environment in which an attempt to reduce runaway inflation is undertaken. Quantity targets (and inevitably the measures taken to achieve them) refer only to the quantity axis of the market, not to the highly relevant price variable. As a measure of the kind of policies pursued by the authorities, they make sense only if demand for money, or for any other monetary variable, is stable or constitutes a stable function of a major economic aggregate.[18] In addition, a nominal credit target is not a very efficient instrument in highly segmented credit markets, owing to the inevitable restriction on the range of credits to which the policy can be applied.

Stable demand for money is neither expected nor is it a target of a stabilization policy designed to reduce inflation. The purpose of this policy is to change the attitude of economic agents to (non-linked) money, that is, to lead to a substantial increase in the demand for various nominal monetary aggregates. Rapidly rising quantity figures are therefore not proper indicators, either of the force or of the direction of the policy pursued by the monetary authorities. If the rate of increase of demand exceeds that of supply, monetary policy could be highly restrictive, even though the quantity measures would indicate high rates of increase of monetary aggregates.

In such circumstances the proper measures for the policy stance within a given time interval are the relevant prices, in this case the medley of real interest rates, supplemented by data on the direction and volume of the flows of short-term funds across the exchanges which are strongly linked to the pattern of these rates (Table 29).[19] The latter were available, with short lags, more or less continuously. Real interest rates are available for a retrospective analysis, but were not available to the authorities for the day-to-day handling of policy. The unpredictability of the fluctuations in the rate of change of prices (underlined by the CPI graph in Figure 10) made monetary management in Israel a difficult proposition in the highly volatile second half of 1985—a factor which may well be present in any attempt to reduce runaway inflation.

Real Interest Rates and Inventories

Having settled on ex post interest rates supplemented by data on capital flows in terms of a real quantity (foreign exchange flows) as the proper gauge for evaluation, the impact of policy on the monetary dimension of the economy is clearly visible from the series in Table 27, Figure 11, and the flow of funds series in Table 29.

The highly negative real interest rates for July, attributable mainly to the error in predicting the size of the price shock at launching, soon changed. By August, the marginal lending rate (and its more representative counterpart—the "effective" rate on overdraft facilities) were sky-high. Also, an annualized real rate of 56 percent for CDs, admittedly ex post, suggests that deposit rates were also high, even if depositors' price expectations at that time were significantly less optimistic than the price pattern in reality. The same statement on the policy stance holds for the two closing months of the first post-stabilization quarter. The "effective" real rates on overdraft facilities, though lower in September than in August, were still three-digit annualized rates, and the real CD rates were still above 20 percent, which is high by any standard.[20] The tightening of credit markets is clearly suggested by the abrupt change in direction of the flow of funds across the exchanges. A total outflow of funds of close to half a billion dollars in the last quarter before the launching of the program was reversed in the first post-implementation quarter, yielding a $140 million inflow (Table 29, column 3).

The much lower average real rate for total credit reveals the segmentation of the credit market described above (Chapter 7). This means that interest rates on some types of credit were significantly lower than those on overdraft facilities. The rise in the average rate in September to an annualized real rate of about 20 percent, when the rates on overdraft credit lines were already dropping, suggests a further tightening of credit markets. This tightening, induced by the central bank, was effected by shifting credit lines from low-interest to high-interest brackets. An inspection of Table 27 suggests that this technique of tightening the credit market was maintained in the second post-stabilization quarter and in the first quarter of 1986.

These two quarters, during which the restrictive policy was not weakened for overall credit (though there was some easing-up at the margin), were the most crucial ones for the success of the program. But the threshold was probably crossed in November: after an unexpected and frustrating jerk of price inflation to 4.7 percent in October, the monthly CPI figure finally dipped below 1 percent for the first time in more than a decade. It was during this short time interval that monetary policy might have been crucial.

The highly restrictive policy undoubtedly had a demonstration effect from the very beginning. Since its implications were directly and continuously felt by households and businesses, its strength and persistence, intensively covered by the media, served as an expression of the government's determination to see the policies through. But the policy was not implemented by the government, which (as is usual in other countries, too) sometimes even tried to distance itself from its immediate consequences.[21] Beyond these public relations effects, however, it had a direct and immediate impact on households and businesses, especially on the trade sector, and thus on the macroeconomics of the system.

As noted, after a pre-stabilization run on the stores, consumers started off with high (i.e., higher than average) inventory-to-income ratios. This anticipatory buying spree, the much higher relative prices (especially relative to the wages/incomes ratio), and the growing uncertainty about employment and income prevailing in the immediate aftermath of implementation, kept consumers out of the stores for some time. But the high liquidity of households in the first place—the obverse of the high domestic public debt noted above—which increased owing to the technical effects of the devaluation, offered households the option of plunging into real markets again; the run on stores of May–June 1985 had been the second in less than a year.[22]

Even a return to the normal flow of purchases would have made life easier for traders, who (relying on past experience) maintained high inventory-to-sales ratios and, in view of the anticipated (July 1) devaluation, had full pipelines of supply. By raising lending rates to an all-time high and simultaneously offering positive real annualized rates in excess of 30 percent on deposits—in stark

contrast to the negative real rates prevalent for many years, even for CDs—
households and middlemen were offered a tempting alternative to real goods.
The effect of this temptation is underlined by retail sales data that show an
aggregate decline of 3.7 percent and a major 8.2 percent drop for durables in
the third quarter of 1985.[23]

This decline in the normal flow of sales, part of which can be attributed to
the high deposit rates, implied a rise in trade inventories. But with real rates on
overdraft facilities at 279 percent (Table 27, part B) this technique of wholesale
and retail trade finance proved expensive. The accepted rule (vindicated throughout 15 years of inflation) that inventories are the safest investment proved wrong
when such high interest rates persisted.[24] By September, trade interests were at
the forefront of the movement against the "atrocious" rates of interest "imposed" by the Bank of Israel.[25]

Though somewhat lower than in the third quarter of 1985, annualized real
rates of almost 120 percent on overdraft facilities and 15 percent on total credit
were maintained through the fourth quarter of 1985. CDs and other deposits still
offered a 10 percent annual rate of return (Table 27). The persistence of these
high rates finally pushed merchandise trade over the brink. For the first time in
many years merchants made a major effort to reduce inventories by lowering
prices. This move was finally felt in November and December price figures, but
it had a much earlier effect on credibility and on the behavior of economic
agents. The media promotion of the sales efforts pulled at least some of the
sting from inertial inflation, leading to a substantial slowdown of price increases,
including even a negative monthly rate of change in January 1986.[26] Lower
prices had already appeared late in September, with minor reductions in elec-
tricity and fuel prices after the collapse of OPEC's control over world oil prices,
but the actual fall in prices reflected first and foremost inventory liquidation
induced by a highly restrictive monetary policy.

Ex post data presented in Table 27 on real interest rates probably overstate
ex ante real rates, which are the ones that affect decisions on inventory accumulation and liquidation.[27] Figure 10, which reveals the substantial lag in adjusting the Bank of Israel's monetary loan rate after prices started slowing down,
offers some insight into the possible lag in adjusting the public's inflationary
expectations. It obviously takes some time and convincing before economic
agents recognize that monthly price increases of 5–10 percent—a prevalent feature in Israel for several years—are a thing of the past. Only after two successive
inflation rates of 3–4 percent (August and September) and the realization that
monetary policy would not be relaxed in spite of strong public criticism, particularly by the business community, did it finally become obvious to the trading
sector—though probably not to the industrial sector—that inventories were be-
coming an embarrassment rather than a goldmine. The push for lower inventories, promoted by price slashing, was then inevitable.

This development, coming as it did toward the end of the second post-
stabilization quarter, was probably the crucial breakthrough on the expectations

front. Yariv's estimates on price expectations, mentioned above, lead to a similar conclusion. Significant supporting monetary evidence is offered by the velocity data presented in Table 30, which show an abrupt decline in the velocity of circulation of demand deposits in the fourth quarter of 1985, to a level 17.2 percent below that in the two previous quarters.[28] The mirror image of this decline in velocity is a leap in demand for (non linked) sheqel assets, which can be seen as evidence of growing confidence in the value of the currency and in the credibility of the program.

Tight Money and Repeal of Price Controls

The positive price signals of the end of 1985, already public knowledge by mid-January 1986, suggested that some relaxation of monetary stringency was feasible. The authorities followed these signals but were reluctant to go as far as suggested by public opinion and political resonance—as indicated by the relevant data.

Real interest rates for the first two quarters of 1986 were significantly lower than the corresponding rates in the preceding quarter. The CD and the treasury bill rates even turned slightly negative in the second quarter of 1986, reducing the incentive to hold nominal sheqel balances. But even these lower marginal lending rates were still high: a monthly average rate of 1.4 percent on overdraft facilities in the second quarter is equivalent to an annualized rate of 18 percent. Although such rates, which mainly affected the activities of firms producing for the domestic market, were by this time already imposing a growing strain on industry, the monetary authorities refused to go further in easing monetary policy. The rationale for this position, and the corresponding extension of the restrictive policy stance for another semester, can be ascribed to the advent of the second stage of the program—the repeal of price controls. The relaxation of the price freeze would inevitably involve some adjustment of relative prices, and thus some upward price push. The high sensitivity of economic agents to prices and price data was a major consideration as long as inflationary expectations were just barely dormant. Relatively tight money thus reduced the danger of rekindling inflation, at a cost, of course, to the real economy.

The repeal of price controls stretched over a period of about 18 months and was carried out successfully in terms of the inflation target. Initiated in January 1986, after two successive months of low price readings, the major steps were over by July of that year.[29] Figure 10 shows a bulge in the CPI curve in the first half of 1986 as relative prices adjusted after decontrol (although seasonal factors inflate the relative size of this bulge). The countervailing restrictive force of high real interest rates, which were by that time creating some slack in the economy, undoubtedly contributed to keeping the price adjustments smaller and allowed the economy to finally settle on a low pattern of inflation—less than 20 percent annually.

Maintaining this monetary policy stance had an obvious cost in terms of unemployment, which rose during the first two quarters of 1986 (Table 21 and Figure 7), The policy would have been more efficient, both in terms of inflation and vis-à-vis employment if real deposit rates had been kept positive throughout and if marginal lending rates had been somewhat lower. A major curtailment of credit market segmentation and a reduction of the monopolistic power of the banking industry could have helped on this score. It was, however, beyond the powers of the central bank to make a major dent in these two structural features that, in any case, were matters of long-term reform.

SOME ISSUES OF MONETARY POLICY TACTICS

The highly restrictive monetary strategy did not represent the judgment and discretion of monetary authorities alone. They were fully in line with the strategy laid out by the informal planning and implementation team working under the aegis of the prime minister and the minister of finance. The data and arguments spelled out in the previous section clearly indicate that if the central bank had strictly adhered to the letter of the plan, the stringency in financial markets during the first four post-stabilization months would have been even greater.

We have already noted why a nominal credit target would have been an inefficient criterion in the specific context of the Israeli stabilization policy. Reluctance to raise real interest rates even further led to the abandonment of this target as a guide to policy. However, reference to the relevant real interest rates (Table 27) raises some questions regarding potency of the monetary measures applied; the high rates on overdraft facilities that for the six months ending in January 1986 were never less than an annualized rate of about 100 percent are an obvious case in point. These rates became the battle cry of the business and political community, whose pressure inevitably spilled over into government circles.

A proper evaluation of the stringency in financial markets should also consider the multidimensional problem facing the day-to-day running of monetary policy, especially in crisis situations, when the short-run stability of factors that can usually be taken for granted does not exist. The demand for monetary assets, the timing, and the strength of the induced (and hoped-for) rise in demand for non-linked sheqel assets is an obvious example in the Israeli case.

The Supply Dimension

Some of the imponderables directly affecting liquidity on the supply side should be considered. It would have been impossible to run a highly restrictive monetary policy if the government budget had not moved from deficits of 9 percent and 4 percent of GNP, respectively, in the first two quarters of 1985 to a deficit of 0.5 percent of GNP in the following quarter and a surplus of 0.5 percent of GNP in the last quarter of 1985. A similar situation occurred in 1986, when the government ran a surplus equivalent to 1.3 percent of GNP.

The overall liquidity of the system was inevitably also affected by government operations in the capital market. Thus, in its attempt to manipulate financial markets the central bank also had to take care of a major redemption of government debt that had been set long before.[30] A refunding operation was designed and implemented but its immediate effect on liquidity depended on the reaction of the holders of that debt, which could hardly be predicted when it counted most. In such circumstances, the natural and deeply ingrained instinct of the monetary authorities—not fully shared usually by treasury officials in Israel or elsewhere—is to assume the worst and operate accordingly.

One possible error that could have led the monetary authorities to adopt a more restrictive stance than necessary in the markets was the difficulty in estimating the net absorption of government and the price pattern. With a lag of at least one month for information on the net liquidity position of the government and on prices, and in view of the special circumstances in the capital market, it was almost inevitable that the central bank would opt for caution in its attempt to guide market rates. The tight posture seen in Figure 10 in the lagged response of the interest rate on the monetary loan to the lower rate of price increase—opening a wide gap between these two rates in the first two post-stabilization quarters—presumably also reflect the difficulties in estimating the rate of price change. Given the inevitable lag in price information, the monetary loan rates of August (and even of September) 1985, about 16 and 12 percent a month, respectively, in nominal terms, which turned out to be high ex post real rates, are explicable. The demonstration effect of a highly restrictive posture, required at the first stage of implementation, was a consideration that justified such high nominal rates, although economic agents at that time were undoubtedly expecting monthly inflation rates to dip to single-digit rates. Although much lower, the nominal rates on the monetary loan—9.5 percent, 7.7 percent, 5 percent, respectively, for October, November, and December—suggest that at that time the Bank of Israel had not yet fully adjusted its policy to the "new 3 percent inflation pattern" or to the even lower level that surfaced after November.

In retrospect, this criticism—voiced several months after the event by the director general of the treasury—sounds convincing.[31] In the circumstances in which decisions on these matters were being made, however, the perspective was altogether different. The first "package deal" at the turn of 1985 succeeded in maintaining much lower price readings than before for two successive months. Based on this experience, it was hardly possible to peg policy at once to a new, lower pattern of inflation. Two price readings did not warrant such a far-reaching premise. The price fluctuations of the second post-stabilization quarter made life particularly difficult. In October 1985 the rate of change of the price index increased abruptly (Figure 10), halving real rates of interest on overdrafts and reducing the average interest rate on total credit to negative values (Table 27). The same can be said for the highly sensitive CD (and other deposit) rates just when the expected steep increase in the liquidity of households and firms may have led them to rush into the commodity markets. Although the Bank cautiously lowered the nominal rate on the monetary loan further, the unexpectedly low price index for the following month (November) sent real interest rates sky-high; the same happened in January 1986.

These events were undoubtedly not intended by the monetary authorities—they simply reflected an error in price prediction. The highly unsettled nature of the markets in the environment of a stabilization policy made price movements, particularly their rate of change, highly volatile. A monetary policy that seeks to create an image of persistent, positive real interest rates across the whole range of rates naturally leans toward caution. Since errors are inevitable, it is safer to err on the high rather than on the low side when stabilization policy is attempted.

The data for longer time intervals, say the first three post-stabilization quarters (Table 27), show a consistently declining trend of real interest rates across the board. These quarterly averages reflect errors in price predictions which, during the fourth quarter of 1985 and the first quarter of 1986, pushed them higher than intended. These longer-term averages are better indicators of the policy pursued by the authorities than are the monthly data, although the latter are the ones that matter most for business and production entities.

The Unpredictability of Demand for Money

The main issue is: should the decline in interest rates have been faster than it was. The foregoing discussion, focused on the supply of money (liquidity) and hence on the controls at the disposal of monetary authorities, omitted a highly relevant factor: the demand for liquidity. Changes in demand (or, more specifically, a rise in demand for nominal money) affect the structure of interest rates. Although the return to the sheqel as the effective ''money'' was an intermediate target of the whole exercise, its timing, and particularly the dimension of the rise in demand for sheqel over a given time interval was hard to predict. The sooner a stabilization program gains credibility, the stronger its impact on the demand for liquidity and thus on interest rates. Stated differently, and from the point of view of the monetary authorities, the greater the expected demand for sheqel credits (in effect, the demand for non-linked money), the greater the permissible expansion of credit if an increase in interest rates is to be prevented. Although the relevant gauges of such a gain in credibility are monetary indicators, such as the velocity of circulation and real interest rates, this information is available only with a time lag. Indeed, factoring in the demand-for-liquidity dimension into the considerations to guiding monetary policy is probably the greatest challenge facing the authorities in charge of a stabilization program.

Some insight into this matter can be gained from the Israeli data. Figure 14, which presents indices of real monetary aggregates, suggests highly diverse changes in the demand for various monetary aggregates. The immediate decline of M3 after the launching of the sheqel program, in contrast to the rapidly increasing values of M2 and M1, underlines the ''upheaval'' in demand for

money. Note, however, that initially it was M2, with its interest-bearing component (CDs and time deposits), that rose at a much higher rate than M1, the
non-interest-bearing component of the more comprehensive aggregate. Yet by
the end of the second post-stabilization quarter the graph indicates an acceleration in the growth of M1, which suggests that the final breakthrough in the
program's credibility may have been reached, reducing the real cost of holding
non-interest-bearing money.

The data on the velocity of circulation of demand deposits presented in Table
30 also support the interpretation that a credibility breakthrough occurred toward
the end of the second post-stabilization quarter. This velocity concept is based
on bank deposits, the dominant component of M1, and is a better indicator of
the demand for money than the value of monetary aggregates in Figure 14 (and
Table 28), since it is less affected by price volatility. It is also less affected than
quantity measures by "supply factors." The quarterly data indicate a substantial
downturn of velocity in the fourth quarter of 1985 and another, even stronger,
downturn of 25 percent in the second quarter of 1986, the fourth post-
stabilization quarter. The obverse of this decline is obviously an abrupt change
in the demand for non-linked, non-interest-bearing money as clearly visible in
Figure 14 which shows the time pattern of real monetary aggregates.[32]

An abrupt rise in the demand for money will affect prices and interest rates
unless the supply of money is adapted pari passu. The abruptness of these
changes during this period was due to the specific economic context of the
stabilization effort. Although relevant data are available with an average lag of
one month, an inspection of the pattern of monthly changes in the upper section
of Table 30 and of the real interest rates in Table 27 suggests that it would have
been quite reasonable not to rely on information for one month only, but to wait
for at least one more reading before a definite pattern was identified. This, of
course, means a lag of a couple of months before monetary management can
be adapted to the changing pattern of demand. It was presumably this difficulty
in predicting changes in the demand for money that led to the revealed preference of the monetary authorities for a slow relaxation of controls toward the
end of 1985, controls that constrained the level of real credit balances throughout
this period to about 6 percent below their level in June 1985 (Table 28), generating quite high interest rates across the board.[33]

Segmentation and Oligopolistic Constraints

The persistence of a restrictive monetary policy through the second quarter
of 1986, though less stringent than initially, was not due only to reasonable
errors in predicting prices or interpreting the abrupt changes in the demand for
money. The reluctance of the authorities—even after five successive readings
of monthly inflation rates of 1–2 percent—to relax monetary policy further in
the fourth post-stabilization quarter was undoubtedly related to the segmentation
feature discussed in Chapter 7. The rise in the average real interest rate on total

credit during the second and third post-stabilization quarters (Table 27) while the effective overdraft rate was declining indicates that some of the "privileged" types of credit were, after many years, moved into higher-cost categories, but substantial differences in interest rates between types of credit remained. Leaders of the business community, supported by statements from government officials, were critical of the cost of overdraft facilities (about an annual real rate of 30 percent in 1986). At the same time, the monetary authorities were justifiably worried by the fact that, although about 15 percent of credit balances carried this high cost, the average real annual interest cost of total credit in 1986 was only about 11 percent, implying that a substantial portion of credits were again bearing real rates of close to zero or even less. The upward adjustment of interest rates that the central bank succeeded in implementing in the first quarter of 1987 (to an average real annual cost of 34 percent for total credit) was undoubtedly partly due to this consideration.

This situation suggests that the image of a highly restrictive policy, conveyed by the rates charged to "nonpreferential credits," is largely a reflection of the limited success achieved in reducing credit market segmentation. It also explains why the very high marginal rates did not result in widespread insolvencies: firms with a credit portfolio similar in composition to the average faced an average interest cost of close to 30 percent in real terms only in one quarter (the first quarter of 1986); the average real cost of credit was only about 14–15 percent in the first two post-stabilization quarters. Firms with a low ratio of privileged credit balances were less fortunate. The fall-out from this financial squeeze, which affected some major business firms, came into the open in 1987, but was not really due only to the high interest rates.

The other, related reason why the authorities resisted calls for further relaxation was the level of deposit rates. The oligopoly-generated, sizable gap between lending and deposit rates, discussed in Chapter 7, meant that the 17 percent real annual rate on overdraft facilities in the second quarter of 1986 involved negative real CD rates (Table 27, part B). The obvious danger of this situation reducing the attractiveness of holding sheqel balances and inducing a move into the goods markets suggested care in further easing monetary policy. The break in the M1 and M2 curves in Figure 14 at that time, and the rapid rise in private consumption expenditures, suggest that the reluctance to go for further monetary ease was warranted. The high lending rates thus also reflect the failure (at that stage) to overcome the monopolistic structure of the banking industry.

A NOTE ON THE 1986–88 MONETARY STANCE

Price data indicate that, if judged by one of its ultimate targets (lowering inflation), the sheqel plan was in good shape by the spring of 1986, the end of the third quarter after its launching. By then, monetary policy was less restrictive than in the previous year; liquidity ratios were reduced in March and May and the rate on the monetary loan, cut in monthly steps, had settled onto a lower plateau in April 1986 (Figure 10).

However, the monetary stance was kept tight by conventional standards through the second half of 1986, and through the two following years. With monthly price inflation in terms of CPI around 1–2 percent for these three successive years, "effective" overdraft rates moving into a nominal 3–4.5 percent range, and the average nominal rate on total credit above 2 percent, this implied annual real interest rates on overdrafts of 30–40 percent and of 10–20 percent for average outstanding credit (Table 24). These rates, and the continuously growing share of non-privileged lines of credit in the total, do not suggest monetary ease.[34]

This relative monetary stringency was maintained in spite of public opinion and the critical attitude in government and parliamentary circles as illustrated by the director general's comments quoted above. Furthermore, the data clearly indicate that the central bank pursued more or less the same policy in spite of a change of leadership in 1986. Indeed, the data on real interest rates for that year reveal no change either in direction or in emphasis. The same is apparent from an inspection of the instruments subject to direct control by the central bank: neither the flat monetary loan rate curve through most of 1986 (Figure 10) nor the stable liquidity ratios from May 1986 through February 1987 (Table 26) enable identification of the timing of the change of leadership at the Bank of Israel. Indeed, the relevant data—interest rates and real M3 figures (Table 28)—suggest some tightening of policy toward the end of 1986.

This evidence and the monetary policy that the data represent are a clear reflection of the nature of the role assigned to monetary policy in these three years. With the support of a tight fiscal policy, especially in 1986 and 1987, this role was to keep the economy "on hold" with respect to inflation. This position was imposed by the failure, after the success with inflation, to achieve a substantial improvement in the fundamentals, especially as regards the wage productivity nexus (reflected in the size of the import surplus) and the absolute size of government. The failure to make some progress in restructuring the fundamentals required the maintenance of a tight policy to support the pegged exchange rate at its level of July 1, 1985. Its role as a nominal anchor as the visible signal of (price) stability—despite the cumulative (still significant) rise in prices and the overvaluation of the currency—forced the hand of the authorities.[35] The change of central bank leadership made no difference on this score.

It has been suggested that one important factor contributing to price developments in this period was the rapid dollar devaluation vis-à-vis the European currencies. In view of the dollar peg, this meant a welcome (from the point of view of the balance of payments) sheqel devaluation vis-à-vis these currencies, with a minimal impact on expectations, but it nevertheless had an unwelcome cost effect on prices. However, with the oil price collapse and lower commodity prices, Israel's terms of trade improved during this period, so that foreign-induced cost-push effects were of minor significance in 1985–86.

A cost effect was nevertheless at work. This pervasive effect, which drove prices during the second year of the plan's implementation, was a major reversal of the trend of real wages. The agreement with the unions (Histadrut), made at the launching of the sheqel program and one of its most important components, stipulated a substantial but temporary cut in real wages. At their trough, toward the end of 1985, real wages in the business sector were down by 14 percent and those in the public sector by almost 25 percent. By July 1986, however, wages in the business sector, though not yet in the public sector, were already back to the level of the previous June.[36] Labor productivity, which did not warrant the real wage rate of June 1985 in the first place, had not, of course, improved sufficiently during this short interval to overcome the real wage-productivity gap (of, say, 10 percent or more) of mid-1985. It was soon obvious that this pattern of wages, which kept rising rapidly through 1986 and 1987, would soon force a realignment of the exchange rate.

Monetary policy toward the end of the last quarter of 1986, with a tightening clearly apparent in the data and the supporting charts, was thus assigned its traditional role of defending the exchange rate before the 10 percent devaluation in January 1987, and of clamping down on demand afterward so as to prevent the reacceleration of prices in the wake of cost effects. The price data for 1986 through 1988 (Tables 26 and 21) indicate that on the whole the line was indeed held in 1987 and 1988, with a broad repetition in the second half of 1988 of developments in the same period of 1986. For better or for worse, the unwar-rantedly prolonged role imposed on monetary policy to hold the fort against inflation was successfully implemented. It had an inevitably dampening effect on the level of activity and on growth. The lack of improvement in the funda-mentals—which made the restrictive stance of monetary policy necessary—was evidently beyond the scope of monetary policy and the responsibility of the monetary authorities, though they could still continue to serve in the role of whipping boy.

NOTES

1. Monthly CPI figures are published on the 15th of each month; the June figure of 14.9 percent (up from the 6.8 percent of May) was thus only available on July 15.

2. The sheqel value of the inflow, of about $1 billion within the first six weeks after implementation, was one and a half times the size of the monetary base at the end of June 1985.

3. The temptation to apply administratively imposed credit ceilings in this kind of situation is obvious. It is fully in line with the "controls" approach—an inherent feature of heterodoxy. It appeared appropriate, particularly in view of the specification of an overall credit target, and was thus favored by some of those involved in the handling and implementation of the program, although the segmentation of the credit market (Ta-ble 23) prevented its application across the board.

An application of an overall quota technique requires the adoption of a rule on "in-terbank" allocation of the total credit quota. This, sooner rather than later, leads to interbank "quota" trading. Bank customers would accordingly pay more for their credit balances, even if the structure of the banking industry were relatively competitive. In a monopolistic environment such as that of Israel's banking system, this would raise credit costs even more (see Chapter 7).

4. Note that a 50 percent liquidity ratio means that to make a profit, banks must charge more than twice the cost of acquiring these marginal deposits. This induces the growth of "grey" money markets, which reduces the effectiveness of monetary controls and increases risks in financial markets.

5. PATAM (foreign-currency-linked) deposits were subject to a 100 percent liquidity ratio. A move from these deposits into sheqel deposits, for which lower liquidity ratios were required, gave the banks leeway for the expansion of sheqel credits. This move into sheqel funds induced by the plan's repeal of interest payments on current PATAM accounts, and the lead- and lag-induced reflow of foreign funds, improved the liquidity of the banking system. This improvement is also indicated by the reduction in the net outflow of funds from the banking system abroad from the second to the third quarter of 1985 (see Table 29). As expected, the non-financial sector changed its position immediately and, in the first post-stabilization quarter, generated an inflow of funds much larger than the outflow of bank funds. The total of these flows involved an inflow of about $140 million. The net reflow of foreign funds and the movement into sheqel funds encouraged by high deposit rates generated the extraordinary increase in the monetary base shown in Table 25.

6. Net sales of treasury bills in July were higher than net redemptions during the whole of the first half of 1985. They were three times higher in the first post-implementation quarter than the redemptions in the first half of 1985 (Bank of Israel, *Annual Report 1985,* table I-3, p. 341).

7. See Bank of Israel, Supervisor of Banking, *Israel's Banking System 1985,* pp. 26–29, especially diagram B-1, p. 28. See also *Israel's Banking System 1986,* pp. 48–51, and diagram B-1, p. 49.

8. The average balance of the monetary loan (i.e., of "borrowed reserves") in this time interval was 15–20 percent of total reserves (Bank of Israel, Supervisor of Banking, *Israel's Banking System 1985,* p. 29, and the same report for 1986, p. 48).

9. The accommodation of any bank at intramarginal interest rates was constrained by the relative level of its deposits. This arrangement did provide an opening to interbank "trade" in reserves acquired at intramarginal rates. A schematic outline of the stepwise technique of accommodation by means of the "monetary loan" is shown below. Initially, the central bank offers the total quantity OA, the sum of OA_1 offered at the lower rate of interest, i_0, and a supplementary, "unlimited" quantity, along the line BC, at a higher rate i_1. The total demand curve of the banking system intersects the BC infinitely elastic section of the supply curve at C, which sets the total volume of borrowed reserves—the monetary loan at OA.

Suppose now that the central bank decides to set a higher rate, say i_2, for borrowed reserves. To establish that rate it can proceed along two alternative, clear-cut routes. One of these is simply to raise the upper step of the supply curve, the BC line, to DE. This would involve an equilibrium quantity OA_2 at E, say, at the bank's presently set marginal cost of funds—the purpose of the exercise, and at the same time would determine the average cost of accommodation. An alternative technique by which the same marginal cost of funds i_2 is set involves reducing the quantity offered at the lower rate i_0, from OA_1 to, say, OA_0. The "new" supply curve would be i_0aFE instead of i_0bDE. The

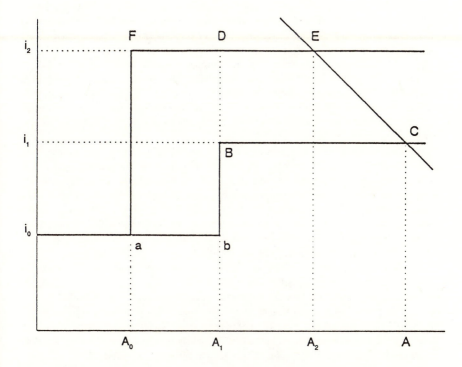

marginal cost of funds would be the same, but the average cost of accommodation to banks would be higher.

Any number of variations of these two extreme cases is possible. What counts, however, is that by operating in this way the bank can tighten (or loosen) the money market without affecting the marginal rate, if it chooses to do so.

10. From November 1984 through July 1985, and again from November 1985 through the end of 1986, banks could benefit from the monetary loan accommodation only if they agreed to offer a minimum rate on short-term time deposits and to charge a maximum prime rate on overdraft facilities (see Table 27, columns 1 and 6). The nominal rates—not the implied real rates presented in the table—were the subject of the Bank's attempt to directly influence interest rates in the money market.

11. The so-called target credit volume was total bank credit (mentioned in the document presented to the government) net of credit for energy (fuel) imports, outstanding diamond industry credits, and credit lines to aviation and shipping. The FC credit series presented in Table 25 offers a good approximation of this concept of credit, while the TC credit series does not exclude the credit balances of the above-mentioned industries. Whether the Bank's adopted series is operationally more meaningful than the TC series is open to debate; the FC series approximates it fairly well.

12. The average real monthly rate for 1984 was 4 percent—an annualized rate of 60 percent. Overdraft facilities in 1984 were, however, less than 10 percent of total outstanding credit (Bank of Israel, *Recent Economic Developments,* No. 44, September 1988, table 21).

13. Yariv's ingenious attempt to trace price expectations in the bond market supports both this interpretation of commercial banks' behavior and that of the monetary authorities, suggesting an optimistic forecasting error of the expected July price index. Yariv uses stock-exchange price quotations of price-linked government bonds due for redemption at the end of the current month, predating the publication of the CPI figure for the previous month, which finally settles their redemption value. His estimate on the expected July 1985 price change as indicated by these bond prices is 21.5 percent. The market's price expectations were also more optimistic for the succeeding three months, according to Yariv's estimate; they put the expected monthly price changes within the 2–3 percent range (Yariv, 1988, table 1).

14. Eighty-nine percent of goods and services on the basis of CPI weights were subjected to price control at the onset of the program. This percentage was maintained through the first two post-stabilization quarters. Similar quantitative information on the scope of controls on commodities, particularly inputs not included in the consumer price index, is not available. However, both the coverage (and especially the timing) of the repeal of controls was similar for all types of commodities and inputs. Information on coverage and timing of the repeal of controls is from a private communication of the Ministry of Trade and Industry, February 1989.

15. Rent controls were included in the controls package. Since Israel features an "owner-occupied" housing market, the rental market is only a small portion. Controls, which were soon repealed, thus did not cause shortages in this sensitive market.

Brazil in particular, but also Argentina, brought price inflation down more rapidly than did Israel. The initial rapid decline of their indices suggests that administratively imposed rapid disinflation, as measured in terms of CPI, hardly reflected the realities in the Brazilian market. See Figure 4, and the corresponding price data in Table 21.

16. The well-known leads and lags in pre- and post-devaluation flows of funds across the exchanges are the obverse of the change in the currency used to finance trade credits.

17. "In cases in which the decreed price freeze created an unreasonable cost-price relationship, permission to adjust prices was granted. This prevented the surfacing of shortages" (Bank of Israel, *Annual Report 1985*, p. 67).

This passage refers to a so-called price committee made up of officials of the Economic Ministries that could grant permits for price adjustments. Note that prices of "essentials" involving 20 percent of the value of the CPI basket ("prices subject to public control") rose over the first quarter at a monthly rate of over 12 percent. This rise, reflecting the major reduction of subsidies, was imposed at once. The rate of price increase of commodities "not subjected to public controls of prices" rose at a monthly rate of only 6.5 percent over the same interval. In view of their nature, and particularly their scope (this group comprised 80 percent of the value of the CPI basket), the process of upward adjustment was naturally slower. It spread over a longer period, spilling over into the following month, thus contributing to the phenomenon labeled "price resistance" in the text.

18. This is Friedman's explicit assumption underlying his well-known proposal for the adoption of a long-run monetary rule. The rationale of his proposed rule reflects obviously his observation of the short-run instability of the demand function for money.

19. I owe the reference to the relevance of the flow of short-term funds across the exchanges to H. Shmidt.

20. Table 27 gives ex post figures. But in view of the abrupt decline of the CPI from 27.5 percent in July to 3.9 percent in August, which became public knowledge in mid-

September, price expectations might have been adapting to the new price environment, so that the ex post figures do not differ significantly from the real situation toward, say, the last week of September. This is supported by Yariv's estimates on price expectations referred to in note 43 in Yariv (1988, table 1).

The real rates on "effective" and marginal overdraft facilities were indeed halved between August and December 1985. But at annualized real rates of 97 percent and over 120 percent for these two types of credit lines, respectively, in December, monetary policy in the second post-stabilization quarter can hardly be described as expansionary.

21. Bank of Israel, *Annual Report 1985* (p. 61), refers to the fact that, excluding the credit target spelled out above, the government did not make any decision or specify any details about the day-to-day management of monetary policy.

22. The imminent redemption of $700 million bank shares—in practice, government bonds—in October 1985 also had an impact on liquidity, even before it occurred.

23. Data on retail sales are from CBS "Indices of Organized Retail Trade" for 1981 through 1985. These are also presented in Bank of Israel, Research Department, *Main Economic Series.*

24. Inventory investment soared in the second quarter of 1985 and kept growing, though at a lower rate, through the third quarter of 1985 (Bank of Israel, *Annual Report 1985,* table B-A-3, p. 46).

25. The president of the Israeli Chamber of Commerce described these rates as "Mafia" interest rates.

26. The effort shows up in the inventory data. Inventories were rapidly depleted in the fourth quarter of 1985—75 percent of the inventory accumulated in the previous three quarters sank in this single quarter (see source in note 24 above). The obverse of this process is the increase in retail sales of durables in particular, clearly indicated by the retail sales data referred to in note 23 above (see also the reference in Bank of Israel, *Annual Report 1985,* to these "sales" and their downward effect on prices, p. 270).

27. According to the Hawtrey proposition on the inventory cycle. For obvious reasons, Hawtrey presented his argument in terms of nominal interest rates.

28. Velocity of circulation of demand deposits which, unlike income velocity figures, are independent of GNP data, and are available on a monthly basis, are the best real-time indicator on the pattern of demand for money.

29. The CPI basket data quoted above (note 14) suggest that about 60 percent of the process of decontrol was completed by that time.

30. This was the redemption of the first block of "bank shares," set for October 1985, for which the government had accepted liability (at a certain minimum dollar price) in 1983. Owing to the specific assets (bank shares which were highly liquid before 1983), the size of the operation ($700 million), and the stabilization plan environment, it was not clear how much of this comparatively large sum could be refinanced in the short interval of a month or two. Thus, although the budget in the fourth quarter was run at a 0.5 percent of GNP surplus, the government's impact on base money—due to its net operations in the capital market, was about 5 percent of GNP, a significant volume by any account. For figures on the government deficit, net sales (redemptions) in the capital market, and net infusion (absorption) of liquidity, see Bank of Israel, *Recent Economic Developments,* No. 44 (September 1988), table 17.

31. In March 1986, when the real marginal rate on overdraft facilities was already down to an annual rate of 44 percent in real terms, with the average rate on total outstanding credit 11 percent and a negative real rate on CDs of 5 percent, the Director

General of the Treasury is reported to have said: " . . . the Central Bank's steered interest rates to exaggerated heights . . . there had been a need for a high interest rate during the first stage of the plan, but soon after that the rates should have been cut abruptly . . . ," *The Jerusalem Post* (March 4, 1987). The passage is from a write-up of an interview with the Director General of the Treasury by A. Temkin and S. Maoz. The date of the report suggests that price figures for February, which show an upturn of the inflation rate from a monthly rate of minus 1.3 percent to 1.6 percent, were not known to the director general when he made these comments.

32. The monthly data in the upper part of Table 30 support the identification of the timing of the abrupt change in velocity to the fourth quarter of 1985. Observations for other periods underline the quality of this variable as a measure of the onslaught of inflation and of its level. The all-time high velocity in June 1985 speaks for itself. Also, a comparison of 1989 with 1980 and 1971 is highly illuminating, though we cannot enter into this matter here.

33. A highly optimistic prediction on improving credibility and of the corresponding rise in demand for nominal money can perhaps explain the highly expansionary stance of monetary policy in Argentina in its fourth post-stabilization quarter, and the consequent demise of the Austral Plan. See Rodriguez (1988).

34. Average quarterly interest rates through 1988 are presented in Table 24.

35. The CPI, reflecting the initial price shock, increased by 48 percent between July 1985 and July 1986, eroding the cushion provided by the 25 percent devaluation at the plan's launching.

36. Real wage data are from the Treasury Memorandum of September 9, 1987. The error in predicting the force of the July 1985 price shock and the exact timing of the downward trend of prices eroded real wages more than expected during the first phase— the first two quarters—of stabilization.

— 9 —

Some Lessons from the Sheqel Plan Experiment

THE FOCUS—INFLATION

At the time of writing, four years after its launching, with annual inflation at 16–20 percent for over three years, the Sheqel Plan can be rated a definite success in terms of its main target—to contain inflation. However, the economy has not yet succeeded in moving on from the stabilization stage to the next one, in which inflation was to be pushed down further—to a single-digit level—and growth was to resume. Nor has it succeeded in reducing the import surplus, although "a significant improvement in the balance of payments" was one of the two targets explicitly spelled out in the program. This failure to wind down inflation and improve the trade account reflects a failure to tackle the fundamentals: the real wage-productivity nexus, the size of government and the onerous taxation levels, some inbred monopolistic features, and protection of some industries that should no longer be treated as "infant industries."

This is not to suggest that all these problems should have been tackled at the stabilization stage; in fact, avoiding a confrontation with *all* the fundamentals at that stage had a major benefit: it made it easier to focus on the most urgent business—the attempt to contain inflation—and in any case it is obviously much easier to deal with the labor market fundamentals in a low inflation price environment. One of the lessons of the Sheqel Plan is therefore that the focus on a single target—inflation—is advisable.

In open economies, the balance-of-payments problem has to be addressed at the launching stage, particularly if the current account is in trouble, as it usually is. Likewise the government deficit; the Israeli experiment shows that the latter can be tackled initially from the revenue, not necessarily from the expenditure side. The latter is, of course, the more relevant dimension for a reform of the fundamentals. But as an instrument whose main purpose in the initial phase is to make a restrictive monetary policy feasible, the reduction of the deficit by increasing net taxes (and thus net government absorption) is as effective as cutting government expenditure on goods and services. The implementation of the program also demonstrated that if the foreign reserve position can be handled by (temporary) foreign aid—in this case, supported by improving terms of trade—the productivity issue can be temporarily shelved. Therefore, at the initial stage of implementation, fiscal and balance-of-payments measures should be considered only as supporting measures.

In what follows, the discussion will focus on the lessons of the Sheqel Plan, essentially conceived as an attempt to rapidly reduce the three-digit annual levels of inflation to the lower rate of 1–2 percent a month.

MONETARY POLICY AND MARKET FORCES

A price freeze and a pegged nominal exchange rate were two elements in Israel's stabilization program. The price freeze was conceived as a temporary measure, and maintaining a pegged nominal exchange rate was subject to holding nominal wages to their planned (and agreed) time pattern. This forced the planning team and the authorities to rely mainly on market discipline, that is, on restraining real aggregate demand and reducing the influence of inertial forces, to put the rate of price changes on a rapidly declining path. The inertial forces were tackled by attempting to influence price expectations immediately. The pegging of the (higher) exchange rate, offering a stable nominal (sustainable) signal, was the main instrument used. A very steep rise in net absorption, substantially reducing disposable income, served as the fiscal peg in cutting aggregate demand. But the role of monetary policy in generating market forces that would clamp down on prices at the crucial time, two to three quarters after launching, is one of the more important messages of the Sheqel Plan. The highly restrictive and long, drawn-out monetary stance, which generated high interest rates, made financial assets comparatively attractive and, after an inevitable delay, forced a well-timed unloading of inventories on "hesitant" markets. The price-depressant features of keeping highly liquid households away from markets and of pushing commodities onto the shelves are obvious.

Reliance on market forces provided better information on the "viability" of the relative prices established in the immediate aftermath of implementation and allowed prompt rectification of substantial distortions. The main benefit of this technique, however, surfaced later, at the repeal stage. Since it was market forces that were initially the factor preventing price hikes, the process of repealing the freeze in the second stage did not make a major difference. The Israeli data clearly show that although repeal was followed by some upward price adjustments, tight monetary and fiscal policies rendered them fairly harmless.

It was obvious that the exchange rate peg, a highly significant signal of stability, might create problems on the trade account. Yet the lead- and lag-induced inflow of funds, supported by special foreign aid, and the foreign credit accommodation attracted by the high interest rates meant that the reserve position was initially strong. The devaluation also improved the trade account in the first stage of implementation. The problems of the export industries surfaced much later as, by previous standards, the very slow yet persistent rise in prices eroded the initial improvement in the real exchange rate. But this became relevant only when the stabilization phase was close to its end.

Reliance on market forces to contain aggregate demand and reduce the momentum of price inflation had to overcome "price resistance." Inflation did not decline immediately to the low rate conceived at the planning stage. This could have undermined the public's faith in the plan at perhaps the most sensitive juncture—the immediate aftermath of implementation, when credibility was at a premium.

Price resistance also had some real effects, higher-than-expected rates of price change affected ex post real wages, especially the real rate of interest, although the latter was more significantly affected by price volatility. This would undoubtedly also have occurred if tight administrative controls had been used to keep prices in line. Reliance on market forces, however, immediately brought these effects into the open.

ON OVERSHOOTING AND PERSEVERANCE

The monetary authorities in Israel have been severely criticized for "overshooting" in their attempt at monetary restraint. Annualized real effective interest rates on overdraft facilities of 320 and 242 percent in August and September 1985, respectively, and a 133 percent rate in January 1986 are obvious evidence for the prosecution. Note, however, that the August and September rates came after a negative effective rate of *minus* 47 percent for July, and that the unexpectedly high January 1986 rate was followed by a sharply lower real effective rate (3.5 percent) in April. Furthermore, at this still positive real rate of interest for overdrafts, the average rate of interest on total outstanding credit was already negative (*minus* 15 percent), and the corresponding rate on CDs was even lower: *minus* 23 percent!

Some overshooting clearly did occur over specific, shorter time intervals, and was due to two different factors. First, price volatility generated a corresponding volatility of real interest rates, if their nominal counterparts were warrantedly, and for obvious reasons, adjusted downward on a stable pattern. Second, it reflected structural phenomena—the segmentation of the credit market and the wide (monopoly-generated) margin between debit and credit rates. The extent of overshooting could have been reduced if the monetary authorities had been given more freedom to simultaneously affect the whole range of lending and deposit rates. The message is quite clear: in order to reduce the extent of overshooting, if at all politically feasible, credit market segmentation and the banking system's monopoly power are to be addressed more forcefully than they were in Israel, as early as possible. It would, however, not be advisable to tackle these issues at the early stages of the process.

Even if the segmentation-monopoly issue could have been eliminated, the unpredictable price volatility would have required some overshooting if monetary policy was to prevent any straying of deposit rates into negative values. In order to ensure that deposit rates offer an economically reasonable alternative to real goods through the entire stabilization period, in which inflationary expectations are still strong, the authorities should aim for real annual rates on deposits of, say, 8–10 percent. With mean monthly inflation rates of 1–2 percent, price volatility would imply that a proximate mean monthly real deposit rate of close to 1 percent could easily move between, say, 0–2 percent. However, a floor for the deposit rate at this level might involve mean annual real lending rates of 15–20 percent, moving—in response to the unpredictable fluctuations in rates of price change—within, say, an annual 10–25 percent range.

This undoubtedly implies some overshooting, but for the initial phase of a stabilization program, in the first three to six or even nine months of implementation, it is acceptable. It is one unfortunate but necessary cost of disinflation borne by the business sector. The suggestion, implied by a device used by the authorities implementing the Cruzado and Austral Plans, that it is possible to "fine tune" nominal interest rates with the fluctuations in price changes in the first stabilization phase, is obviously a pipe dream. The only warranted error during the first stage of implementation, when so much is at stake, is therefore on the upside rather than on the downside of the interest-rate spectrum.

Thus, the lesson from the Israeli experiment is that overshooting is inevitable in the first stage of stabilization. The policy pursued by the authorities, namely, systematically, yet more slowly than the mean rate of price decline, reducing the nominal rate of the "monetary loan," was bound to result in overshooting. In fact, it was beneficial. Furthermore, it was perseverance, through the first half of 1986 and beyond, that made the difference, and undoubtedly helped to hold the line on inflation.

The Israeli experiment also offers another message. While, say, 6 or even 12 months of high interest rates are unfortunately warranted if the target—to reduce runaway inflation to lower, more bearable low rates—is to be achieved, the extension of a comparatively restrictive policy for another two to three years exacts major (perhaps intolerable) costs for the real economy. It not only nips in the bud growth-inducing investment, but the resulting prolonged financial strain could become unbearable even for viable firms, and could push weaker firms to the brink of collapse and beyond.

ON ORTHODOXY AND HETERODOXY

If a heterodox stabilization program is defined as a program involving an incomes policy, the Israeli program indeed belongs in this category. This formulation covers the feature that identifies heterodoxy to most people—a price freeze enforced by controls. Both the freeze and the controls were items in the formal policy outline, but it was the image of the controls rather than their implementation that counted. If the price freeze could be maintained only by controls, and thus involve rationing, its function of demonstrating stability day in, day out, would have been an exercise in futility.

This applies even more strongly to the most prominent of all so-called nominal anchors—the pegged exchange rate. If the rate were to be maintained by controls involving foreign currency quotas, its assigned role as the dominant signal of stability would have been useless. However, the peg was supported by market forces: the inflow of funds attracted by the high interest rates that were induced by restrictive monetary policy, and the confidence stimulated by the announcement of special U.S. aid and by an improvement in the trade account. Rising reserves and the collapse of the black-market dollar premium were the market signals indicating that the exchange-rate peg was there to stay.

However, if market forces mainly enforced the price discipline, what was the purpose of the freeze and controls? The answer has more to do with politics and social psychology than with economics. The launching of the Sheqel Plan undoubtedly depended on an incomes policy, not in an abstract sense (the Cruzado Plan in Brazil was also based on an incomes policy), but with a specific content. It was based on a very substantial, albeit temporary (for 6–12 months) cut in real wages, which required the agreement of labor and the support of public opinion. The unions (Histadrut) consented to the lowering of real wages subject to several conditions; the relevant condition in this context was a universal price freeze and, inevitably, price controls. Thus, whether the freeze is an effective instrument for neutralizing the inertial driving force of inflation or not, any stabilization policy involving a significant cut in real wages cannot take off without a price freeze and controls as an integral item of the formal plan.

In view of the welfare goal of minimizing the cost of a stabilization program in terms of foregone output and employment, the addition of one more instrument to the traditional set of fiscal and monetary tools was also warranted by theoretical considerations. If the level of activity cannot be taken as residual, even in the short run, the inclusion of an incomes policy that helps reduce pressures on economic activity by a preordained price adjustment makes economic sense.

One can hardly imagine a situation in which an incomes policy involving a cut in real wage rates would not be absolutely necessary for the success of a stabilization policy. Nor would it be feasible to reduce real wages and incomes by a cut in nominal rates. Instead, the mechanism would usually have to involve cost-push pressures generated by devaluation and taxation not (fully) compensated by an adjustment of nominal wages. In these circumstances, a price freeze and controls are not only a claim made by representatives of labor. They appear to be fair. If the plan involves measures applied to control aggregate demand— a proper fiscal policy and, initially, a highly restrictive monetary stance—the control element might do little harm, and the freeze component might contribute to weakening inertial forces.

However, the inclusion of a control element also has a cost. The cost is a reflection of the fact that a stabilization policy is first and foremost a political act and is thus directly dependent on the attitude, mood, and decisions of the political community and, no less important, on public opinion as reflected in, and influenced by, the media. The credence now placed on legislation and public control means that this program's price freeze and controls may not be considered merely a technical device, on equal footing, say, with the fiscal and monetary instruments. To many in the political arena, it is an expression of a philosophy that on more than one occasion has led governments to opt for the apparently easy line—doomed to failure—of attempting to stop inflation by administrative fiat.

The sophisticated argument in favor of controls considers them a temporary device, helping to reset relative prices, weakening the impact of inflationary price expectations, and reducing the real cost of the policy to some segments of the population. Yet the short-term orientation of the political arena and the emphasis on the control element of a stabilization program, underlined by the recent creation of a specific term: "heterodoxy," could easily clog the wheels of a stabilization policy. The suggestion that a heterodox program is altogether different (as it dispenses with the requirement to impose tight fiscal and monetary discipline) is usually welcome in the political arena. The freeze and controls are thus soon visualized as a target rather than an instrument, with a revealed preference to keep them in place.

The Israeli experiment suggests that this preference for controls emerges at the very stage when controls should be on their way out. In practice, the repeal of controls was hampered by the political process, as the political players preferred the status quo to a possible immediate and politically unwelcome rise in prices. Furthermore, the loss of power, which was the inevitable result of the abolition of controls, was proved resented by leading politicians. This reluctance to abolish controls, or at least some of them, has obvious long-run consequences.

The message conveyed by the comparative performance of the three programs—the Austral, Cruzado, and Sheqel programs—on this matter is quite clear. Freezes, pegs, and controls alone cannot do the job. Persistent restrictive monetary and fiscal policies, supported by a stable exchange rate as a highly visible nominal anchor, and a substantial, though temporary, erosion of real wages succeeded in containing runaway inflation.

___ 10 ___

Inflation and Stabilization:
The Message

AN OVERVIEW

"Stabilization"—the catch phrase for what historical experience has shown to be a series of (usually repetitive) attempts to pull the sting of inflation—follows every inflationary experience as day follows night. This, of course, begs the question: why step onto the slips in the first place? The experience of the twentieth century suggests that governments in industrialized countries eventually overcome their reluctance and make a go at "stabilization," in spite of the considerable short-run economic and social cost, so that the sequence of events described above would seem the height of folly. Yet, what to all appearances is patently absurd, in hindsight, does not necessarily seem so when events unfold in real time.

The universality of the inflation phenomenon that surfaced in most industrialized countries in the aftermath of World War I, and its recurrence in the four decades following World War II, suggests the presence of an underlying common motif. It points to the prevalence of structural features that make it easy to start and sustain an inflationary process, sometimes unwittingly. Even if this is not so, and accelerating inflation is more or less deliberate, its universality suggests the existence of similar initial conditions which facilitate the surfacing of that phenomenon. A misreading of the signals of inflation's immediate effects, especially on expectations, and of its ultimate, though delayed consequences, has probably also had an effect on the behavior of governments. Similarly, the very fact that governments sooner or later accept that there is no alternative but to restrain the upward momentum of prices—even at the cost of putting their political survival on the line—indicates the presence of some similar factors which ultimately force their hand.

The surfacing of major inflations in the twentieth century is obviously linked to the existence of a highly relevant initial condition, the universal adoption of "paper standards," which made it much easier for governments to inflate the money supply. Although a necessary condition for inflation, this precondition was neither a sufficient nor, indeed, a necessary and sufficient one for the appearance of inflation. The great diversity of inflation rates among industrial countries, all of which were effectively on a paper standard since World War II, is a case in point. Heavy wartime demands inevitably followed by efforts at rapid reconstruction and attempts to placate the electorate in peacetime, are both usually identified as sufficient conditions for an inflationary process to surface. The paper standard adopted by industrialized (and semi-industrialized countries in Latin America) meant that major budget deficits created by expansionary fiscal policies could easily be monetized, thereby offering the option of an inflation tax to substitute for statutory taxes levied to finance real government activity. Ultimately, of course, the inherent dynamics of an inflation tax leads to its own erosion, due to its generation of ever-rising deficits and introducing increasingly violent gyrations into the economic system. This is finally followed by loss of control, whereupon inflation itself becomes a major political issue. Thus, the temptation of opting for an expedient inflation ultimately comes home to roost, leading to the demise of the administration that relied on it.

This leads back to the above query about the (long-run) rationality of such behavior. The answer usually involves reference to the difference, often a sizeable one, between political and economic horizons, where the former is usually conceived as being much shorter than the latter. Even in peacetime, when populist demands for a "forward-looking" social policy might force the government's hand even though the economy is operating at full employment, the long lag (in political terms) between the appearance of a budget deficit, its monetization, and (finally) the pressure exerted by the inflated money supply on both prices and the current account can explain why an ultimately self-defeating policy of initiating inflation was pursued. An attempt to stem the tide of inflation, once it gets going, requires a reversal of the (expansionary) policy which brought it into being. But this is obviously self-defeating in political terms. The option of allowing the economy to be borne along on an inflationary current, buying (political) time, is the "easy" way out: true, the resultant trade deficit serves as a temporary safety valve, easing part of the demand pressure on the more visible and (politically more damaging) domestic price level. In a widely open economy with a sizeable foreign trade (thus imports) component in terms of the size of domestic product, the trade balance operates as a shock-absorber, granting government a temporary reprieve, until the point of no return is reached and the economy spins out of control. The loss of control is manifested by an expectations-driven acceleration of price inflation interacting with the exchange rate with no input from the fundamentals, in what apparently is a race with no end in sight.[1]

An ensuing attempt at *stabilization* is usually initiated by a new government, which can blame its predecessor for having mishandled the economy.[2] To succeed, such a policy must involve, first and foremost, an attempt to deflate aggregate demand, of both the public sector and businesses and households. A rapid and significant reduction of the budget deficit, so as to support a protracted (in terms of the political horizon), highly restrictive monetary policy, is therefore a necessary condition for implementing such a policy.

The upheaval resulting from such a clamping down on demand and the related adjustment of the (official) exchange rate, in an environment of sticky real wages, naturally generates an upsurge in unemployment. The restrictive monetary policy forces up the interest rates, raising correspondingly the carrying costs of inventories, reducing the (expected) profitability of investment, straining the liquidity of businesses and the solvency of firms with low equity/liability ratios. All these developments operate in the same direction—they have a negative effect on economic activity and employment. Stabilization attempts are therefore a highly delicate exercise in political management. They require persistence, thus political stamina, and a wide and sustained public opinion and parliamentary support, say, for one to two years at least. In democratic countries this might seem an eternity in political terms. It is, however, clearly a necessary condition for success.

The Israeli case offers a clear message on the conditions and factors that push industrial countries run by a democratically elected governments to succumb to a take-off of inflation, which eventually runs out of control, and on attempting to stop it in its tracks. In more than one sense Israel served as a laboratory experiment and thus provides an interesting lesson on the interplay of factors that generate a take-off of inflation, and ultimately interact as an attempt is made to quench its fires.

THE STATUS AND ROLE OF THE CENTRAL BANK

There is no doubt that full employment prevailed in the Israeli economy when the first stage of the take-off took place. Government finances were strained to the utmost by defense-related expenditures—the cost of the War of Attrition along Israel's eastern borders and along the Suez Canal in the summer of 1970. The economic boom which in 1969/70 gathered momentum, due to the rapid buildup of defense works following the formal ceasefire with Egypt (August 1970) and the de facto ceasefire with Jordan (October 1970), fanned smoldering social tensions into life, revealing dissatisfaction with an apparent bias in income distribution along ethnic lines. The government responded by initiating a major move in the field of social policy, even though its budget was under enormous strain, caused both by defense expenditures and by absorption costs of immigrants as a new wave of immigration was swelling up. The new policy was implemented by significantly expanding social security: transfer payments doubled to 3.6 percent of GNP in the 45-month interval of the take-off (1970–1973). And while part of this leap in public sector expenditure was financed by a hefty increase in tax absorption (from 34 percent of GNP in 1969 to 42 percent in 1972), this still meant that the public sector deficit was well beyond 10 percent of GNP through September 1973 with full employment (by 1972, overfull employment). This deficit was financed mainly by (base) money creation.

The magnitude of these deficits clearly reveals the dominance of the treasury in its inevitable conflict with the central bank. The argument between these two protagonists in the macroeconomic arena was no secret, and was thoroughly covered in the media. But the Bank of Israel Law, which effectively gave the government direct access to central bank accommodation (subject only to the approval of the Knesset finance committee), meant that the monetary authority had almost no control over the volume of base money, and very little discretion with respect to the second component of the money supply—bank credit. On this second point, the Bank was restricted by the rule imposed by legislation that changes in commercial bank liquidity ratios were not at its ultimate discretion. Whenever the Bank of Israel wished to change these liquidity ratios, it had to go through the economic committee of the cabinet, where the governor of the Bank was a non-voting member.

Moreover, although the governor of the Bank, appointed for a five-year term, was not an outright government appointee, the central bank was in a very weak position for lack of a strong board of directors that could, after deliberation, spell out a considered central bank stance on the macroeconomic situation and the appropriate policy options.[3] This weakened the stance of the governor's position in the inevitable tug-of-war with the ministry of finance and other spending ministries, all of which were represented by their ministers in the cabinet's economic committee. The legislation that granted the government direct (and virtually unlimited) access to central bank accommodation and restricted the central bank's effect on commercial bank liquidity, combined with the segmentation of the commercial bank credit market, involving quotas of privileged credits the scope of which was set by the government's economic committee (chapters 2-5, 3-5, and 8-3), rendered the central bank effectively impotent.[4] The small size of the capital market and the traditional vehement opposition of the treasury to higher rates of return on government paper restricted the scope of open-market policy, the only tool the central bank could (formally) wield without the approval of the economic committee, in an attempt to counteract an expansionary fiscal policy. The deluge of money and inflation was the inevitable result.

Israel's monetary dilemma thus offers the first message: long-run considerations suggest that in "paper-standard environments" the legal stance and political stature of the central bank should be strong and strengthened. In practice, this means first and foremost that the Bank of Israel Law should explicitly prohibit central bank accommodation of any entity—government and/or business. Reasonable budget deficits, if any, should be financed by resort to the capital market, thereby inevitably affecting market interest rates and forcing the government to face up to market realities, which would clearly publicize the party responsible for pushing up the interest rates. Legislation should ensure that the central bank be master in its own house, which means that it should have sole discretion in matters of (commercial bank) liquidity ratios. Finally, the segmentation of the (bank) credit market by a quota system of privileged access to cheap credit should be avoided at all cost.

The lesson taught by the Bank's utter failure to prevent the rapid inflation of the money supply, first during the take-off and later on while inflation accelerated, is not just a matter of theory. One of the main items in the 1985 stabilization program was the elimination of the article in the Bank of Israel Law that allowed direct government access to central bank credit.[5] This amendment, passed just before the program was launched, was followed from 1987 onward, by a gradual elimination of privileged credit quotas until they were finally abolished. That allowed thereafter a corresponding, gradual extension of the scope of monetary policy across the board, allowing it to affect the volume of credit in toto and hence the supply of money. Were it not for these two changes—in the monetary legislation and the rules of the game in the bank credit market—the 1985 stabilization effort would have been doomed from the start.

THE COMPOSITION OF FISCAL POLICY: ITS LONG-RUN RELEVANCE

Fiscal policy played a major role in generating the take-off, and was a crucial element in the stabilization program. The former was due to the highly expansionary policy pursued in the early 1970s, and the success of the latter depended on the policy's volte-face in the mid-1980s retaining its newly restrictive stance. It is therefore obvious that the single operative magnitude in both contexts was the size of the deficit. But the opening (and later closure) of the gap between tax receipts and public sector expenditures could be implemented by a mix of measures operating on both the inflow to and outflow from the government's coffers. The precise composition of this expenditure-absorption mix is of very little interest from the monetary point of view. In the long run, however, the fiscal policy tools used—whether a reduction or expansion in the deficit is achieved by applying higher tax rates and absorption levels or by reducing (expanding) real government demand and transfer payments—does make a difference.

It was clearly the highly expansionary fiscal policy of the early 1970s, generated by a major leap of expenditures far greater than the corresponding rise in tax absorption, that pushed the system over the brink. In the full employment environment of the time, comparative price stability and budget deficits of around 5–10 percent of GDP were manifestly untenable. The huge deficits soon eroded the inflation tax inflows, as inflation took off and dragged the system into a vicious circle of rising prices, self-fulfilling inflationary expectations, and growing nominal budget deficits "papered over" by the printing press. The swelling flood of money accelerated the rising trend of domestic prices and of the exchange rate.

This lesson is suggested not only by the unfolding of events during the take-off of Israel's great inflation. It is also the message broadcast by the contrast between the (comparative) success of Israel's 1985 stabilization program and the dismal failure of similar stabilization efforts implemented by Argentina and Brazil at approximately the same time (see Chapter 6). The implementation of the Israeli program hinged on strict fiscal discipline being enforced from the very beginning. It involved a rapid reduction of the budget deficit to less than 1 percent of GDP in the program's first year. Although deficit levels were allowed to grow slightly, to about 2 percent of GDP, tight fiscal discipline was generally maintained. In contrast, the two Latin American economies succumbed within six months to the "old-time religion" and by the end of the 1980s the inflationary consequences had moved past the brink of hyperinflation.[6]

Another lesson offered by Israel's (and in the early 1990s also Argentina's) technique of reducing the budget deficit refers to the short- and long-run implications of the alternative mix of measures applied to reach that goal. As noted above, the mix of techniques chosen makes little difference from the monetary point of view; any reduction in the deficit, which means less (base) money creation and/or a lower volume of public sector borrowing in the capital market, makes it easier to pursue a highly restrictive monetary policy. This was indeed what happened in Israel, as indicated both by the fiscal data and by the two-digit real interest rates on bank credit, maintained for almost two years after the 1985 stabilization effort was launched.

In the long run, though, the composition of restrictive *fiscal* policy tools does make a difference. Tightening the tax screws rather than reducing government expenditure in an effort to reach a given level of fiscal deficit affects the behavior of businesses and households. Higher tax rates and expanding absorption levels mean greater government involvement in the economy, with unfavorable effects on efficiency and a smaller contribution of potentially rising productivity to the attempt to lead the economy onto a threshold of a stable price pattern. The failure to reduce the impact of government demand, while the reduction of aggregate demand is sine qua non for the success of a stabilization program, obviously requires a correspondingly greater reduction in the real demand of households and of the business sector, that is, of consumption expenditure and real business and household investment. This, in turn, means that the success of the stabilization effort requires a prolonged period of highly restrictive monetary policy, the close substitute of a restrictive, expenditure-dominated fiscal policy.

This was the strategy applied in the Israeli case, and succeeded in first reducing, then holding inflation down to the first target of (annual) 16–20 percent through 1989 and beyond. But this success took its toll in terms of the real economy. Initially, unemployment rose by a mere one percent or so (to 7 percent, which, for Israel, was quite high), but after two years the aftershock began to be felt in the business sector, involving the collapse of firms with household names, and major failures in the farming sector. Unemployment reached an unprecedented level of 9 percent in 1989.

This shows that the impact of a major reduction of inflation on the real economy is far stronger and more lasting than predicted by (extreme) monetarists. The Israeli experience suggests that in spite of a substantial though temporary cut of real wages across the board in 1985–86, implemented with the consent of labor, the upheaval in the business sector was inevitable in a system that had been operating in a highly inflationary environment for many years. The reason lies in inflationary expectations, which induced firms operating in an inflation-ridden environment to reduce the share of equity in their capital structure and rely more and more on bank credit to finance their activity. But this business strategy, clearly a clever one when inflation was accelerating and the real value of debt was continuously being eroded by rising prices, backfired when stabilization set in, when the real cost of debt was deliberately pushed up, and real interest rates abruptly soared from negative to very high positive rates. Hence, the longer demand is restricted by means of very tight monetary policy, the greater the strain on business, the more business failures, and the worse the employment consequences.

This, of course, means that the exact prescription and dosage of restrictive fiscal policy applied in the context of a stabilization policy does count. Its composition is not neutral in its effect on the level and structure of economic activity and thus on the long-run success of the policy itself. The message of the Israeli experience is that the greater the reduction in public sector expenditure in the mix designed to reduce the budget deficit, the less strict the required stringency of monetary policy in terms of both the level of interest rate and the duration of the monetary squeeze. In other words: the greater the reduction in government demand for real resources, the lower the required contribution of the business sector and households to the restraint of aggregate demand; hence, too, the lower the probability of business failures and the smaller the required reduction in business and household investment. This has obvious consequences for both employment and production in the short run, and for productivity and growth in the long run.

THE COST OF INFLATION

The above considerations are obviously linked to another, highly relevant issue—the real cost of inflation—which is evidently much higher than the so-called "shoe-leather cost" (the cost to households and businesses of negotiating more financial transactions because of rapid inflation).[7] Although part of this "shoe-leather" component can be relatively easily approximated, its quantitative significance is usually of secondary importance. The main component of the cost of high and accelerating inflation is due to the persistent misallocation of labor capital and enterprise induced by the chaotic nature of relative prices, which confounds any attempt at prediction, even in the short run. This distorted price structure, including the level and the structure of real interest rates and the exchange rate, sends confusing signals to operators and therefore breeds a major misallocation of resources. The results do not surface immediately after the launching of a stabilization program; as noted above, in Israel, the magnitude of these costs became apparent only about three to four years after the stabilization program was launched, once inflationary expectations had finally settled down to a relatively low two-digit level while real interest rates in the money and short-term capital market remained in the two-digit (annual) range.[8] The steep drop in inflation rates, which allowed much more stable prices and price relatives, combined with high real interest rates, drove some well-known firms to the wall. Several of these highly leveraged firms, which had been operating with next to no equity—a profitable strategy in an era of high and accelerating inflation—soon began to feel the pinch. As the ''sellers' markets'' which they had enjoyed for over a decade slipped away, and with the cost of maintaining inventories rising continuously, they began to close down production lines and to shed labor. The beginning of this shake-up was put off for a couple of years because most of these large firms enjoyed considerable privileged bank credit quotas that reduced average interest cost. But as such privileged credit quotas were continuously reduced, to give greater scope to (restrictive) monetary policy, these firms had to move into the ''free'' (and more expensive) credit market to maintain both their inventory/output ratios and their level of activity. The emergence of buyers' markets and the leap in the (interest) cost of inventories meant that the capital gains, from which these firms had been benefiting for years, began slipping away and that the profitability of investment projects was eroded by higher marginal interest rates. The shelving of investment projects and a reduction of the level of activity, thus the shedding of labor, which began in earnest in 1988, were the inevitable consequences, even among firms that had successfully weathered the storm. Other firms collapsed entirely, and sacked their entire labor force.[9]

Thus, the immediate claim made by the authorities about the ''successful stabilization'' program—the taming of inflation at minor costs in terms of employment—had to be qualified. The small rise in unemployment, from 6 to 7 percent of the labor force immediately after the launching of the program, followed even by a small reduction (in 1987 and the beginning of 1988) to around 6 percent, was soon overtaken by events. In 1989, after major tremors in manufacturing and farming, unemployment had climbed beyond 9 percent, a level unheard of in Israel for almost 25 years. Between 1987 and 1989 about 3–4 percent of the total number of employees were forced to leave firms that either went out of business altogether or substantially reduced their volume of operations.[10]

The message broadcast by these developments in Israel's real economy is clear: stabilization sooner or later causes a major shake-up of the branch and firm structure and pushes up unemployment rates. It is, however, also clear that a less restrictive monetary policy, which would have allowed lower real interest rates by, say 1988, would also have eased the pressure on the business sector, thus encouraging a more early revival of investment and the level of activity. The inability of government to curtail its demand for real resources, which would have forced the public sector to reduce invisible unemployment by shedding labor, required a more stringent monetary policy whose impact, in terms of much tighter money and capital markets, was inevitably felt in the business sector, which was eventually forced to release more labor. The price of avoiding unemployment in the public sector in the immediate wake of stabilization was thus paid in the business sector, and ultimately took the form of a delay in the restructuring of employment and of the labor market. Inevitably, it also reduced the growth rate of productivity.

THE IMPLICATIONS OF THE ROBUST DEMAND FUNCTION FOR MONEY

Another interesting feature of the great inflation in Israel was the robustness of the demand for money. Several studies on the demand for money, whose results were discussed in chapters 2 and 3, found that the demand function for money was not affected by the rising rate of inflation during the whole take-off period.[11] On the other hand, these same studies show that later, as inflation was moving up from a 20 percent annual average at the (end of) take-off stage to about 40 percent (in 1974–77), the demand for money began to decline. This development, apparently induced by expectations, and well past the take-off interval, provided additional fuel for the inflationary process. The robustness of the demand for money during a lengthy interval of about 45 months, during which inflation rose from an annual rate of about 2–3 percent to 20 percent, suggests that single-digit inflation rates and even somewhat higher rates do not significantly affect the demand for money. This probably holds only for a relatively brief period of time, say, two to three years.[12]

This feature offers a reasonable explanation of the propensity of the political community operating in a "paper (money) standard" environment to opt for a highly expansionary fiscal policy even in a full employment context. During a time interval of such a length, which, in terms of the political horizon, might seem close to eternity, that same behavioral feature that expresses the "consumer surplus" of holding and using of money also offers governments an opportunity to finance the budget deficit by resorting to the printing press. Prosperity in the markets, fueled by the induced low nominal interest rates owing to the (temporary) stability of the demand function for money, surfaces immediately, whereas inflation appears only after a substantial lag; in a widely open economy, inflation is further delayed by the endogenously created trade deficit. The combination of a paper standard environment and a robust demand function for money—at inflation rates of, say, 10 percent or somewhat more—is thus a strong temptation and a perfect scenario for the political community to inflate the system.

When this natural tendency to follow political instincts also seemed warranted by economic considerations, the option adopted by governments in democratic countries was obvious. The economic justification for an expansionary fiscal policy in a full employment context rested on the notion of the Phillips Curve trade-off which was at the height of its popularity in the 1960s and early 1970s.[13] This notion suggested an explicit menu, which was apparently just what government sought; they could opt for a higher level of activity at the cost of somewhat higher inflation. The implication was that the rate of inflation was considered to be fully under the control of government. This implicit line of reasoning inevitably excluded the reaction of the public—businesses and households—to a prolonged and quantitatively meaningful inflationary process.[14] Nor did it take into consideration potential cost-push factors that could accelerate the "chosen" inflation rate and thus activate (hitherto) dormant expectations of business and households.

THE LINKAGE CONTRAPTION

Furthermore, the belief that government could prevent runaway inflation is one of the reasons why the political community attempted to control its symptoms rather than its causes. Hence, the propensity to implement linkages—wages to prices, prices to "costs," debt to prices or to the rate of exchange and vice versa, and, finally, taxes to prices. These were, of course, not adopted all at once. The Israeli comprehensive linkage system—a nightmare for the designers of the 1985 stabilization program and one of the hardest nuts that had to be cracked by those responsible for its implementation—was not the result of a comprehensive design. It was erected bit by bit over almost 40 years, some of its elements having been set up in the 1940s and 1950s. Yet sooner rather than later, inflationary expectations lock onto the linkage system, which emerges as an autonomous mechanism—an automatic pilot driving inflation with no necessary reference to fiscal and or monetary stimuli.

The Israeli experience manifested all of these features—a paper standard, an initial robust demand function for money, a tangle of linkages made up of a comprehensive and complicated network—and also underlines another crucial fact. The loss of a nominal anchor, the inevitable result of surging inflation and expectations driven by rising prices and a complicated setup of linkages, makes it very difficult to design a stabilization policy that can be implemented at low cost in terms of the level of activity, employment, and growth. Though an instantaneous cut of the Gordian knot—an immediate abolition of all linkages neutralizing inflationary expectations—would have made a significant difference to the success of the stabilization program of 1985, both in terms of the length of time it would take to reach the (low) inflation target and in terms of the (low inflation) target itself. Such a move was not on the agenda. The reason is obvious: the faith in a government that can stick to its guns on economic matters is inevitably low after a long phase of inflation; economic agents are reluctant to abandon their own defenses—their specific linkage—though they would be happy if others would. This offers another message, perhaps the most important one: the successful implementation of a stabilization program requires an early (if not immediate) positive change in the credibility of government, which undoubtedly is a difficult feat in such a context.

NOTES

1. If the government attempts to maintain an "official rate," that race between domestic prices and the exchange rate is manifested in the black-market rate, an inherent phenomenon in such a situation.

2. In most cases it involves a government reshuffle at the personal level and usually also on the political plane. A wider parliamentary basis of a government, which attempts to quench inflation, is almost a sine que non of such an exercise.

3. The revolving door feature of the central bank governor's office, characteristic of Latin American countries, does not apply to Israel. In the 40-year history of the Bank of Israel, it had only six governors, the last of whom had not yet completed his first five-year term of office. The absence of a strong board of directors clearly restricts the power of the Bank as an autonomous actor in the realm of money, and broadcasts weakness. The so-called advisory committee, whose members are appointed simultaneously to a two-year term of office, is evidently neither purported to be nor is it in practice a substitute for a board of directors. The simultaneous appointment of the committee and its chairman inevitably reduces its power vis-à-vis the government.

4. Israel's central bank law, prepared in the early 1950s, was finally enacted in 1954. To a very great extent it reflected the mood of the times, wedded to the oversimplified, "diagonal cross" Keynesian model of saving and investment that, to many members of the profession, suggested that "money is not relevant." This, on the whole, was the feature of several central bank laws enacted at that time in Latin America and countries that had gained independence in the late 1940s and early 1950s, such as India.

This attitude toward the monetary dimension of macroeconomics, though widespread, was not all-embracing. The Bundesbank Law, enacted in 1957, which established it statutorily as the "protector of the currency," leaned the other way. The transformation in attitudes on this matter gained momentum in the wake of M. Friedman's presidential address (to the American Economic Association) in 1968, where he made the modest claim that "money is relevant."

5. The involvement of the State Department delegation in the preparation of the 1985 stabilization program, supported by a $1.5 billion grant (in two tranches spread over two years), was probably crucial in the government's concession to the demand for a change in the central bank legislation. This change substantially altered the balance of power in the monetary arena between the ministry of finance and the Bank of Israel in favor of the latter.

6. In 1989, four years after the launching of the previous attempt, the new Menem administration had to start from scratch. Menem's stabilization effort, launched in the summer of 1989 after his election to the presidency, succeeded (after two initial failures) in reducing Argentina's price inflation to a low two-digit rate by the middle of 1991, and to a single-digit rate in 1993/4. This involved, of course, a major reduction in the budget deficit and a structural change in the constitution of the central bank. According

to the new central bank law it was virtually transformed into a currency board, thus effectively preventing the creation of base money on the basis of explicit government credit (Barkai, 1993).

7. An indicator of these costs is the significant expansion of the banking sector in terms of employment and other inputs in a period of rapid inflation. Kleiman (1984) offers a crude estimate of this kind of cost of inflation in Israel. Although his estimate was made when inflation was close to its peak, later events show that his technique of estimating that type of extra cost proved very useful. As inflation came down and settled in the low two-digit range from 1986 onward, the banking system reduced the number of its branches by about 6 percent and shed about 15 percent of its labor force within three years. (*Bank Supervisor Statistical Bulletin* 1994, table II-1)

8. Real interest rates on short-term, non-privileged bank credit exceeded 20 percent through 1988, and were still about 10 percent in 1989. The net cost to business, liable to income tax was lower—about 10 percent through 1988 and about 5 percent in 1989 (*Report 1989*, table VII-9, p. 278). Eligibility for a quota of privileged bank credit naturally reduced the average cost of credit to the firm. The size of the quota was consequently a major determinant of the average cost of credit, and thus of enterprise profitability. It goes without saying that the quota had a property value, and could be (indirectly) traded in the market.

9. In the farm sector, where operators were entitled to relatively high credit quotas (in terms of output), the squeeze generated by the continuous erosion of these quotas (finally eliminated by 1989) was enormous. Many farmers were forced to suspend activities in farming, and others accumulated mountains of debt. The high indebtedness of this sector required a major bailout at the cost of the taxpayer in the early 1990s.

10. These figures refer to only major firms in which the trimming down of the work force due to a reduction of lines (or their going out of business) can be easily traced. The significance of the 3–4 percent figure is much greater than the number itself suggests, since the overhaul in the structure of employment was borne entirely by the business sector. This sector was at that time responsible for the employment of only 70 percent of the total work force. Furthermore, this figure does not include the loss of employment in farming.

11. See Chapter 2, pp. 33–34 and notes 19–21, and Chapter 3, pp. 53–54 and note 10.

12. This proposition probably does not hold in a secular context—if inflation proceeds indefinitely at similar low rates. The Israeli experience does not warrant the claim that in the case of secular process of inflation at, say, 10–20 percent, the demand function for money would not be affected. We have no observation for an interval longer than about 45 months. Yet this interval is undoubtedly long in terms of the political horizon.

13. In spite of Friedman's (1968, p. 11) presidential address to the American Economic Association, in which he argued that the Phillips Trade-off was, at most, relevant in the short run only, many members of the profession in the early 1970s, probably most of them, were still referring to the feasibility of a Phillips Curve trade-off without qualifications. The impact of that message on the political community and on public opinion was quite obvious.

14. In technical terms this means that the accepted notion of the Phillips Curve hypothesis focuses on the slope of the curve, to the exclusion of factors that determine its location in the plane. This location is, however, not determined by factors exogenous to the system; it is affected by (endogenous) expectations of labor households and businesses, among others.

Figures and Tables (Part II)

Figure 4
Price Patterns (CPI) (average monthly rate of change, percent)

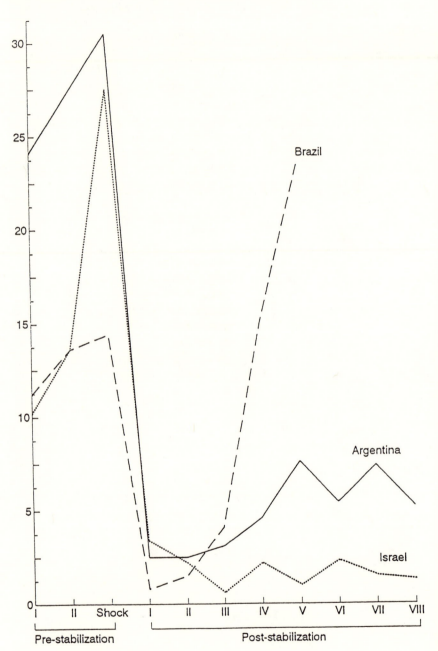

Source: Table 21.

Figure 5
Official and "Parallel" Exchange Rates (average monthly rate of change, percent)

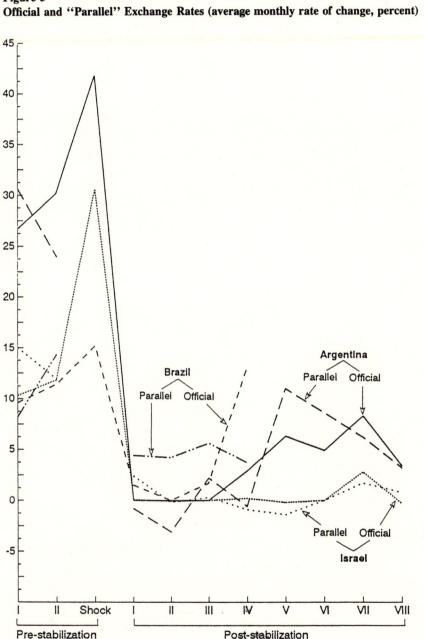

Figure 6
Premium on Unofficial Exchange Rate (ratio of parallel to official exchange rate)

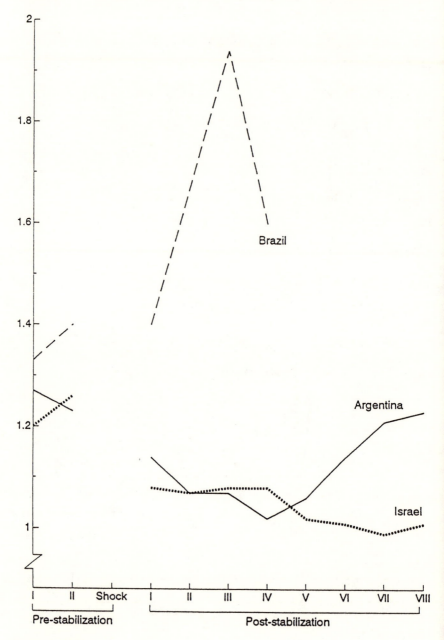

Source: Table 21.

Figure 7
Unemployment Levels (percent)

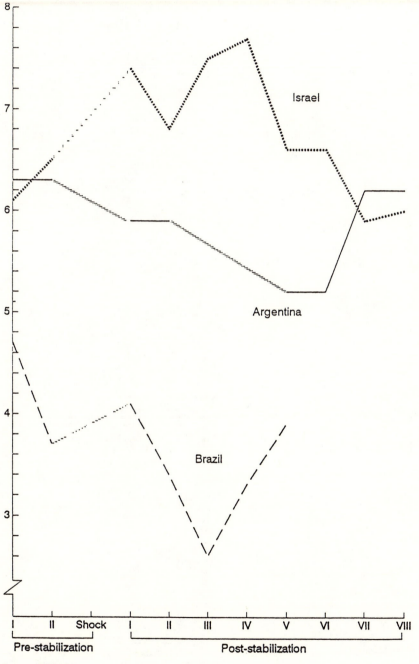

Figure 8
Public Sector Deficit (percent of GDP)

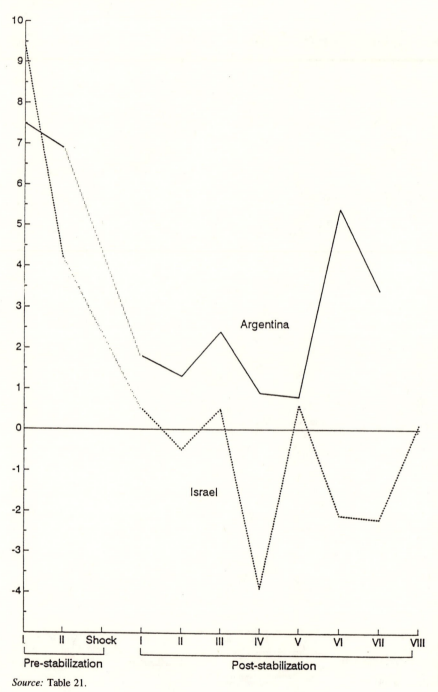

Source: Table 21.

Figure 9
Real Interest Rates (annualized lending rates, percent)

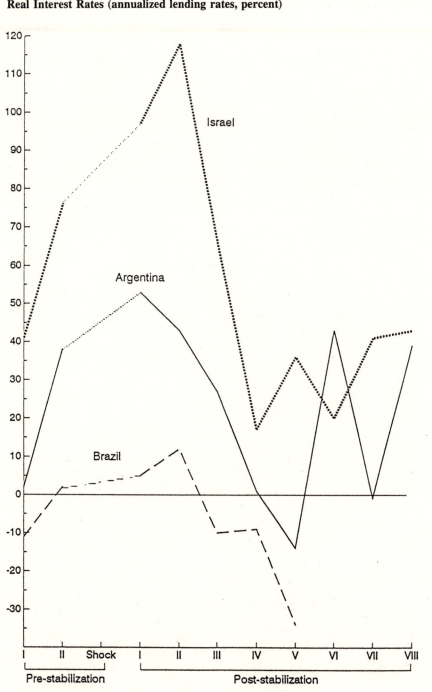

Source: Table 21.

Figure 10
Bank of Israel Marginal Interest Rates (monthly rates, percent)

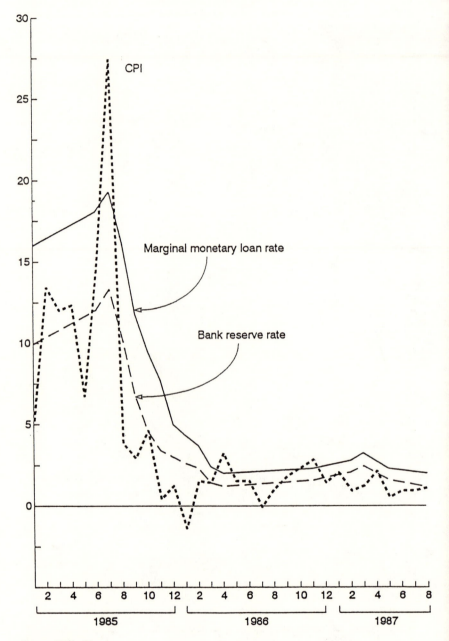

Source: Table 26.

Figure 11
Real Monthly Interest Rates: Israel (percent)

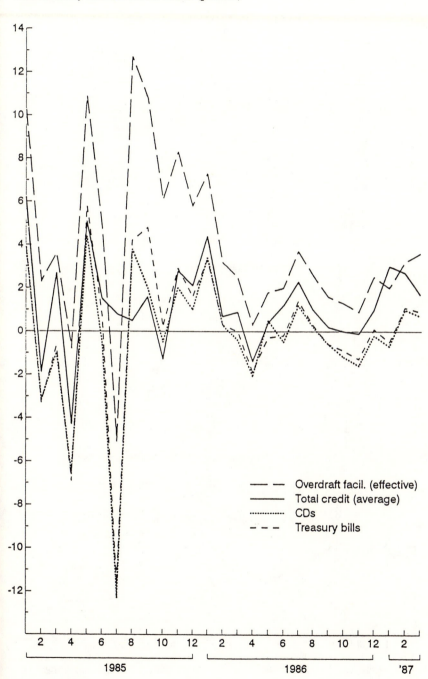

Figure 12
Selected Lending Rates: Israel (quarterly data; percent)

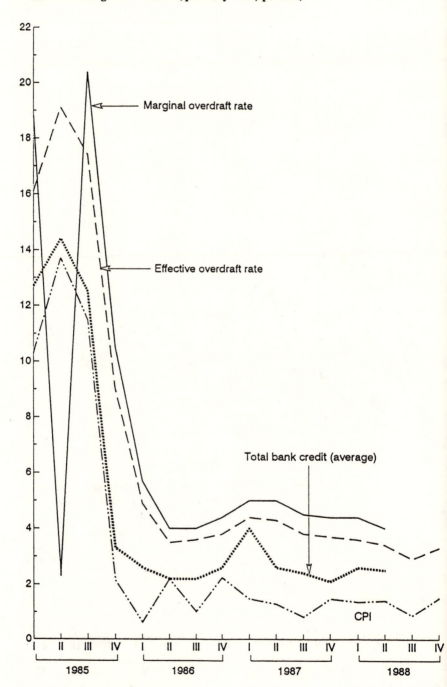

Source: Table 24 and underlying sources.

Figure 13
Selected Deposit Rates: Israel (monthly data; percent)

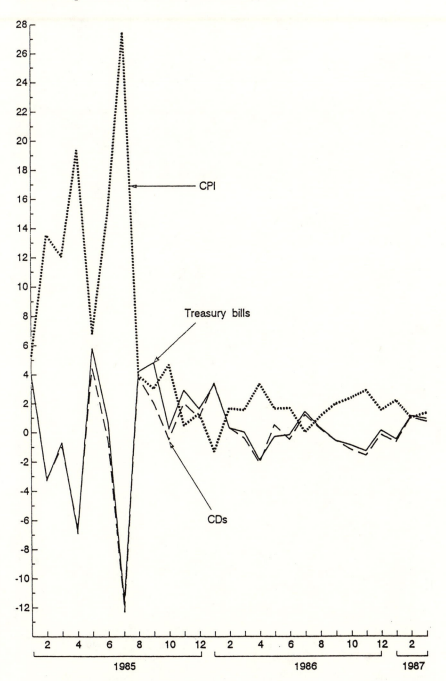

Figure 14
Real Monetary Aggregates: Israel (Index: June 1985 = 100)

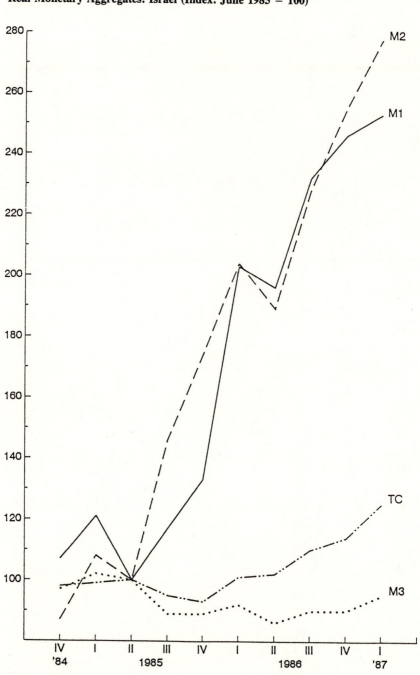

Source: Table 28.

Table 21
Argentina, Brazil, Israel: Pre- and Post-Stabilization Quarterly Indicators

	Pre-stabilization		Shock	Post-stabilization							
	I	II		I^a	II	III	IV	V	VI	VII	VIII
A. Prices CPI (average monthly rates of change—percent)											
1. Argentina	24.1	27.3	30.5	2.5	2.5	3.1	4.6	7.6	5.4	7.4	5.2
2. Brazil[b]	11.2	13.6	14.4	0.8	1.5	4.1	15.0	23.4	...	...	...
3. Israel	10.2	13.6	27.5	3.4	2.2	0.6	2.2	1.0	2.3	1.5	1.3
B. Exchange rates (average monthly rates of change—percent)											
1. Argentina i) Official	26.7	30.2	41.8	0.0	0.0	0.0	2.9	6.3	4.9	8.3	3.4
ii) Parallel	30.6	24.0	—	-0.8	-3.1	2.2	-0.6	11.0	8.6	6.2	3.2
iii) Ratio[c]	1.27	1.23	—	1.14	1.07	1.07	1.02	1.06	1.14	1.21	1.23
2. Brazil i) Official	9.6	11.4	15.2	1.5	0.0	1.7	13.0	...	...	...	...
ii) Parallel	8.2	14.3	—	4.4	4.2	5.6	3.7	...	...	...	...
iii) Ratio	1.3	1.4	—	1.40	1.67	1.94	1.6	...	...	...	...
3. Israel i) Official	10.3	11.8	30.6	0.1	-0.1	0.0	0.2	-0.2	0.0	2.8	-0.3
ii) Black market	15.0	11.9	—	2.4	-0.2	0.3	-0.9	-1.4	0.0	1.7	0.8
iii) Ratio	1.20	1.26	—	1.08	1.07	1.08	1.08	1.02	1.01	0.99	1.01
C. Unemployment (rates—percent)											
1. Argentina[d]	6.3 (7.5)			5.9 (7.4)		n.a. (6.4)		5.2 (7.3)		6.2 (8.2)	
2. Brazil	4.7	3.7		4.1	3.4	2.6	3.3	3.9	...	...	...
3. Israel	6.1	6.5		7.4	6.8	7.5	7.7	6.6	6.6	5.9	6.0

Table 21 (Continued)

D. Deficit of public sector (% of GNP)

1. Argentina[e] a)	7.5	6.9	1.8	1.3	2.4	0.9	0.8	5.4	3.4	...
b)	11.9	11.9	3.0	2.2	4.2	2.2	2.1	7.6	5.3	...
2. Israel[f]	9.4	4.2	0.5	-0.5	0.5	-3.9	0.6	-2.1	-2.2	0.1

E. Real interest rates (annual lending rates—percent)

1. Argentina i) Regulated	-30	-26	15	26	18	2	-18	18	-16	14
ii) Unregulated	2	38	53	43	27	1	-14	43	-1	39
2. Brazil — overnight rate[g]	-11	2	5	12	-10	-9	-34	...	...	...
3. Israel[h] i) Overdraft facilities	41[i]	76	97	118	66	17	36	20	41	43
ii) Total bank credit	4[i]	9	12	15	26	1	15	4	34	17

Sources:

A. Line 1: Canavese and Di Tella (1988), pp. 174–75; line 2: Modiano, 1988, table 5A-3, p. 247; line 3: Bank of Israel, *Recent Economic Developments*, No. 44, September 1988, table 21; line 3.iii: Liviatan (1986), p. 21, table 5.

B. Line 1: Canavese and Di Tella (1988), table 4A-2, pp. 174–75, and Machinea and Fanelli (1988), table 3.14, p. 143; line 2: Modiano (1988), table 5A-10, p. 254; line 3: unpublished data from the Bank of Israel.

C. Argentina: Argentine National Statistical Office; Brazil: Banco Central do Brasil, Boletim Mensal, 3/88, table 2.2.11; Israel: Bruno (1985), table 10.

D. Line 1: Machinea and Fanelli (1988), table 3.10, p. 137; line 3: Bruno (1985), table 17, columns 5 and 6.

E. Line 1: Machinea and Fanelli (1988), table 3.9, p. 135; line 2: see footnote g; line 3: Bruno (1985), table 21, columns 1, 5, 11.

[a] Refers to price and exchange-rate changes in two out of the three months of the quarter. It thus excludes the premediated price and exchange-rate shocks in the first month of implementation. In Argentina and Israel the entry accordingly excludes the price change of July 1985, and in Brazil, that of February 1986. These are entered in the "shock" column (for Argentina the "shock" column represents June 1985).

The Argentina plan was launched in the middle of June. Its June price figure presumably reflects a component of the implementation price shock and the June price data are excluded from the last quarter before implementation.

[b] The Cruzado Plan was launched in February 1986. The pre-stabilization quarters accordingly refer to August-October 1985 and to November 1985-January 1986. The entries for the first post-stabilization quarter are the average price and exchange-rate changes for the March–June 1986 four-month interval.

[c] Mean quarterly ratio of parallel market dollar exchange rate to official rate.

[d] Unemployment data for Argentina are semiannual estimates. For 1985, they were available for May and November; in 1986, for June and November; in 1987, for April and October. The figures in the table accordingly apply to two quarters: the top line represents the national average unemployment rate, figures in parentheses are "underemployment rates" for Buenos Aires, which offer additional relevant information on the stage of the labor market.

[e] (a) Deficit of the non-financial public sector, cash basis. (b) Total deficit including the "central bank deficit."

[f] Deficit of the non-financial public sector, cash basis. Interest payments on domestic national debt are included in the expenditures.

[g] The Brazilian series was derived from a series of overnight rates and a corresponding series of inflation rates in terms of CPI. Both series are from data of Central Bank of Brazil and from Getulio Vargas Foundation, *Conjuntura Economica*. This interest-rate series sets the floor to the interest rate structure. The very great variance of Brazilian inflation, and an interest rate sometimes leading and sometimes lagging after prices, generate substantial monthly changes in real rates, the variance of which is not fully revealed by the quarterly average of ex post real interest rates. The ex ante (and economically more relevant) rates therefore presumably varied considerably.

[h] The series represents interest rates on bank credit. The overdraft series is a weighted mean of rates charged for overdrafts, and penalty rates for exceeding the "agreed" limits of such facilities. It is therefore a close approximation to the marginal rate of interest, though somewhat lower than that rate. The total bank credit series represents a weighted average of interest rates charged on short- and medium-term bank credit. It is significantly lower than the corresponding overdraft rates, since overdrafts were (initially) only about 10–11 percent of total outstanding bank credit.

[i] Mean of February–March, 1985.

Table 22
Selected Monetary Indicators (percent)

| | Ratio of "money" to nominal domestic uses[a] | | | | Foreign currency financial asset ratio[c] |
| | M1 | M2 | M3 | M3–M2[b] | |
	(1)	(2)	(3)	(4)	(5)
1966	14.9	n.a.	n.a.	n.a.	n.a.
1970	11.9	22.2	25.6	3.4	n.a.
1976	7.6	13.3	18.2	4.9	n.a.
1980	4.3	5.7	18.5	12.8	n.a.
1981	3.5	5.2	17.2	12.0	n.a.
1982	3.0	5.4	16.9	11.6	14.5
1983	2.5	5.5	17.9	12.4	22.5
1984	1.7	4.8	20.4	15.6	32.1
1985	2.2	8.8	22.7	13.9	—
1st half	1.5	4.6	...	...	36.6
2nd half	2.9	13.2	...	...	28.3
1986	3.5	12.2	20.8	8.6	—
1st half	2.9	10.6	19.6	9.0	26.5
2nd half	4.1	13.6	21.7	8.0	24.0
1987	4.3	16.1	21.7	5.6	18.4
1988	4.9	16.9	21.7	4.8	19.8

Sources: Bank of Israel, *Annual Report 1986*. Columns (1) through (3): table H-8, p. 249; data for 1987 and 1988 are from the same table in *Annual Report 1987* and *1988*, p. 242 and p. 247, respectively; column (5), table H-13, p. 289 (Hebrew).

[a]Domestic uses = GDP *plus* import surplus. Since the M_1 figures—from which the annual corresponding "money" entries were calculated—were means of monetary data, the ratios entered in the table refer approximately to the middle of each period.

The definitions of M1 and M2 are the conventional definitions. M2 is "non-linked sheqel money"—currency and bank deposits including CDs. M3 is the sum of M1 and PATAM (foreign-currency-linked) deposits, which from 1977 onward were highly liquid. The value of the M3 ratios also depends on the comparative movement of prices and the nominal official exchange rate.

[b]The ratio of foreign-currency-linked "money" to domestic uses.

[c]Ratio of (net) assets linked to foreign currency (excluding bank shares) to net financial asset portfolio of the non-financial sector. The data refer to end-of-period balances.

Table 23
Composition of Commercial Bank Credit, 1984–88ᵃ (percent)

		1984	1985	1986	1987	1988
1.	Free	44.6	54.5	71.0	80.4	85.8
	a. Linked	25.2	22.1	23.3	27.3	30.1
	b. Non-linked	19.4	32.3	47.7	53.2	55.7
2.	Directed	55.4	45.6	29.0	19.6	14.2
	a. Exports	37.8	34.9	25.1	16.2	12.2
	b. Fuel	17.6	10.7	3.9	3.4	2.0
3.	Total	100.0	100.1	100.0	100.0	100.0

Sources: Bank of Israel, *Annual Report 1988*, table 8A-2, p. 252 (English); and similar tables in
   Annual Reports, 1985–87.
ᵃEnd-of-year balances.

Table 24
Selected Commercial Bank Interest Rates and Financial Margins, 1985–88 (average monthly rates, percent)

	1985				1986				1987				1988			
	I	II	III	IV	I	II	III	IV	I	II	III	IV	I	II	III	IV
1. Average rate on total bank credit	12.7	14.4	12.5	3.3	2.6	2.2	2.2	2.6	4.0	2.6	2.4	2.1	2.6	2.5	…	…
2. Rates of overdraft facilities																
a. Effective[a]	16.1	19.1	17.4	9.0	4.9	3.5	3.6	3.8	4.4	4.3	3.8	3.7	3.6	3.4	2.9	3.3
b. Marginal	18.8	2.3	20.4	10.5	5.7	4.0	4.0	4.4	5.0	5.0	4.5	4.4	4.4	4.0	…	…
3. CD rates	10.1	12.4	8.2	3.0	1.7	1.1	1.2	1.3	1.8	1.5	1.0	1.1	1.0	0.8	0.8	1.0
4. Financial margin[b] (2a. – 3.)	6.0	6.7	9.2	6.0	3.2	2.4	2.4	2.5	2.6	2.8	2.8	2.6	2.6	2.6	2.1	2.3

Sources: Bank of Israel, *Recent Economic Developments*, No. 43, March 1988, and No. 44, September 1988, table 21.
[a]Weighted mean of interest on overdraft facilities and a penalty rate for exceeding the approved credit line.
[b]Since corresponding average interest rates on total bank credit were significantly lower than overdraft rates, the financial margins calculated here exaggerate banks' profit margins.

Table 25
Rates of Change of Selected Monetary Aggregates[a]

		H (1)	M1 (2)	M2 (3)	M3 (4)	M3[a] (5)	TC (6)	FC (7)	CPI (8)
		(Annual rates—percent)							
1984		454	354	421	485	486	487	494	445
1985		667	257	470	163	159	172	184	185
1986		34	121	75	21	23	46	68	19.6
1987		44	51	48	25	28	60	78	16.1
1988		-24	11	-1	14	15	42	48	16.4
		(Monthly rates—percent)							
1985	I	11.9	15.0	18.6	12.4	12.8	10.6	10.7	10.3
	II	8.7	6.6	10.6	12.7	12.1	13.9	14.1	13.7
	July	163.3	18.4	57.5	16.0	14.2	17.5	14.0	27.5
	III	49.5	16.9	25.9	6.7	6.3	8.9	10.0	3.5[b]
	IV	8.3	6.7	8.2	2.1	2.1	1.7	2.0	2.1
1986	I	3.1	15.7	6.1	1.9	2.2	3.4	5.3	0.6
	II	-2.5	0.9	-0.4	-0.2	-0.8	2.4	4.1	2.2
	III	8.2	7.0	7.6	2.6	3.2	3.6	4.4	1.0
	IV	1.2	4.2	6.0	2.0	2.4	3.3	3.8	2.2
1987	I	7.2	2.4	4.5	3.3	3.1	4.6	4.9	1.5

Memorandum item (CPI percent):

1985	Apr.	May	June	July	Aug.	Sept.	Oct.	Nov.	Dec.
	19.4	6.8	14.9	27.5	3.9	3.0	4.7	0.5	1.3

Sources: Column (1): Bank of Israel, *Annual Report 1985*, table H-6a, p. 306; and the same tables for *1986–88*, in corresponding *Annual Reports*; Columns (2)–(5): Bank of Israel, *Annual Report 1985*, table H-5a, p. 306, and table H-7a, p. 308, the same tables from *Annual Report 1986–88*, pp. 262 and 264 and *Recent Economic Developments*, No. 44, September 1988, table 19; Columns (6)–(7): *Annual Report 1987*, table 20; Column (8): *Annual Report 1987*, table B, p. 10 and *Recent Economic Developments*, No. 41, table B. Entries for 1988, according to Bank of Israel, *Annual Report 1988*, table H-10, p. 281.

[a]H—"Wide monetary base"—is slightly different from the so-called narrow base. See definition and data in Bank of Israel, *Annual Report 1985*, table H-6a, p. 307, and similar tables in later *Annual Reports*. The definitions of M1 and M2 are the conventional definitions, M3 is the sum of M2 and PATAM (foreign-exchange-linked) deposits: M3[a] is M2 *plus* total PATAM deposits exclusive of a specific component of the total—deposits originating from "restitution payments." TC is total bank credit. FC is the "free" credit component of total bank credit. See Table 3 and Chapter 7—Credit market segmentation. The rates of change were derived from end-of-period data.

[b]Average of August and September 1985 only.

Table 26
Some Indicators of Bank of Israel Monetary Controls

A. Required liquidity ratios (percent) on:

	1985					1986		1987	
	June	Jul. 4	Jul. 11	Jul. 25	Aug. 1	Mar. 13	May 15	Feb. 12	Apr. 1
1. Current accounts	35	35	35	45	50	45	38	30	34
2. Time deposits[a]	8	12	23	33	36	25[b]	20	20	20
3. Certificates of Deposit	9	13	28	38	43	43	38	30	34

B. Interest rates on (monthly, percent):

	1985								1986					1987			
	1	6	7	8	9	10	11	12	1	2	3	4	11	2	3	5	8
1. Monetary loan:[c]	16.0	18.1	19.3	16.1	11.8	9.5	7.7	5.0	4.3	3.7	2.4	2.0[e]	2.3	2.8	3.2	2.3	2.0
2. Reserves[d]	10.0	12.1	13.3	10.3	6.8	4.6	3.4	3.0	2.6	2.3	1.4	1.2[e]	1.6	2.1	2.5	1.7	1.2
Memorandum item:																	
CPI	5.3	14.9	27.5	3.9	3.0	4.7	0.5	1.3	-1.3	1.6	1.5	3.3	2.9	1.0	1.3	0.6	1.2

Sources: Liquidity ratios are from Bank of Israel, *Annual Report 1985*, table I-2, and the same table from succeeding *Annual Reports*. Data on interest rates on monetary loans and reserves are from *Recent Economic Developments*, No. 44, table 21.

a Liquidity ratio on time deposits for one month.
b Reduction effective January 16, 1986.
c Marginal rate.
d Interest rates paid by the bank on highest reserve bracket. The first bracket of required reserves does not carry any interest.
e This rate was maintained for the coming six months, through September 1986.

Table 27
Estimates of Ex Post Real Interest Rates, 1985(I)–87(I)

	Monthly rates[a]						Annualized rates			
	Overdraft facilities		Total credit (average)	CDs	Treasury bills	Time deposits[b]	Over-draft facilities (effective)	Total credit (average)	CDs	Treasury bills
	Effective	Marginal								
A. Monthly rates—percent										
1985										
Jan.	10.3	12.8	6.2	3.9	3.9	4.0	224.3	105.8	58.3	58.3
Feb.	2.3	4.6	-1.9	-3.2	-3.3	-3.2	31.4	-25.3	-45.9	-47.8
March	3.6	6.1	2.7	-1.0	-0.7	-1.2	52.9	37.6	-12.6	-8.7
April	-0.8	2.6	-4.3	-6.6	-6.9	-7.0	-10.0	-65.7	-115.3	-122.7
May	10.9	14.1	5.1	4.4	5.8	4.2	246.7	81.6	67.7	96.7
June	4.8	8.5	1.5	-0.6	0.7	-0.4	75.6	19.6	-7.4	8.7
July	-5.1	-2.2	0.8	-12.3	-11.7	-12.8	-81.6	10.0	-302.3	-277.3
Aug.	12.7	15.9	0.5	3.8	4.2	2.7	319.8	6.2	56.4	63.8
Sept.	10.8	12.9	1.6	2.0	4.8	1.8	242.4	20.9	26.8	75.5
Oct.	6.1	8.2	-1.3	-0.5	0.2	-0.8	103.5	-16.7	-6.1	2.4
Nov.	8.3	9.7	2.8	2.0	2.9	2.3	160.3	39.9	26.8	40.9
Dec.	5.8	6.8	2.1	1.0	1.6	1.0	96.7	28.3	12.7	20.9
1986										
Jan.	7.3	8.2	4.4	3.4	3.3	3.4	132.9	67.7	49.4	47.6
Feb.	3.2	4.1	0.7	0.3	0.3	0.2	45.9	8.7	3.7	3.7
March	2.5	3.1	0.9	-0.4	0.0	-0.5	34.4	11.4	-4.9	0.0
April	0.3	0.7	-1.4	-2.1	-1.9	-2.1	3.5	-15.1	-22.8	20.9
May	1.8	2.3	0.4	0.5	-0.3	-0.5	23.5	4.8	5.7	-3.5
June	2.0	2.5	1.2	-0.5	-0.2	-0.4	26.4	15.1	-5.7	-2.3
July	3.7	4.1	2.3	1.2	1.4	1.3	54.6	31.4	15.4	18.2
Aug.	2.6	3.0	1.0	0.2	0.3	0.3	35.6	12.5	2.4	3.6
Sept.	1.6	2.0	0.2	-0.6	-0.6	-0.5	20.6	2.4	-6.8	-6.8
Oct.	1.3	1.7	0.0	-1.2	-0.9	-0.9	16.3	0.0	-13.2	-10.1
Nov.	0.9	1.4	-0.1	-1.6	-1.3	-1.3	11.4	-1.2	-20.9	-16.8
Dec.	2.5	3.2	1.0	-0.2	0.1	0.1	34.4	12.7	-2.4	1.2
1987										
Jan.	2.0	2.5	3.0	-0.7	-0.5	-0.5	26.8	42.6	-8.7	-6.1
Feb.	3.2	3.8	2.7	1.0	1.1	1.3	45.9	37.7	12.7	14.0
March	3.6	4.1	1.7	0.7	0.9	1.1	52.9	22.4	8.7	11.4
B. Quarterly average of monthly rates—percent										
1985 I[c]	3.0	5.4	0.4	-2.1	-2.0	-2.1	42.6	4.9	-28.3	-26.8
II	4.8	8.3	0.7	-1.0	-0.3	-1.2	75.5	8.7	-12.6	-3.7
July	-5.1	-2.2	0.8	-12.3	-11.7	-12.8	-81.6	10.0	-302.3	-277.3
III[d]	11.7	14.4	1.0	2.9	4.5	2.3	277.2	12.7	40.9	69.6
IV	6.7	8.2	1.2	0.8	1.5	0.8	117.8	15.4	10.0	19.6
1986 I	4.3	5.1[e]	2.0	1.1	1.2	1.0	65.7	26.8	12.7	15.4
II	1.3	1.8	0.1	-1.0	-0.8	-1.0	16.7	1.2	-12.7	-10.0
III	2.6	3.0	1.2	0.3	0.4	0.4	36.1	15.3	3.7	4.9
IV	1.5	2.1	0.3	-1.0	-0.7	-0.7	19.6	3.7	-12.7	-8.7
1987 I	2.9	3.5	2.5	0.3	0.5	0.6	40.9	34.4	3.7	6.2

Sources: Bank of Israel, *Recent Economic Developments*, 44, September 1988, table 21.
[a]Estimated on the basis of nominal rates and CPI.
[b]Rate for two-week time deposits.
[c]Average of February and March rates only.
[d]Average of August and September rates only.
[e]New method of estimation from 1986 on.

Table 28
Real Money Aggregates, 1985–87ᵃ (June 1985 = 100)

		"Money"				Credit		Infla-tion
		$\frac{M1}{p}$	$\frac{M2}{p}$	$\frac{M3}{p}$	$\frac{M3^a}{p}$	$\frac{Tc}{p}$	$\frac{Fc}{p}$	
		(1)	(2)	(3)	(4)	(5)	(6)	(7)
1984	December	107	87	97	97	98	97	51
1985	March	121	108	102	104	99	99	68
	June	100	100	100	100	100	100	100
	September	117	146	89	88	95	97	136
	December	133	174	89	88	93	97	145
1986	March	203	204	92	92	101	111	148
	June	196	189	86	85	102	118	158
	September	232	228	90	90	110	130	163
	December	246	255	90	91	114	136	174
1987	March	253	278	95	95	125	151	182

Sources: As in Table 26.
ᵃEnd-of-period balances deflated by the CPI.

Table 29
Short-Term Capital Flows, 1985(I)–87(I)[a]

		Non-financial sector ($US mill.) (1)	Commercial banking sector ($US mill.) (2)	Total ($US mill.) (3)	% real exchange rate change[b] (4)
1985	I	−88	−98	−186	0.0
	II	177	278	455	1.6
	July	...	...	...	−2.4
	III	−277	139	−138	1.4
	IV	−43	−323	−366	2.2
1986	I	−247	−39	−286	0.6
	II	−45	−73	−118	1.9
	III	−152	200	48	1.2
	IV	−337	−107	−444	2.2
1987	January	...	...	...	−3.5
	I	−96	251	155	−1.3

Sources: Bank of Israel, *Recent Economic Developments*, No. 44, September 1988, tables 7 and 21.
[a]A negative sign indicates inflow of funds; positive figures are outflows.
[b]Quarterly mean of monthly rate of change of real exchange rate; depreciation (−). Nominal exchange rate against the U.S. dollar deflated by the CPI. Deflation by a labor cost deflator would show a more substantial devaluation of the sheqel initially, and a slower rise of the real exchange rate later. The depreciation of the U.S. dollar against other major currencies, which began in 1985(III) and accelerated through 1986, meant that the sheqel's real revaluation vis-à-vis the dollar, from 1985(III) through 1986(IV), involved a continuous real devaluation vis-à-vis European currencies and the yen.

Table 30
Velocity of Circulation of Demand Deposits, 1971–89

	1971	1980	1984	1985	1986	1987	1988	1989
January	22	75	284	412	433	267	195	200
February	22	82	307	386	369	294	175	164
March	23	88	270	342	341	256	164	164
April	24	91	224	420	270	258	154	149
May	23	99	299	390	285	269	181	...
June	22	99	336	567	310	220	166	...
July	22	113	387	520	268	220	154	...
August	23	115	354	455	231	250	159	...
September	24	120	458	476	235	250	151	...
October	24	122	489	382	233	183	151	...
November	22	132	428	385	221	167	153	...
December	24	158	443	407	271	195	196	...
Quarterly averages								
I	22	88	287	380	380	273	178	176
II	23	99	319	459	288	249	166	...
III	23	120	400	483	245	240	156	...
IV	23	116	447	390	244	182	166	...

Sources: Bank of Israel, Supervisor of Banks, *Current Banking Statistics*, 1985, 1986, 1987,
1988, and 1989, table XII-2.

References

OFFICIAL REPORTS AND STATISTICS

Bank of Israel (various years). *Annual Reports.*
——— (various years). *Economic Reviews.*
——— (periodic issues). *Recent Economic Developments.*
——— (periodic issues). Research Department. *Main Economic Series.*
———. Supervisor of Banking. *Annual Report.*
——— (various issues). Supervisor of Banking, *Israel's Banking System.*
Central Bureau of Statistics (various issues). *Monthly Bulletin.* Jerusalem.
Central Bureau of Statistics. *Monthly Bulletin* (various years). "Indices of Organized Retail Trade."
——— (various years). *Statistical Abstract of Israel.* Jerusalem.
"Comprehensive Economic Stabilization Program, A." Memo, June 1985, Ministry of Finance (Hebrew).
International Monetary Fund (various issues). *International Financial Statistics.*

BOOKS AND PERIODICALS

Barkai, H. (1976). "The Pattern of Oil Prices from the End of World War II through the Yom Kippur War," Part I. *The Economic Quarterly,* nos. 88–89 (April): 2–3. Hebrew.
——— (1977). "The Pattern of Oil Prices from the End of World War II through the Yom Kippur War," Part II. *The Economic Quarterly,* nos. 92–93 (April): 25–45. Hebrew.
——— (1987). "The Defense at a Crossroads." *Monthly Survey,* IDF Chief Education Officer, 34 (no. 9): 35–48. (Reprinted as Falk Institute Research Paper No. 197.)
——— (1993). *Contours of Argentina's Macroeconomic Stabilization, 1989–1992.* WP Series no. 135. Washington, D.C.: InterAmerican Development Bank.

Barkai, Haim, Y. Ben-Porath, M. Bruno, E. Kleiman, M. Michaely, and D. Patinkin (1975). *Economic Panel,* ed. N. Gross. Reprint of weekly Friday column in *Ma'ariv.* Hebrew. Jerusalem: University Publishers Ltd.

Beenstock, M. (1991). "Business Sector Production in the Short and Long Run in Israel: A Cointegration Analysis." D.P. 91-10, Bank of Israel, Research Dept.

Beenstock, M., Y. Lavi, A. Offenbacher, and D. Singer (1990). "To Hyperinflation and Back: Israel's Monetary Sector 1960–1988." Bank of Israel, Research Dept.

Ben-Bassat, A., and A. Marom (1988). "Is the Demand for Money in Israel Stable? (1965–1983)." *Bank of Israel Economic Review,* no. 60 (January): 52–71. English.

Ben-Porath, Y., ed. (1986). *The Israel Economy: Maturing Through Crises.* Cambridge, Mass.: Harvard University Press.

Ben-Shahar, H., S. Bronfeld, and A. Cukierman (1972). *The Capital Market in Israel.* Jerusalem: Shocken. Hebrew.

Ben-Zion, U., J. Minzli, and U. Spiegel (1986). "The Variance of Relative Prices in an Inflationary Situation and Its Impact on Interest Rates in Israel," in Z. Sussman et al., eds., *Iyunim be-Kalkala, 1982, 1984* [Economic Issues]. Jerusalem: The Israel Economic Association, pp. 107–21. Hebrew.

Bruno, M. (1985). "Stabilization of the Economy: The First Steps of the Emergency Program." *Economic Review,* no. 126 (October): 213. Hebrew.

——— (1986). "External Shocks and Domestic Response: Macroeconomic Performance, 1965–1982," in Y. Ben-Porath, ed. (1986), pp. 276–302.

Bruno, M., and S. Fischer (1986). "The Inflationary Process: Shocks and Accommodation," in Y. Ben-Porath, ed. (1986), pp. 347–75.

Bruno, M., G. Di Tella, R. Dornbusch, and S. Fischer, eds. (1988). *Inflation Stabilization: The Experience of Israel, Argentina, Brazil, Bolivia, and Mexico.* Cambridge, Mass.: MIT Press.

Canavese, A. J., and G. Di Tella (1988). "Inflation Stabilization or Hyperinflation Avoidance," in Bruno et al., eds. (1988), pp. 153–90.

Cardozo, E. A. (1988). "Comment" to M. H. Simonsen, in Bruno et al., eds. (1988), pp. 287–94.

de Pablo, J. C. (1988). "Comment" on Canavese and Di Tella, in Bruno et al., eds. (1988), pp. 195–201.

Dornbusch, R., and S. Fischer (1990). *Macroeconomics,* 5th ed. New York and London: McGraw-Hill.

Friedman, M. (1968). "The Role of Monetary Policy." *American Economic Review* 58, no. 1: 1–17.

Halevi, N. (1983). "The Structure and Development of Israel's Balance of Payments." Jerusalem: The Maurice Falk Institute for Economic Research, Discussion Paper No. 83.02.

Halevi, N., and Y. Kop, eds. (1976). *Israeli Economic Papers, 1976.* Jerusalem: The Maurice Falk Institute for Economic Research in Israel. Hebrew.

Kleiman, E. (1984). "The Costs of Inflation," in *The Economic Quarterly,* no. 30: 859–64. Hebrew.

———. (1986). "Indexation in the Labor Market," in Y. Ben-Porath, ed. (1986), pp. 302–20.

Kop, Y., ed. (1989). *Allocation of Resources to Social Services* (1981/84). Jerusalem: Center for Research on Social Policy.

Lach, S., and D. Tsiddon (1992). "The Behavior of Prices and Inflation: An Empirical Analysis of Disaggregated Price Data." *Journal of Political Economy* 100, no. 2: 349–89.

Leiderman, L., and A. Maron (1988). "New Estimates of Demand for Money in Israel." *Bank of Israel Economic Review*, no. 60 (January): 19–35.

Liviatan, N. (1984). "A Policy for Lowering Inflation with Reference to Past Experience." Israeli Center for Social and Economic Progress, September. Hebrew.

———. (1986). "Inflation Stabilization in Israel." IMF, WP/86/10, November 4.

Liviatan, N., and S. Piterman (1986). "Accelerating Inflation and Balance of Payments Crises, 1973–1984," in Y. Ben-Porath, ed. (1986), pp. 320–46.

Liviatan, O. (1987). "The Development of the Cost of Living Wage Allowance Arrangements." Bank of Israel, Research Dept. Discussion Paper No. 8, pp. 2–9, September. Hebrew.

Lucas, R. (1973). "Some International Evidence on Output-Inflation Tradeoffs." *American Economic Review* 63 (June): 326–34.

Macedo, R. (1988). "Comment" to M. H. Simonsen, in Bruno et al., eds. (1988), pp. 295–96.

Machinea, J. L., and J. M. Fanelli (1988). "Stopping Inflation: The Case of the Austral Plan in Argentina, 1985–87," in Bruno et al., eds. (1988), pp. 141–42.

Melnick, R. (1988). "Two Aspects of the Demand for Money in Israel, 1970–1981." *Bank of Israel Economic Review*, no. 60 (January): 36–51.

Meridor, L. (February 1988). "The Role of the Public Sector in the Israeli Economy 1960–1986." WP 1–88 Program for the Study of the Israeli Economy, MIT.

Metzer, J. (1983). "The Slowdown of Economic Growth in Israel: A Passing Phase or the End of a Big Spurt?" Jerusalem: The Maurice Falk Institute for Economic Research in Israel, Discussion Paper No. 83.03.

Modiano, E. M. (1988). "The Cruzado First Attempt: The Brazilian Stabilization Program of February 1986," in Bruno et al., eds. (1988), pp. 215–58.

Piterman, S. (1988). "The Irreversibility of the Relationship between Inflation and Real Balances." *Bank of Israel Economic Review*, no. 60 (January): 72–83.

Plozker, S. (1987). "How the Program Was Saved." *Al-Hamishmar*, September. Hebrew.

Rodriguez, C.A. (1988). "Comment," in Bruno et al., eds. (1988), pp. 202–9.

Sanbar, M., and Sh. Bronfeld (1973). "Monetary Thought, Policy and Development, 1948–1972," Parts I and II. *The Economic Quarterly*, no. 77: 3–16, and no. 78–79: 217–36. Hebrew.

Simonsen, M. H. (1988). "Price Stabilization and Incomes Policies: Theory and the Brazilian Case Study," in Bruno et al., eds. (1988), pp. 257–86.

Sokoler, M. (1987). "The Inflation Tax on Real Balances, the Inflation Subsidy on Credit and the Inflationary Process in Israel." *Bank of Israel Economic Review*, no. 59 (April): 1–26.

Tooke, T. (1838, 1848, 1857). *History of Prices and the State of Circulation* (6 vols.). London: P. S. King & Son.

Urrutia, M. (1988). "Comment" to M. H. Simonsen, in Bruno et al., eds. (1988), p. 302.

Yariv, D. (1988). "Publication of the CPI and a Test of the Efficiency of Israel's Stock Market." Jerusalem: Bank of Israel Research Department, Discussion Paper 88.04, June. Hebrew.

Yashiv, E. (1990). "Long-run Money Demand in Israel: A Co-Integration Analysis." MIT, Program for the Study of the Israeli Economy, No. 14–20, August.

Index

About the Author

HAIM BARKAI is Sapir Professor of Economics at the Hebrew University, Jerusalem. He has served as Chairman of the Department of Economics and as Dean of the Faculty of Social Sciences. He was also a fellow of the Falk Institute of Economic Research in Jerusalem. From the late 1960s until the early 1980s, he was a board member and later Chairman of the Advisory Committee and Board of the Bank of Israel. He also served as Chairman of the Committee on Public Sector Salaries and as a member of the Bank of Israel Committee on Banking Policy.

ISBN 0-275-95146-4

90000>

EAN

9 780275 951467

HARDCOVER BAR CODE